Creating
2D Animation

WITH THE ADOBE CREATIVE SUITE

Creating
2D Animation

WITH THE ADOBE CREATIVE SUITE

Debbie Keller

DELMAR
CENGAGE Learning

Australia • Brazil • Japan • Korea • Mexico • Singapore • Spain • United Kingdom • United States

DELMAR
CENGAGE Learning®

Creating 2D Animation with the Adobe Creative Suite
Debbie Keller

Vice President, Career and Professional Editorial:
Dave Garza

Director of Learning Solutions: Sandy Clark

Senior Acquisitions Editor: Jim Gish

Director, Development-Career and Computing:
Marah Bellegarde

Senior Product Development Manager: Larry Main

Product Managers: Jane Hosie-Bounar, Meaghan Tomaso

Editorial Assistant: Sarah Timm

Vice President Marketing, Career and Professional:
Jennifer Baker

Brand Manager: Kay Stefanski

Associate Market Development Manager:
Jonathan Sheehan

Senior Production Director: Wendy Troeger

Production Manager: Andrew Crouth

Senior Content Project Manager: Kathryn B. Kucharek

Developmental Editor: Barbara Waxer

Technical Editor: Sarah Gosser

Director of Design: Bruce Bond

Cover Design: Riezebos Holzbaur/Tim Heraldo

Cover Photo: Riezebos Holzbaur/Andrei Pasternak

Text Designer: Liz Kingslein

Production House: Integra Software Services Pvt. Ltd.

Copy Editor/Proofreader: Kim Kosmatka

Indexer: Alexandra Nickerson

Technology Project Manager: Jim Gilbert

For product information and technology assistance, contact us at **Cengage Learning Customer & Sales Support, 1-800-354-9706**

For permission to use material from this text or product, submit all requests online at **www.cengage.com/permissions**

Further permissions questions can be emailed to **permissionrequest@cengage.com**

Adobe® Premiere Pro®, Adobe® Premiere Elements®, Adobe® After Effects®, Adobe® Soundbooth®, Adobe® Bridge®, Adobe® Encore®, Adobe® Photoshop®, Adobe® InDesign®, Adobe® Illustrator®, Adobe® Flash®, Adobe® Dreamweaver®, Adobe® Fireworks®, and Adobe® Creative Suite® are trademarks or registered trademarks of Adobe Systems, Inc. in the United States and/or other countries. Third party products, services, company names, logos, design, titles, words, or phrases within these materials may be trademarks of their respective owners.

Adobe product screenshot(s) reprinted with permission from Adobe Systems Incorporated.

Library of Congress Control Number: 2011945481

ISBN-13: 978-1-133-69348-2
ISBN-10: 1-133-69348-2

Delmar
5 Maxwell Drive
Clifton Park, NY 12065-2919
USA

Cengage Learning is a leading provider of customized learning solutions with office locations around the globe, including Singapore, the United Kingdom, Australia, Mexico, Brazil, and Japan. Locate your local office at: **international.cengage.com/region**

Cengage Learning products are represented in Canada by Nelson Education, Ltd.

To learn more about Delmar, visit **www.cengage.com/delmar**

Purchase any of our products at your local college store or at our preferred online store **www.cengagebrain.com**

Notice to the Reader
Publisher does not warrant or guarantee any of the products described herein or perform any independent analysis in connection with any of the product information contained herein. Publisher does not assume, and expressly disclaims, any obligation to obtain and include information other than that provided to it by the manufacturer. The reader is expressly warned to consider and adopt all safety precautions that might be indicated by the activities described herein and to avoid all potential hazards. By following the instructions contained herein, the reader willingly assumes all risks in connection with such instructions. The publisher makes no representations or warranties of any kind, including but not limited to, the warranties of fitness for particular purpose or merchantability, nor are any such representations implied with respect to the material set forth herein, and the publisher takes no responsibility with respect to such material. The publisher shall not be liable for any special, consequential, or exemplary damages resulting, in whole or part, from the readers' use of, or reliance upon, this material.

Printed in China
1 2 3 4 5 6 7 17 16 15 14 13

Revealed Series Vision

The Revealed Series is your guide to today's hottest multimedia applications. For years, the Revealed Series has kept pace with the dynamic demands of the multimedia community, and continues to do so with the publication of 13 titles covering the Adobe Creative Suite products. Each comprehensive book teaches not only the technical skills required for success in today's competitive multimedia market, but the design skills as well. From animation, to web design, to digital image editing and interactive media skills, the Revealed Series has you covered. We recognize the unique learning environment of the multimedia classroom, and we deliver textbooks that include:

■ Comprehensive step-by-step instructions
■ In-depth explanations of the "Why" behind a skill
■ Creative projects for additional practice
■ Full-color visuals for a clear explanation of concepts
■ Comprehensive online material offering additional instruction and skills practice
■ Video tutorials for skills reinforcement as well as the presentation of additional features

—The Revealed Series

About This Edition

This one of kind new text will give you the ability to create and edit two-dimensional animations using the Adobe Creative Suite, while also exploring story and character development, and the history of animation.

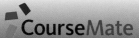

A CourseMate is available to accompany *Creating 2D Animation with the Adobe Creative Suite* which helps you make the grade! This CourseMate includes:

■ An interactive eBook, with highlighting, note-taking, and search capabilities
■ Interactive learning tools including:
    ■ Chapter quizzes
    ■ Flash cards
    ■ Instructional video lessons from Total Training, the leading provider of video instruction for Adobe software. These video lessons are tightly integrated with the book, chapter by chapter, and include assessment.
    ■ And more!

Go to login.cengagebrain.com to access these resources you have purchased.

AUTHOR'S VISION

Wow! This book went from concept to reality in what seems like a blink of an eye. My approach on this book was to expose students to animation concepts to help them as they begin to develop their own characters and stories. My goal was to teach the software skills they would need in a short amount of time so they could spend more time on the end-of-chapter projects. The goal of the end-of-chapter projects is to allow them to practice those skills with not much "hand holding" and to create their own stories and characters.

Thank you so much to Meaghan Tomaso for being there when I needed to vent. This book was definitely a challenge and I would not have been able to get to the end without you.

And of course, thank you to my husband, Glenn, for his continued love and support. I'm not sure I could teach high school fulltime and write books if he wasn't there to support me. We are about to celebrate our 10th anniversary in just a few days, and fortunately all of the chapters have been written, which means I can finally give him my undivided attention for at least one day!

—Debbie Keller

Introduction to Creating 2D Animation with the Adobe Creative Suite

Welcome to *Creating 2D Animation with the Adobe Creative Suite*. This book offers creative projects, concise instructions, and complete coverage of basic drawing, image-editing, and animation skills, helping you to create polished, professional-looking illustrations and animations. Use this book both in the classroom and as your own reference guide.

The text is written with an integrated approach to each of the three applications: Adobe Illustrator, Photoshop, and Flash. A chapter is dedicated to each application to help you gain familiarity with the program.

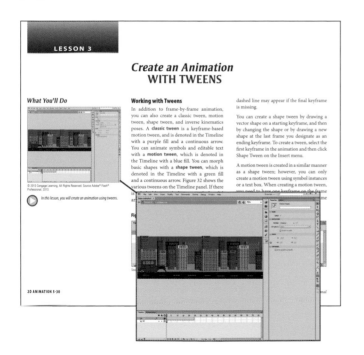

What You'll Do

A What You'll Do figure begins every lesson. This figure gives you an at-a-glance look at what you'll do in the chapter, either by showing you a screen from the current project or a tool you'll be using.

Comprehensive Conceptual Lessons

Before jumping into instructions, in-depth conceptual information tells you "why" skills are applied. This book provides the "how" and "why" through the use of professional examples. Also included in the text are tips and sidebars to help you work more efficiently and creatively, or to teach you a bit about the history or design philosophy behind the skill you are using.

Step-by-Step Instructions

This book combines in-depth conceptual information with concise steps to help you learn about working with 2D animation in Adobe Creative Suite. Each set of steps guides you through a lesson where you will create, modify, or enhance a file. Step references to large colorful images and quick step summaries round out the lessons. The Data Files for the steps are available online at www.cengagebrain.com.

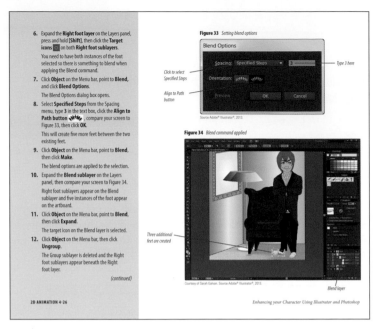

6. Expand the **Right foot layer** on the Layers panel, press and hold [**Shift**], then click the **Target icons** on both **Right foot sublayers**.
You need to have both instances of the foot selected so there is something to blend when applying the Blend command.

7. Click **Object** on the Menu bar, point to **Blend**, and click **Blend Options**.
The Blend Options dialog box opens.

8. Select **Specified Steps** from the Spacing menu, type **3** in the text box, click the **Align to Path button**, compare your screen to Figure 33, then click **OK**.
This will create five more feet between the two existing feet.

9. Click **Object** on the Menu bar, point to **Blend**, then click **Make**.
The blend options are applied to the selection.

10. Expand the **Blend sublayer** on the Layers panel, and compare your screen to Figure 34.
Right foot sublayers appear on the Blend sublayer and five instances of the foot appear on the artboard.

11. Click **Object** on the Menu bar, point to **Blend**, then click **Expand**.
The target icon on the Blend layer is selected.

12. Click **Object** on the Menu bar, then click **Ungroup**.
The Group sublayer is deleted and the Right foot sublayers appear beneath the Right foot layer.

(continued)

Figure 33 *Setting blend options*

Click to select Specified Steps

Align to Path button

Type 3 here

Source Adobe® Illustrator®, 2013.

Figure 34 *Blend command applied*

Three additional feet are created

Blend layer

Courtesy of Sarah Galvan. Source Adobe® Illustrator®, 2013.

Enhancing your Character Using Illustrator and Photoshop

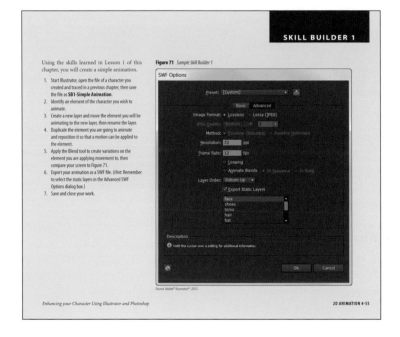

SKILL BUILDER 1

Using the skills learned in Lesson 1 of this chapter, you will create a simple animation.

1. Start Illustrator, open the file of a character you created and traced in a previous chapter, then save the file as **SB1-Simple Animation**.

2. Identify an element of the character you wish to animate.

3. Create a new layer and move the element you will be animating to the new layer, then rename the layer.

4. Duplicate the element you are going to animate and reposition it so that a motion can be applied to the element.

5. Apply the Blend tool to create variations on the element you are applying movement to, then compare your screen to Figure 71.

6. Export your animation as a SWF file. (*Hint:* Remember to select the static layers in the Advanced SWF Options dialog box.)

7. Save and close your work.

Figure 71 *Sample Skill Builder 1*

SWF Options

Source Adobe® Illustrator®, 2013.

Enhancing your Character Using Illustrator and Photoshop

Projects

This book contains a variety of end-of-chapter materials for additional practice and reinforcement. The chapter concludes with three projects: two Skill Builders and one Portfolio Project. The Skill Builders require you to apply the skills you've learned in the chapter. The Portfolio Project encourages you to address and solve challenges based on the content explored in the chapter, and to develop your own portfolio of work.

Capstone Projects

Included at the end of Chapter 6 are three Capstone projects. These projects are designed as scenario-based projects, so you can let your creativity take control and create your own animations from beginning concept to completion. Each project provides specifications and requires you to use all the essential skills you have learned within the previous chapters.

What Instructor Resources Are Available with This Book?

The Instructor Resources are Delmar's way of putting the resources and information needed to teach and learn effectively into your hands. All the resources are available for both Macintosh and Windows operating systems. These resources can be found online at: **http://login.cengage.com**. Once you login or create an account, search for the title under 'My Dashboard' using the ISBN. Then select the instructor companion site resources and click 'Add to my Bookshelf.'

Instructor's Manual

The Instructor's Manual includes chapter overviews and detailed lecture topics for each chapter with teaching tips.

Sample Syllabus

The Sample Syllabus includes a suggested syllabus for any course that uses this book.

PowerPoint Presentations

Each chapter has a corresponding PowerPoint presentation that you can use in lectures, distribute to your students, or customize to suit your course.

Data Files for Students

To complete most of the chapters in this book, your students will need Data Files, which are available online. Instruct students to use the Data Files List at the end of this book. This list gives instructions on organizing files.

To access the Data Files for this book, take the following steps:

1. Open your browser and go to http://www.cengagebrain.com.
2. Type the author, title, or ISBN of this book in the Search window. (The ISBN is listed on the back cover.)
3. Click the book title in the list of search results.
4. When the book's main page is displayed, click the Access button under Free Study Tools.
5. To download Data Files, select a chapter number and then click the Data Files tab on the left navigation bar to download the files.
6. To access additional materials, click the additional materials tab under Book Resources to download the files.

Solutions to Exercises

Solution Files are Data Files completed with comprehensive sample answers. Use these files to evaluate your students' work, or distribute them electronically so students can verify their work. In cases where the end-of-chapter projects are open ended, we have provided rubrics to help in grading your students' work.

Additional Resources

To access additional materials for this book, take the following steps:

1. Open your browser and go to http://www.cengagebrain.com.
2. Type the author, title, or ISBN of this book in the Search window. (The ISBN is listed on the back cover.)
3. Click the book title in the list of search results.
4. When the book's main page is displayed, click the Access button under Free Study Tools.
5. Click the Additional Materials tab under Book Resources to download the files.

Test Bank and Test Engine

ExamView is a powerful testing software package that allows instructors to create and administer printed and computer (LAN-based) exams. ExamView includes hundreds of questions that correspond to the topics covered in this text, enabling students to generate detailed study guides that include page references for further review. The computer-based and LAN-based/online testing component allows students to take exams using the EV Player, and also saves the instructor time by grading each exam automatically.

BRIEF CONTENTS

CONTENTS

CHAPTER 1: CREATING A CHARACTER USING ADOBE ILLUSTRATOR

CHAPTER 2: CREATING A COMIC BOOK USING ADOBE ILLUSTRATOR

CHAPTER 5: CREATING BASIC ANIMATIONS IN FLASH PROFESSIONAL

CHAPTER 6: ANIMATING WITH ILLUSTRATOR AND PHOTOSHOP FILES IN FLASH PROFESSIONAL

Intended Audience

This book is designed for students who have some experience with Illustrator, Photoshop, and Flash and focuses on the skills necessary for creating digital illustrations and animations. The book is written in a project-based format to provide basic and in-depth material that not only educates, but also encourages you to explore the nuances of each of the applications discussed in this book.

Approach

The text is designed so you can work at your own pace through step-by-step tutorials. A concept is presented and the process explained, followed by the actual steps. To take advantage of what this text has to offer, you should work as follows:

- Read the introduction for each chapter to understand the overall concept that is being used to teach the tools and techniques the applications have to offer.

- The introduction for each lesson provides greater explanation than the actual steps. Refer to the introduction while working on the steps.
- As you work on the steps, pay attention to what you are doing and why; do not just go through the motions of following directions.
- After completing a set of steps, ask yourself if you could use these skills without referring to the steps. If you feel you could not, review the steps.

Icons, Buttons, and Pointers

Symbols for icons, buttons, and pointers are shown each time they are used in the steps. Try to become familiar with their names and their location.

Data Files

To complete the lessons in this book, you need the Data Files located online at www.cengagebrain.com. Your instructor will tell you where to store the files as you work, such as to your hard drive or network server. The instructions will refer to the drive and folder where these Data Files are stored.

Building an Electronic Portfolio

It is suggested you work on the chapters in the book in consecutive order so that as your skills are developed you are able to utilize them in later chapters. Students will also have the opportunity to continue to create their own original work and continue to develop that work in the end-of-chapter exercises.

Windows and Macintosh

The Adobe applications work virtually the same on both the Windows and Macintosh operating systems. In those cases where there is a difference, the abbreviations (Win) and (Mac) are used.

Windows

- Intel® Pentium® 4 or AMD Athlon® 64 processor
- Microsoft® Windows® XP with Service Pack 3 or Windows 7 with Service Pack 1. Adobe® Creative Suite® 5.5 and CS6 applications also support Windows 8. Refer to the CS6 FAQ for more information about Windows 8 support.*
- 2GB of RAM (3GB recommended) for 32 bit; 2GB of RAM (8GB recommended) for 64 bit
- 11GB of available hard-disk space for installation; additional free space required during installation (cannot install on removable flash storage devices)
- 1280 × 800 display (1280 × 1024 recommended) with 16-bit color and 512MB of VRAM
- OpenGL 2.0–capable system
- DVD-ROM drive compatible with dual-layer DVDs
- Java™ Runtime Environment 1.6 (included)
- QuickTime 7.6.6 software required for HTML5 media playback and multimedia features
- Adobe® Flash® Player 10 software required to export SWF files
- This software will not operate without activation. Broadband Internet connection and registration are required for software activation, validation of subscriptions, and access to online services.†Phone activation is not available.

Mac OS

- Multicore Intel processor with 64-bit support
- Mac OS X v10.6.8 or v10.7. Adobe Creative Suite 5, CS5.5, and CS6 applications support Mac OS X Mountain Lion (v10.8) when installed on Intel based systems.**
- 2GB of RAM (8GB recommended)
- 9.5GB of available hard-disk space for installation; additional free space required during installation (cannot install on a volume that uses a case-sensitive file system or on removable flash storage devices)
- 1280 × 800 display (1280 × 1024 recommended) with 16-bit color and 512MB of VRAM
- OpenGL 2.0–capable system
- DVD-ROM drive compatible with dual-layer DVDs
- Java Runtime Environment 1.6
- QuickTime 7.6.6 software required for HTML5 media playback and multimedia features
- Adobe Flash Player 10 software required to export SWF files
- This software will not operate without activation. Broadband Internet connection and registration are required for software activation, validation of subscriptions, and access to online services.†Phone activation is not available.

*Adobe Photoshop® Extended 3D features and some GPU-enabled features are not supported on Windows XP.

CHAPTER 1

CREATING A CHARACTER USING
ADOBE ILLUSTRATOR

1. Review the Illustrator workspace
2. Work with the drawing tools
3. Master the Pen tool
4. Understand character development
5. Review drawing tips
6. Trace scanned images

CREATING A CHARACTER USING
ADOBE ILLUSTRATOR

A quality comic book or animation begins with character development and a story. You may first decide to develop a character and then write a story. On the other hand, you may first have a story you want to tell and then need to develop the characters to tell that story. Either way is fine. First, though, it is important to understand what character development is and what a story is. In this chapter, you will focus on character development. In Chapter 2, you will learn about story and the story development process.

The creation process begins with determining the information and characteristics about the character you wish to create. Once you have an idea about who you want your character to be, you can begin to sketch and refine that character on paper. You can then scan the final drawing and trace it digitally using a vector-drawing program.

Adobe Illustrator CS6 is a professional vector-drawing application with precision drawing tools. You can purchase Illustrator as a standalone application or as part of the Adobe Design & Web Premium, Adobe Design Standard, Adobe Master Collection Creative Suites, and the Adobe Creative Cloud.

In this book, it is assumed that you have basic knowledge of the following Adobe applications: Illustrator, Photoshop, and Flash. You will first review the Illustrator workspace and some of the most basic tools.

When working with Illustrator, you will create vector drawings by tracing scanned images using a variety of tools. In this chapter, you will review the Illustrator interface, practice using the drawing tools, master the Pen tool, and create a character.

TOOLS YOU'LL USE

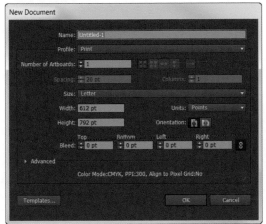

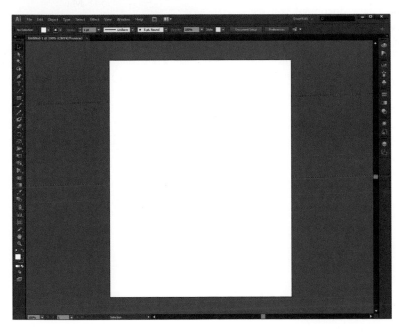

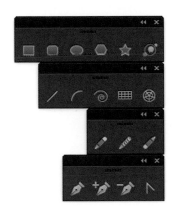

Source Adobe® Illustrator®, 2013.

Review the Illustrator
WORKSPACE

What You'll Do

Source Adobe® Illustrator®, 2013.

In this lesson, you will review the Illustrator workspace.

Exploring the Illustrator Workspace

You should already have some familiarity with Illustrator before beginning this chapter, but you will first briefly review some of the key elements of the Illustrator workspace. When you create a new document you see the **application window**, which is the main window comprised of various panels. The arrangement of panels in the application window is known as the **workspace**. Illustrator offers several preformatted workspaces that are designed for specific tasks. Figure 1 shows the default workspace, called **Essentials**. The Essentials workspace, as its name implies, displays the essential panels needed to create a document. You will be using this workspace throughout this book.

QUICK TIP

The Welcome Screen has been removed in CS6. If you would like to view your recent files, click File on the Menu bar and point to Open Recent Files; to select a template, click File on the Menu bar, and then click New from Template; and to choose a specific New Document Profile, select an option on the Profile menu in the New Document dialog box.

You can move individual panels by clicking and dragging the panel tabs. **Panel tabs** display the panels' names and are found at the top of a panel. When you drag a panel, it is

Creating a Character Using Adobe Illustrator

removed from the dock and you can place it anywhere on the screen or in a different panel group. When moving a panel to another panel group, a **drop zone** appears, shown as a blue highlighted area, indicating where the panel will be placed when you release the mouse.

You can move a panel group by dragging the title bar for the group. The title bar is the gray area to the left of the panel menu. A collection of panels or panels groups is called a **dock**. The expanded panel dock is shown in Figure 2.

You can resize panels by dragging any side of the panel or collapse panels by double-clicking the active panel tab. At the top of a dock are the Collapse panel and Expand panel icons. These icons allow you to either collapse

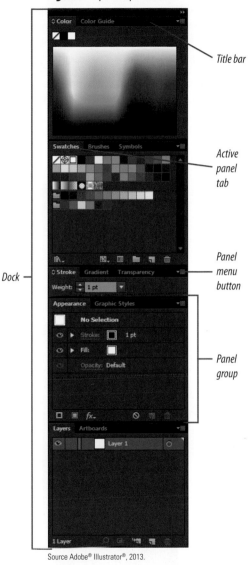

Figure 2 *Expanded panel dock*

Title bar

Active panel tab

Dock

Panel menu button

Panel group

Source Adobe® Illustrator®, 2013.

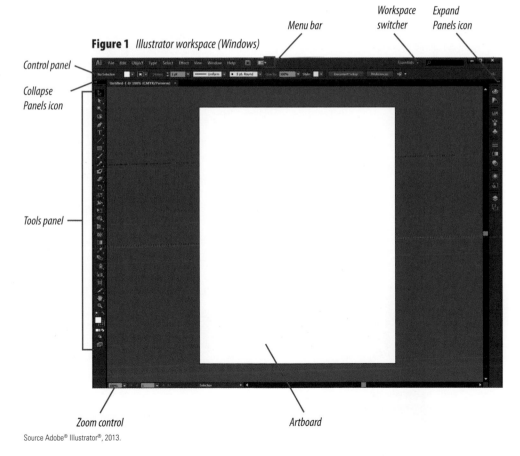

Figure 1 *Illustrator workspace (Windows)*

Menu bar

Workspace switcher

Expand Panels icon

Control panel

Collapse Panels icon

Tools panel

Zoom control

Artboard

Source Adobe® Illustrator®, 2013.

the dock to icon view or expand the dock to panel view. When in icon view, you can resize the panel to display or hide the panel names, as shown in Figure 3. In icon view, only one expanded panel is visible at a time.

If you want to save a custom workspace, you can do so by clicking the New Workspace command on the Workspace menu, or by clicking the Save Workspace command on the Workspace switcher on the Menu bar. The **Workspace switcher** is a menu on the Menu bar. A **custom workspace** is one that has been created by the user and saved with a unique name.

If you want to open or move panels while you are working, you can reset the workspace back to the Essentials workspace using the Workspace switcher.

Understanding the New Document Dialog Box

When you create a new document, the New Document dialog box opens. The New Document dialog box is where you specify the settings for an Illustrator document, as shown in Figure 4.

The New Document Profile menu allows you to select a preset that creates a document

Figure 3 *Panel dock in icon view*

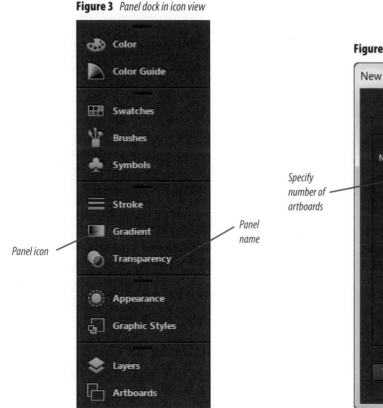

Panel icon

Panel name

Source Adobe® Illustrator®, 2013.

Artboard layout options

New document profile list arrow

Figure 4 *New Document dialog box*

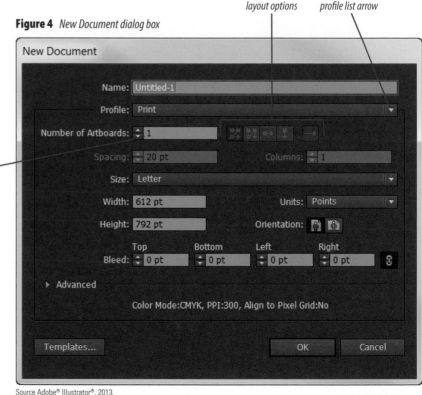

Specify number of artboards

Source Adobe® Illustrator®, 2013.

Creating a Character Using Adobe Illustrator

profile designed for the final output. **Final output** is how you intend to use the document when you are finished. You should decide on the final output before beginning your project: Is the design for print, video, or the web? The appropriate values are automatically set to the proper setting for that particular output. For example, if you are designing for the web, the preset will change the color mode to RGB and the units to pixels. If you are designing for print, the color mode will be set to CMYK and the units will be points. If you plan on working with the artwork in Flash, you will need to set the document's color mode to RGB, since Flash is used to create animations for the web and mobile devices. (*Note*: If you make any changes to the available options, the profile will automatically change to Custom.)

An **artboard** is the printable region of your document. You can designate the number of artboards for your document in the New Document dialog box, shown in Figure 4, or create additional artboards after you have created your document. You will learn more about artboards in Chapter 2.

Understanding RGB vs. CMYK

The color modes **RGB** (red, green, and blue) and **CMYK** (cyan, magenta, yellow, and black) are both available in Illustrator. RGB, the color mode used on computer displays, television screens, and mobile devices such as smartphones and tablets, uses red, green, and blue in various combinations to create the colors you see. When creating an illustration for print, the color mode CMYK uses cyan, magenta, yellow, and black to create various colors.

Start Illustrator, create a new document, and explore the workspace

In this exercise, you will explore the Illustrator workspace.

1. Click the **Start button** 🌀 on the taskbar, point to **All Programs**, then click **Adobe Illustrator CS6** (Win), or open the **Finder** from the dock, click **Applications** from the sidebar, click the **Adobe Applications folder**, then click **Adobe Illustrator CS6** (Mac).

   You may need to look in a subfolder if you have installed the Creative Suite.

2. Click **File** on the Menu bar, then click **New**.

   The New Document dialog box opens.

TIP Pressing and holding [Alt][Ctrl][Shift] (Win) or [option] ⌘ [Shift] (Mac) while starting Illustrator, restores the default preference settings.

3. Type **Illustrator Workspace** in the Name text box, select **Print** from the Profile menu, then compare your dialog box to Figure 5.

   While you can name the document here, the document will not be created until you save it.

4. Click **OK** to close the New Document dialog box.

5. Click the **Workspace switcher** on the Menu bar, then click **Essentials** if necessary.

   The Essentials workspace appears in its original configuration. If a workspace is already selected, you can click the name to reset the workspace.

6. Click the **Expand Panels icon** ◀◀ at the top of the panel dock.

   The panel dock expands from icon view to panel view.

(continued)

Figure 5 *Naming a document in the New Document dialog box*

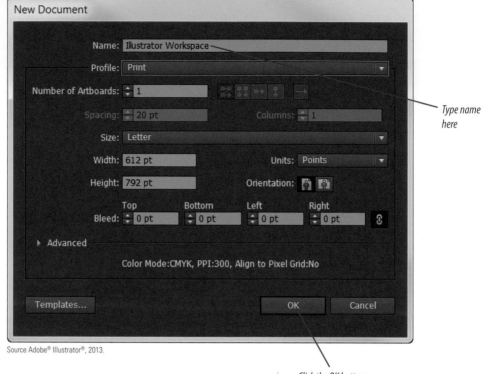

Source Adobe® Illustrator®, 2013.

Type name here

Click the OK button

Figure 6 *Type tool options on the Control panel*

Source Adobe® Illustrator®, 2013.

Font list arrow   *Font Size list arrow*

Understanding the Illustrator Options Dialog Box

When you click Save in the Save As dialog box, the Illustrator Options dialog box opens, as shown in Figure 7. While you can select several saving options, you should be primarily concerned with two options. First, you can choose to make the document compatible with a previous version of Illustrator. It is important to use caution when doing this and to be sure to read the warnings that appear at the bottom of the dialog box. For example, not all options are backwards compatible and may result in you losing some of your design. The second option you should consider is whether to embed any artwork you may have linked in the document. This may be important when you save a copy of the file to a flash drive or plan on sharing it with another person. If the linked artwork is not embedded, it will not be available when the file is opened from another location. As a result, embedding artwork makes the document file size larger.

Figure 7 *Illustrator Options dialog box*

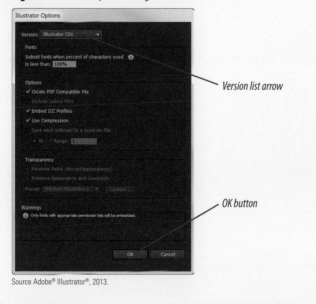

Version list arrow

OK button

Source Adobe® Illustrator®, 2013.

7. Click the **Expand Panels icon** at the top of the Tools panel.

   The Tools panel changes from a single column to a double column.

8. Click the **Type tool** on the Tools panel.

   The Control panel appears with options associated with the selected tool, as shown in Figure 6.

9. Position the pointer near the middle of the artboard, click the **mouse**, then type **your name**.

10. Highlight the **text**.

11. On the Control panel, click the **Font list arrow**, then click a different font.

12. Click the **Font Size list arrow**, then click a larger size.

13. Click the **Selection tool** on the Tools panel, then drag the **name block** to the top of the artboard.

14. Click **File** on the Menu bar, then click **Save**.

    The Save As dialog box opens, where you can select where to save the file.

15. Click **Save**.

16. Click **OK** to accept the default settings in the Illustrator Options dialog box.

17. Click **File** on the Menu bar, then click **Exit**.

Lesson 1   Review the Illustrator Workspace

Work with the
DRAWING TOOLS

What You'll Do

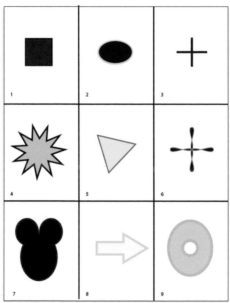

 In this lesson, you will work with the drawing tools.

Using Illustrator Drawing Tools

Illustrator has a variety of drawing tools available for creating graphics. These tools are explained in Table 1. In this lesson, you will create characters for use in a comic book you are writing. You will also trace hand drawn sketches. Therefore, it is important to become proficient in using these tools before you can bring your character to life in Illustrator. Being able to draw with shapes and customize them can be a real time-saver when you begin to trace your hand drawn sketches. Figure 8 shows how working with only the Ellipse tool, the Line Segment tool,

Figure 8 *Examples of Illustrator drawing tools*

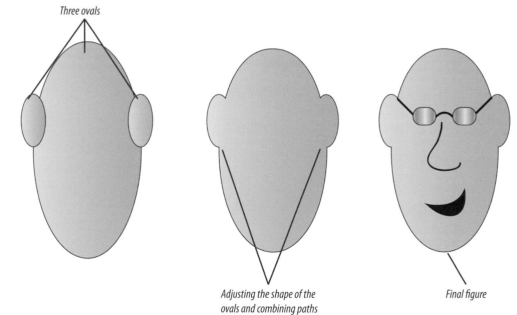

Three ovals

Adjusting the shape of the ovals and combining paths

Final figure

Creating a Character Using Adobe Illustrator

and the Brush tool, you can quickly create the face for your character. (*Note*: The Paintbrush tool is considered a painting tool, which you will learn about in Chapter 2.)

When drawing in Illustrator, you create vector graphics. You can enlarge a vector drawing without a loss of quality in the image. A **vector drawing** is made up of **objects**, which are created by a series of paths. **Paths** are a sequence of line and curve segments that have anchor points at either end. An **anchor point** is the point between each line segment that can either be a smooth anchor point or a corner anchor point; the anchor point determines whether the line is straight or curved.

TABLE 1 ILLUSTRATOR DRAWING TOOLS			
Name	**Tool**	**Description**	**Location**
Line Segment tool		Uses the stroke color to draw straight line segments	Default tool on the Tools panel
Arc tool		Uses the stroke color to draw curved line segments that can be either concave or convex. (*Note*: You can apply a fill color that will color in the area of the curve.)	Found under the Line Segment tool
Spiral tool		Uses the stroke color to draw spirals clockwise or counterclockwise. (*Note*: You can apply a fill color that will color in the area of the spiral.)	Found under the Line Segment tool
Rectangle tool		Draws rectangles and squares; allows you to apply a stroke and/or fill color	Default tool on the Tools panel
Rounded Rectangle tool		Draws rectangles and squares with rounded corners; allows you to apply a stroke and/or fill color	Found under the Rectangle tool
Ellipse tool		Draws ovals or circles; allows you to apply a stroke and/or fill color	Found under the Rectangle tool
Polygon tool		Draws a multi-sided figure including triangles; allows you to apply a stroke and/or fill color; you can specify the number of sides in the Polygon dialog box or by using the up and down arrow keys while drawing the shape	Found under the Rectangle tool
Star tool		Draws multi-point stars; allows you to apply a stroke and/or fill color; the number of sides can be specified in the Star dialog box or by using the up and down arrow keys while drawing the star	Found under the Rectangle tool
Pencil tool		Uses the stroke color to draw lines similar to drawing with a pencil on paper	Default tool on the Tools panel
Smooth tool		Smooths the path of already drawn path segments	Found under the Pencil tool
Path Eraser tool		Erases anchor points from a path or an object	Found under the Pencil tool

Figure 9 shows an example of vector drawings in Outline mode. The object is made up of a series of paths. The selected path shows anchor points as blue outlined squares, with the line segment in between the anchor points.

Figure 9 *Viewing a vector drawing in Outline view*

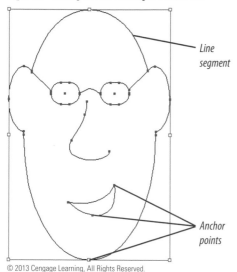

Line segment

Anchor points

Creating vector shapes and paths is done with the variety of tools found on the Tools panel. A small triangle on a tool indicates there are

Figure 10 *Working with the Tools panel*

Hidden tools panel

Rectangle Tool	(M)
Rounded Rectangle Tool	
Ellipse Tool	(L)
Polygon Tool	
Star Tool	
Flare Tool	

Click to create a floating tools panel

Floating tools panel

additional tools in the tool group underneath. To view the tool group, point to the visible tool, then click and hold the mouse. To keep a hidden tool panel displayed as a floating panel, click the small triangle on the bar at the right side of the hidden tool panel, as shown in Figure 10.

Viewing Modes in Illustrator

You can use two viewing mode options on the View menu to view artwork: Preview and Outline.

Preview mode is the default setting and displays visible paths, colors, patterns, and gradients the way the artwork will look when it is printed. When you are working in Preview mode, Illustrator redraws the artwork every time you make a change. Depending on your computer, this may take extra time while you are working and slow you down.

Outline mode displays every path that makes up the artwork, including paths that may be hidden. Working in Outline mode may increase how quickly you can work depending on the complexity of your image. Outline mode also makes it easier to work with paths when you are trying to edit a path with the Direct Selection tool or the Scissors tool.

Creating a Character Using Adobe Illustrator

One way of using a tool is to place the pointer where you want to begin drawing, click and drag the tool on the artboard where you want the shape or path segment to end, and then release the mouse. If you place the pointer at a location on the artboard and release the mouse before dragging, a tool options dialog box opens. The tool options dialog box is where you can specify a specific size for the shape or path segment.

Comparing Vector and Bitmap Images

A vector image is created with mathematical calculations and can be enlarged without a loss of quality. A **bitmap** image, technically known as a raster image, is represented by pixels in a grid layout; each pixel contains color information for the image. When you enlarge a bitmap, the quality of the image is lost because the pixels are visible, often resulting in jagged edges, as is shown in Figure 11.

Example of a vector image

Example of a bitmap image

Figure 11 *Comparing a vector and bitmap image*

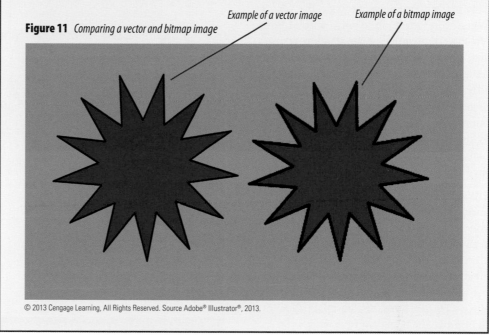

Working with the Selection Tools

Illustrator has three selection tools: the Selection tool, the Direct Selection tool, and the Group Selection tool, explained in more detail in Table 2.

The Selection tool selects the entire object allowing you to move or scale the object. When you select an object, a solid-lined rectangle known as a **bounding box** appears around the selection. If you want to select multiple objects at the same time, you can do so by creating a selection marquee around the objects. A **selection marquee** creates a single bounding box around the selected objects, as shown in Figure 12. To create a selection marquee, click and drag the pointer around the shapes that you want to select.

The Direct Selection tool selects individual anchors and path segments, which allows you to customize a shape or edit a path segment. This tool can be tricky to use, but is a valuable skill to have because it helps you create professional looking graphics. You can use the Direct Selection tool to create custom shapes, custom fonts, or adjust path segments to improve the quality of your work.

Figure 12 *Creating a bounding box*

Bounding box with only the head selected

Bounding box with all objects selected

© 2013 Cengage Learning, All Rights Reserved. Source Adobe® Illustrator®, 2013.

TABLE 2 ILLUSTRATOR SELECTION TOOLS			
Name	**Tool**	**Description**	**Location**
Selection tool		Selects a single object by clicking the object or multiple objects by clicking and dragging a marquee around the objects	Default tool on the Tools panel
Direct Selection tool		Selects individual anchor points or path segments allowing you to delete or alter the selection	Default tool on the Tools panel
Group Selection tool		Selects an object inside a single group, or a single group inside a multiple group, or a set of groups	Found under the Direct Selection tool

© 2013 Cengage Learning, All Rights Reserved. Icons: Source Adobe® Illustrator®, 2013.

Figure 13 shows a path created with the Pencil tool; each hollow square represents an anchor point. The green line with a green dot on the end that extends from an anchor point is called a **direction handle** and is comprised of a direction line and a direction point. The blue line is called a **direction line**. The blue dot at the end of the line is the **direction point**.

You can change the shape of a curve by dragging a direction point. An anchor point with a direction handle is classified as either a smooth point or a corner point. A **smooth point** has two direction lines. When you move one of the direction points, both direction lines move together. A **corner point** may have one, two, or no direction lines. If the corner point has two direction lines, when you move a direction point, it will only adjust the curve on the same side as the direction point being adjusted. When you adjust a direction line, it changes the curve's slope or height. To change the slope of the curve, adjust the angle of the direction line. To change the height of the curve, adjust the length of the direction line. Making the direction line longer, creates a taller curve; making the direction line shorter, creates a shallow curve.

> **QUICK TIP**
>
> If you want to move only one side of a curve on a smooth point, press and hold [Alt] (Win) or [option] (Mac), then drag the direction point.

If the path does not have enough anchor points to customize the shape, you can use the Add Anchor Points command to create a series of anchor points on the path automatically.

Figure 13 *Working with the Direct Selection tool*

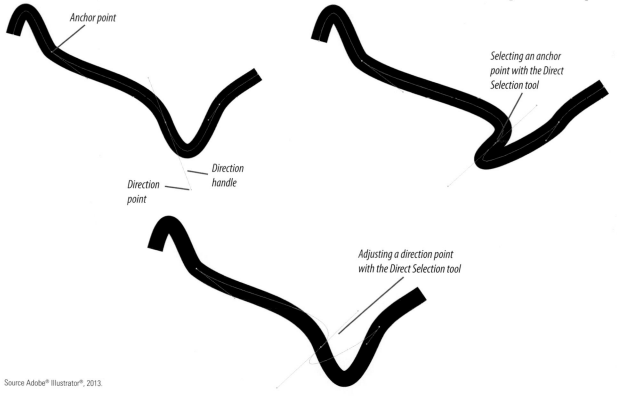

Anchor point

Direction point

Direction handle

Selecting an anchor point with the Direct Selection tool

Adjusting a direction point with the Direct Selection tool

The Add Anchor Points command, located on the Object, Path menu, creates anchor points at the midpoint of each of the already existing anchor points, as shown in Figure 14.

Figure 15 shows how you can use the Direct Selection tool to modify a circle with eight anchor points into a different design. The anchor points at 2 o' clock, 5 o' clock, 7 o' clock, and 11 o' clock are moved to the center of the circle, creating the loop shape.

Exploring the Pathfinder Panel

The Pathfinder panel is another method to combine objects. The Pathfinder panel can create paths, compound paths, and compound shapes. A **compound path** appears in the Layers panel as <Compound Path> and

Figure 14 *Adding anchor points*

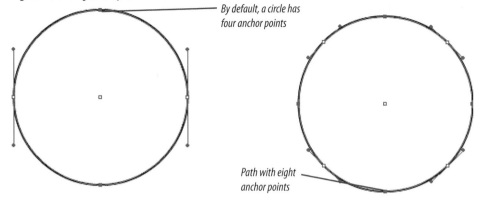

By default, a circle has four anchor points

Path with eight anchor points

© 2013 Cengage Learning, All Rights Reserved. Source Adobe® Illustrator®, 2013.

Figure 15 *Customizing a shape*

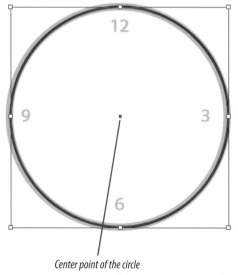

Center point of the circle

© 2013 Cengage Learning, All Rights Reserved. Source Adobe® Illustrator®, 2013.

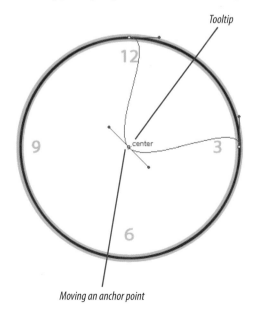

Tooltip

center

Moving an anchor point

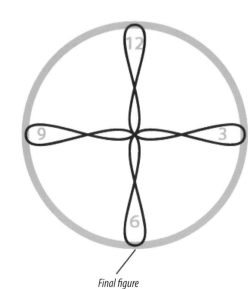

Final figure

Creating a Character Using Adobe Illustrator

is created by two or more paths; a hole appears where the shapes overlap. A **compound shape** is displayed in the Layers panel as <Compound Shape> and is created by two or more objects.

The Pathfinder panel has two rows, as shown in Figure 16. The four options in the top row are known as **shape modes**, which create compound paths. The six options in the bottom row are known as pathfinders. **Pathfinders** create new shapes from overlapping objects. (*Note*: Additional Pathfinder commands can be found on the Effect menu.)

When creating a custom shape, look at the shape you are trying to create and see if you can break it down into basic shapes, as shown in Figure 17.

Working with Color

When you start Illustrator, the default colors are set to a white fill and a black stroke. You can change stroke and fill colors on the Control panel, at the bottom of the Tools panel, or in the Color panel. The Fill color is designated by a solid square of the selected color. The Stroke color is designated by a square with a white fill and a stroke of the selected color.

The Swatches panel displays a color library based on the color mode of the document.

You can find additional Swatch Libraries from the Swatches panel menu and by making a selection from the Open Swatch Library menu.

If you choose to change either the fill or stroke color from the Control panel, click the arrow to the right of the color swatch to open the

Figure 16 *Pathfinder panel*

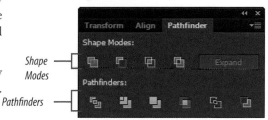

Shape Modes

Pathfinders

Figure 17 *Shape mode and pathfinder examples*

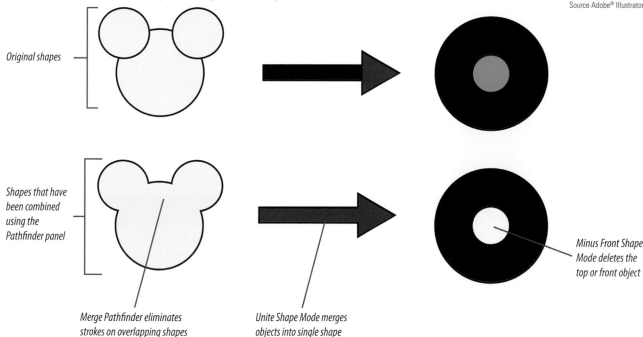

Original shapes

Shapes that have been combined using the Pathfinder panel

Merge Pathfinder eliminates strokes on overlapping shapes

Unite Shape Mode merges objects into single shape

Minus Front Shape Mode deletes the top or front object

default Swatch library, as shown in Figure 18. To change the fill or stroke color on either the Tools panel or the Color panel, double-click the color swatch you want to change. The Color Picker dialog box opens, as shown in Figure 19. To select a color, adjust the arrows on the color spectrum, then move the selection circle in the color field. Finally, you can also change the color by clicking a color in the Swatches panel or in a Swatch library. When you select a color on the Swatches panel, it is important to pay attention to whether the Fill icon or the Stroke icon is in front on the Tools panel or the Color panel. The color of whichever icon is in front will be changed. (*Note*: Once you select a color from a Swatch library, it is automatically added to the Swatches panel.)

Figure 18 *Opening the Swatch library*

Fill color   Stroke color

Click the arrow to open the default swatch library

Source Adobe® Illustrator®, 2013.

Figure 19 *Color Picker dialog box*

New color

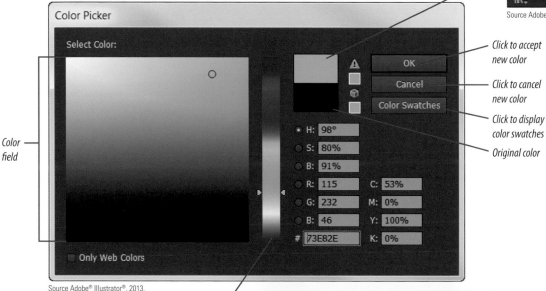

Color field

Color spectrum

Click to accept new color

Click to cancel new color

Click to display color swatches

Original color

Source Adobe® Illustrator®, 2013.

Using Tips When Drawing Shapes

When creating shapes, if you press and hold [Shift] while drawing, you can constrain the shape's proportion. For example, to create a square using the Rectangle tool, press and hold [Shift] while you draw. Similarly, to create a circle, select the Ellipse tool, then press and hold [Shift] while you draw.

To create a shape from the center point, press and hold [Alt] (Win) or [option] (Mac) while you draw the shape; the shape will draw from the center point outward.

Figure 20 *Rectangle dialog box*

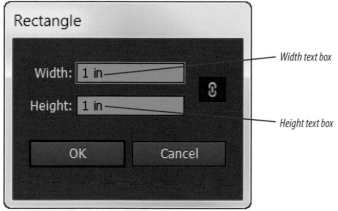

Width text box

Height text box

Use the Illustrator Drawing tools

In this exercise, you will use the various shape tools to trace objects.

1. Open 2D 1-1.ai, then save it as **Illustrator Drawing Practice**.

    TIP Click OK to close the Illustrator Options dialog box.

2. Click the **Fill box** ⬜ on the Control panel, then click the **None button** ⧄.

    These settings create shapes with a stroke and no fill color.

3. Click the **Rectangle tool** ▣ on the Tools panel, place the **pointer** –⁝– over the top-left corner of the square in square #1, then click the **mouse** when the word "anchor" appears.

    The Rectangle dialog box opens.

4. Type **1 in** in the Width text box, type **1 in** in the Height text box, as shown in Figure 20, then click **OK**.

    A rectangle at the same location and size as the one on the template appears on the artboard.

5. Click and hold the **Rectangle tool** ▣ , click the **Ellipse tool** ⬭ , place the **pointer** –⁝– over the center of the ellipse in square 2, press and hold **[Alt]** (Win) or **[option]** (Mac), then drag the **pointer** –⁝– to create an ellipse that is the same size as the one on the template.

    The Ellipse tool is a hidden tool under the Rectangle tool.

6. Click the **Line Segment tool** ⁄ , place the **pointer** –⁝– over the top of the vertical line in square 3, press and hold **[Shift]**, then click and drag the **pointer** –⁝– to create a line the same size as the vertical line on the template.

    (continued)

Pressing and holding [Shift] constrains the Line Segment tool to draw a straight line.

7. Repeat step 6 for the horizontal line in square 3.

8. Click the **Star tool** , place the **pointer** –¦– in the white space above the left side of the star in square 4, then click the **mouse**.

    The Star tool is a hidden tool under the Ellipse tool. The Star dialog box opens.

9. Type **1 in** in the Radius 1 text box, type **.5 in** in the Radius 2 text box, type **11** in the Points text box as shown in Figure 21, then click **OK**.

    A star that is the same size and has the same number of points as the original appears on the artboard. You will adjust the location of the star in the next set of steps.

10. Click the **Polygon tool** , place the **pointer** –¦– over the center of the triangle in square 5, drag the **pointer** –¦–, press the **down arrow key** until the shape has three sides, then drag and rotate the **pointer** –¦– until the triangle is the same size as the triangle on the template.

    The Polygon tool is a hidden tool under the Star tool.

11. Save your work.

Work with the Selection tools

1. Verify that Illustrator Drawing Practice.ai is open.

2. Click the **Selection tool** , then click the **starburst** in square 4 that you created in the previous set of steps, as shown in Figure 22.

(continued)

Figure 21 *Star tool dialog box*

Radius 1 text box
Radius 2 text box
Points text box

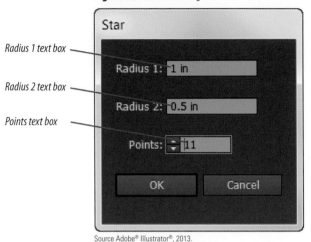

Figure 22 *Making a selection with the Selection tool*

The hollow squares are called bounding box handles

Selected starburst; your location might differ

The red square is called the bounding box

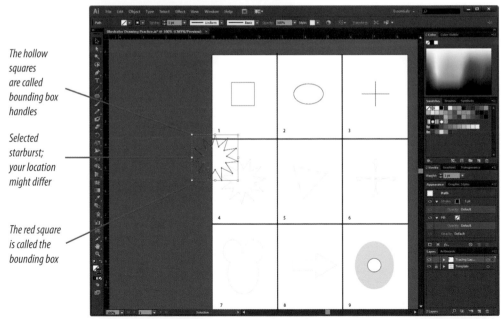

Creating a Character Using Adobe Illustrator

Figure 23 *Aligning the starbursts*

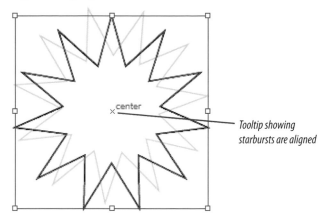

×center

Tooltip showing
starbursts are aligned

Figure 24 *Drawing a circle*

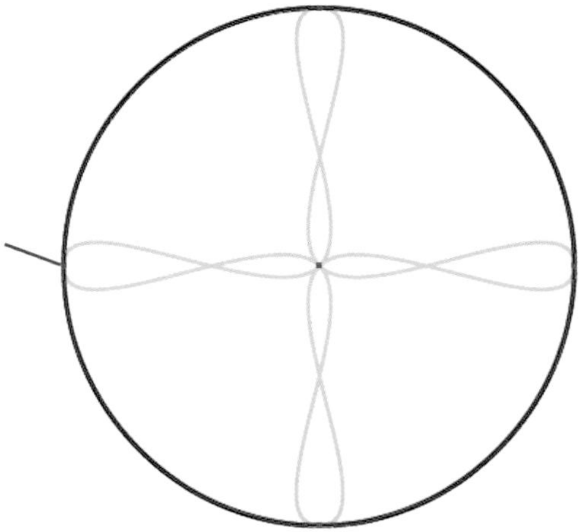

Circle anchor points
should touch all
four outside edges
of the shape

3. Drag the **starburst** over the template until the word "center" appears, as shown in Figure 23.

   Note that the centers are aligned, but the points of the starburst are not.

4. Position the **pointer** over the **outside edge** of a bounding box handle until it changes to a curved **double-headed arrow** , then rotate the shape to line up the starbursts.

TIP After you rotate the shape to the correct position, you can use the arrows on the keyboard to nudge it into place.

5. Click the **Ellipse tool** , place the **pointer** – ¦ – over the center of the graphic in square 6, press and hold **[Alt][Shift]** (Win) or **[option] [Shift]** (Mac), then drag the **pointer** – ¦ – to create the circle shown in Figure 24.

   Pressing and holding [Shift] constrains the proportions of the ellipse to create a perfect circle.

TIP Make sure the circle extends around the shape.

6. With the circle still selected, click **Object** on the Menu bar, point to **Path**, then click **Add Anchor Points**.

   Four additional anchor points are added to the circle in between the original existing anchor points.

(continued)

7. Click the **Direct Selection tool** 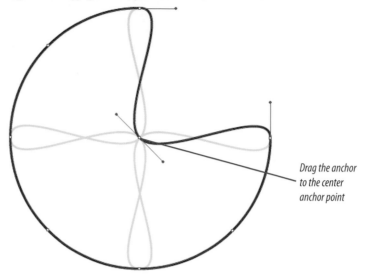, click the **anchor point** near the 2 o'clock position on the circle to select it, then drag the **anchor point** to the center of the circle, as shown in Figure 25.

TIP   If the entire circle moves, press and hold [Ctrl][Z] (Win) or ⌘ [Z] (Mac) to undo, then try again.

8. Repeat step 7 for the anchor points located near the **5, 7**, and **11 o'clock positions**, then deselect the shape, as shown in Figure 26.

9. Save your work.

Work with Shape Modes on the Pathfinders panel

In this exercise, you will create custom shapes using the Shape Modes buttons on the Pathfinder panel.

1. Verify that Illustrator Drawing Practice.ai is open.

2. Click the **Ellipse tool** , place the **pointer** –¦– over the center of the largest ellipse in square 7, press and hold **[Alt]** (Win) or **[option]** (Mac), then drag the **pointer** –¦– to create an ellipse that is the same size as the large one on the template.

TIP   Estimate the center of the largest ellipse, not the shape.

3. Repeat step 2 for the two smaller ellipses. (*Note:* Use the Selection tool as needed to resize the ellipses.)

(continued)

Figure 25 *Dragging an anchor point with the Direct Selection tool*

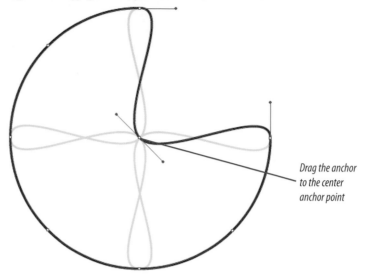

Drag the anchor to the center anchor point

Figure 26 *Completed circle figure*

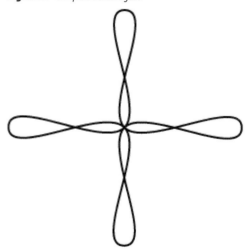

Creating a Character Using Adobe Illustrator

Figure 27 *Completed ellipse figure*

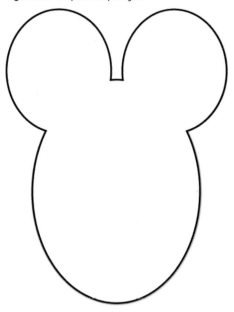

Figure 28 *Drawing a rectangle*

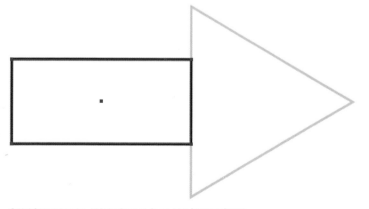

4. Click the **Selection tool** , then draw a **selection marquee** around the three ellipses.

5. Click **Window** on the Menu bar, click **Pathfinder**, then click the **Unite button** on the Shape Modes row.

   The three ellipses merge into a single path, as shown in Figure 27.

6. Save your work.

7. Click the **Rectangle tool** , place the **pointer** – ¦ – over the top-left corner of the rectangle in square 8, then drag the **pointer** – ¦ – to the bottom-right corner of the rectangle, as shown in Figure 28.

8. Click the **Polygon tool** , place the **pointer** – ¦ – over the center of the triangle, then drag and rotate the **pointer** – ¦ – until the triangle is the same size as the triangle on the template.

   Press the down arrow key to modify the polygon to three sides, if necessary.

TIP Use the Selection tool to resize the triangle.

9. Click the **Selection tool** , then draw a **selection marquee** around the two shapes.

10. Click the **Unite button** on the Shape Modes row of the Pathfinder panel.

    The shapes are merged into a single path, creating an arrow.

11. Click the **Ellipse tool** , place the **pointer** – ¦ – over the center of the ellipse in square 9, press and hold **[Alt]** (Win) or **[option]** (Mac), then drag the **pointer** – ¦ – to trace the larger ellipse on the template.

(continued)

12. Repeat step 11 for the smaller ellipse.

13. Click the **Selection tool**, click the **smaller ellipse** if necessary, press and hold **[Shift]**, then click the **larger ellipse**, as shown in Figure 29.

14. Click the **Minus Front button** on the Shape Modes row of the Pathfinder panel.

    The smaller ellipse created a hole in the center of the larger ellipse.

15. With the shape still selected, click the **Fill box** on the Control panel, then click a **light gray swatch**.

16. Save your work.

Work with color

In this exercise, you will add fill and stroke colors to objects.

1. Verify that Illustrator Drawing Practice.ai is open.

2. Click the **Fill box** on the Tools panel.

3. Click the **Selection tool**, click the **square** in square 1, click the **Fill box** on the Control panel, then click a **red swatch** in the Swatches panel.

4. Click the **Selection tool**, click the **ellipse** in square 2, double-click the **Fill box** on the Tools panel, click a **deep shade of red** in the Color Picker dialog box, then click **OK**.

5. Open the **Swatches panel**, click the **Panel menu button**, point to **Open Swatch Library**, then click **Celebration**.

    The Celebration Swatches panel opens.

(continued)

Figure 29 *Both ellipses selected*

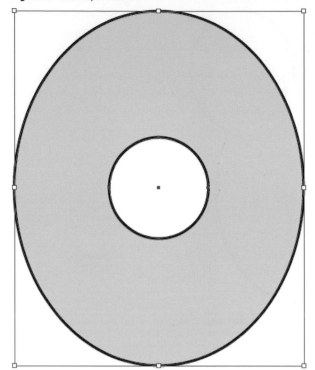

Figure 30 *Sample completed shapes*

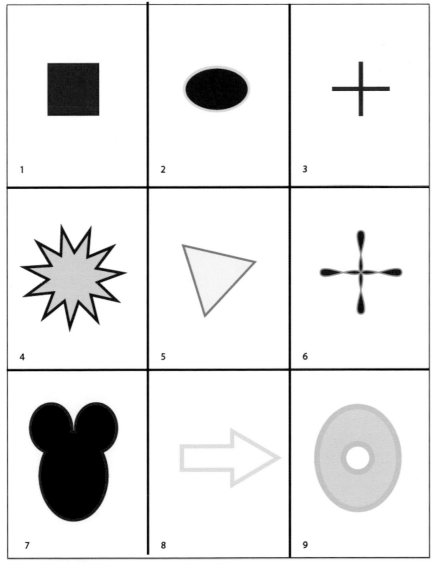

6. Click the **shapes** in squares 4 through 9, then change the fill color using the colors of your choice on the Celebration Swatches panel.

TIP Because the shape in square 3 was made with the Line Segment tool, the fill color will have no effect.

As you use a color, the swatch is added to the Swatches panel.

7. Open the Color panel.

8. Click the **Stroke box** on the Tools panel to make it active.

9. Click the **shapes** in each of the squares, modify each shape's **stroke color** using the colors of your choice from the Celebration Swatches panel, click the **Stroke Weight list arrow**, click a **stroke width**, then compare your shape to Figure 30.

TIP You can modify the stroke weight in either the Control panel or the Stroke panel.

10. Save and close your work.

Master the PEN TOOL

What You'll Do

 In this lesson, you will create straight and curved lines using the Pen tool.

Working with the Pen Tool

The Pen tool can be challenging to use when you first work with it. However, it is likely the most important tool to learn and master. The Pen tool allows you to elevate the appearance and creativity of your vector illustrations and designs.

You can use the Pen tool to create open and closed paths with straight lines and curves, and work with both fill and stroke colors. Each line or curve begins and ends with an anchor point; each click of the mouse will create an anchor point.

QUICK **TIP**

When working with the Pen tool, it is sometimes easier to work with only a stroke color and then add the fill color when you have completed the closed path.

Creating Straight Lines with the Pen Tool

To create a straight line with the Pen tool, click the artboard, move to another location on the artboard, then click a second point. Anchor points created when drawing straight lines are corner points, as you learned about in Lesson 2.

QUICK **TIP**

To create a 90-degree angle from an anchor point, press and hold [Shift], then click the mouse.

To close the shape, place the Pen tool pointer over the first anchor point that you created, then notice a small circle next to the pointer. When you click the mouse, the anchor point closes the path, as shown in Figure 31.

The figures you create with the Pen tool are fully editable even after you complete your illustration. You use the Pen tool to edit paths, just as you can use the Direct Selection tool to edit shapes created with drawing tools.

While drawing with the Pen tool, you can remove any previously created anchor point. When you place the pointer over an anchor point, the pointer changes to a minus sign, as shown in Figure 32. Click the anchor point to delete it. (*Note*: If you delete an anchor point that is in the middle of a path, the remaining points are connected automatically.) Table 3 describes the Pen tool pointer.

If you decide to edit your figure after you have finished drawing it, you can add, delete, and convert the anchor points with the tools in the Pen tool group. These tools behave in

Figure 31 *Closing a figure with the Pen tool*

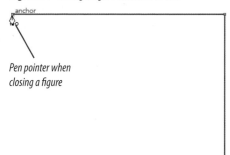
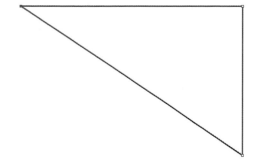

Pen pointer when closing a figure

Figure 32 *Deleting an anchor point*

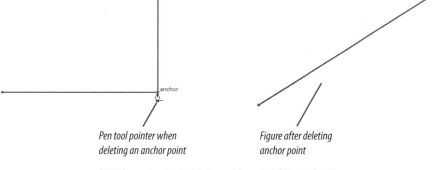

Pen tool pointer when deleting an anchor point

Figure after deleting anchor point

TABLE 3 PEN TOOL POINTERS	
Pointer	**Description**
	Beginning a path
	While creating or editing a path
	Mouse is clicked
	Hover over path section; adds an anchor point to path
	Hover over anchor point; removes anchor point from path
	Hover over beginning point of path to close path
	Hover over endpoint of existing path to continue path
	Hover over end anchor point to remove handle

Note: The crosshair appears when the Caps Lock key is active.

a similar manner as the Pen tool does when you are initially drawing the figure. Refer to Table 4 to learn about the hidden tools under the Pen tool.

Creating Curves with the Pen Tool

To create a curve with the Pen tool, click and hold the mouse, then drag the pointer in any direction. (*Note*: Clicking and dragging the first anchor point creates a direction handle, sets the initial slope of the curve, and creates a smooth anchor point; clicking without dragging creates a corner anchor point. Anchor points created in this manner are smooth points, as you learned in Lesson 2.) When creating a path, the fewer points on the path, the smoother and neater the path will look.

You can remove anchor points as you create your drawing, just as you can do when you create straight lines. In addition, you can press and hold [Alt] (Win) or [option] (Mac) to adjust the length or angle of the handle. The pointer changes to the Convert Anchor Point tool pointer, as shown in Table 4. The direction and length of a handle will affect the shape of the next curve.

When your illustration is complete, you can adjust the anchor points and curves using the Direct Selection tool. In addition, you can move the direction lines to change the angle of curves, as shown in Figure 33. A smooth anchor point displays a direction handle and direction points when selected. If you want

to convert a smooth anchor point to a corner anchor point, select the Convert Anchor Point tool, then click the anchor point. When you click a corner anchor point, it is converted to a smooth anchor point.

The best way to learn the Pen tool and become proficient with it is to practice. You will complete some practice exercises to better familiarize yourself with the Pen tool.

Figure 33 *Adjusting a curve*

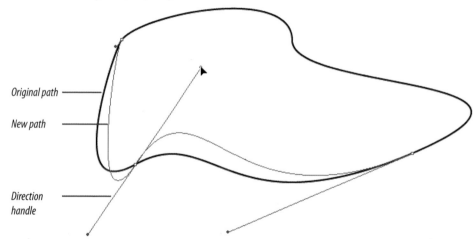

Original path

New path

Direction handle

TABLE 4 TOOLS IN THE PEN TOOL GROUP		
Name	**Tool**	**Description**
Pen tool		Draws straight and curved lines by clicking and creating points
Add Anchor Point tool		Adds additional anchors to an existing path; displays the Pen tool with the plus sign
Delete Anchor Point tool		Removes anchor points from an existing path; displays the Pen tool with the minus sign
Convert Anchor Point tool		Converts an anchor point from an existing path from a corner point to a smooth point or from a smooth point to a corner point

Creating a Character Using Adobe Illustrator

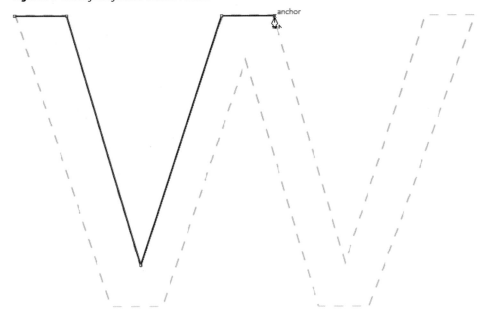

Figure 34 *Creating straight lines with the Pen tool*

anchor

© 2013 Cengage Learning, All Rights Reserved. Source Adobe® Illustrator®, 2013.

Create straight lines with the Pen tool

In this exercise, you will use the Pen tool to trace dashed lines using the red dots as guides to create corner anchor points.

1. Open 2D 1-2.ai, then save it as **Illustrator Pen Practice 1**.

TIP Click OK to close the Illustrator Options dialog box.

2. Set the Fill color to **None**, then set the Stroke color to **black**.

3. Click the **Pen tool** , click the **red dot** next to 1, then click the **red dot** next to 2.

TIP Press and hold [Shift] to constrain the angle to 45 degrees.

4. Click the remaining **red dots** in numerical order, until you reach **5**.

5. Click the **Selection tool** , then deselect the **zigzagged line**.

The Pen tool is no longer active, which allows you to begin a new path with the Pen tool.

6. Click the **Pen tool** , then repeat the process in steps 3 and 4 to trace the **star** in the right corner of the template.

7. When you reach 11, click the **beginning point** to close the path.

8. Click the **Selection tool** , then deselect the **star**.

9. Click the **Pen tool** , then trace the **W** at the bottom of the template, as shown in Figure 34. (*Note:* There are no red dots to help you on this shape.)

10. Save and close your work.

Create curved lines with the Pen tool

In this exercise, you will use the Pen tool to trace dashed lines using red dots and blue squares as a guide to create smooth anchor points.

1. Open 2D 1-3.ai, then save it as **Illustrator Pen Practice 2**.

TIP Click OK to close the Illustrator Options dialog box.

2. Set the Fill color to **None**, then set the Stroke color to **black** if necessary.

3. Click the **Pen tool** , click and hold the **red dot** next to 1 in the circle, drag the **pointer** to the blue square next to 2, then release the mouse.

4. Repeat step 3, dragging the **pointer** from the red dot to the associated blue square until you reach 8.

5. Click and drag the **pointer** from anchor point 1 to the blue square next to 2 to complete the circle.

   The Pen tool pointer contains a small circle when you close the path at 1.

6. Click the **Selection tool** , then deselect the **circle**.

7. Click the **Pen tool** , press and hold **[Shift]**, click and drag the **pointer** from red dot 1 to blue square 2 on the wavy line in the top-right corner of the template, then release the **mouse**.

8. Click and drag the **pointer** from red dot 3 to blue square 4.

   An arc forms between red dot 1 and red dot 3.

9. Repeat steps 7 and 8 for numbers 5–8 to trace the **wavy line**.

10. Click the **Selection tool** , then deselect the **wavy line** as shown in Figure 35.

(continued)

Figure 35 *Sample completed simple curved path*

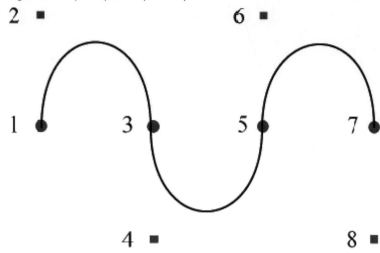

Creating a Character Using Adobe Illustrator

Figure 36 *Selecting a direction handle*

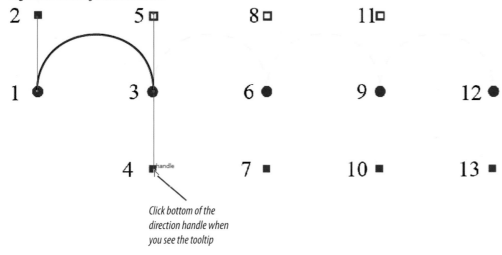

Click bottom of the
direction handle when
you see the tooltip

Figure 37 *Dragging a direction handle*

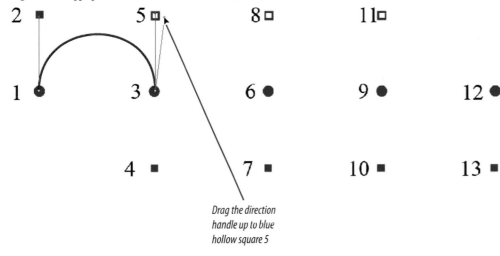

Drag the direction
handle up to blue
hollow square 5

11. Click the **Pen tool** , then click and drag the **pointer** from red dot 1 to blue square 2 on the wavy line in the bottom-left corner of the template.

12. Click and drag the **pointer** from red dot 3 to blue square 4, press and hold **[Alt]** (Win) or **[option]** (Mac), click the **handle** on blue square 4, as shown in Figure 36, drag the **handle** to hollow blue square 5, then compare your screen to Figure 37.

    You adjusted the location of the handle so the next curve will go in the correct direction.

13. Repeat steps 11 and 12 beginning with red dot 3 until you reach blue square 13.

(continued)

14. Click the **Selection tool** 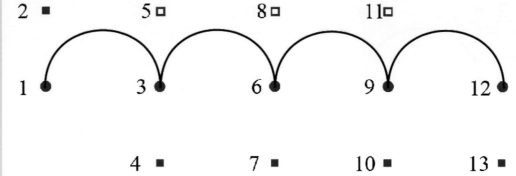, then deselect the **wavy line**, as shown in Figure 38.

15. Click the **Pen tool** , click and drag the **pointer** from red dot 1 to blue square 2, then release the **mouse**.

16. Click **hollow red dot 3**, then release the **mouse**.

17. Click and drag the **anchor point** next to hollow red dot 3 to blue square 4, then release the **mouse**.

(continued)

Figure 38 *Sample completed curved path*

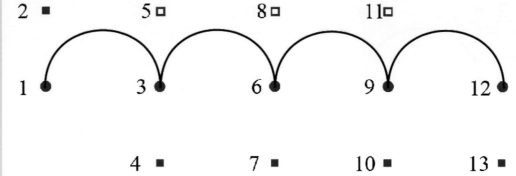

Creating a Character Using Adobe Illustrator

Figure 39 *Sample completed wavy path*

18. Repeat this process starting with hollow red dot 3 until you reach blue square 8.

19. Click the **Selection tool** , then deselect the **wavy lines**, as shown in Figure 39.

20. Save and close your work.

Understand Character DEVELOPMENT

What You'll Do

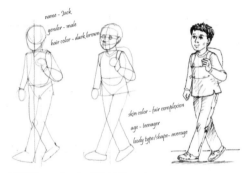

 In this lesson, you will develop a character using the character development process.

Developing a Character

The process of developing a character is referred to as **character development**. It is important when creating a character to identify a name, physical characteristics, personality, and a backstory. The more detail that you can create to describe the character, the easier it will be for you to write for that character.

The character you create will determine the character arc. A **character arc** is the path of growth a character develops as the story is told and follows the flow of the story structure. The arc reveals when a character has learned something. For example, in most stories it was when a character learns to care or learns to have courage. If you manage to create a character that you feel connected with, the character will virtually come to life and help you tell the story. You will begin to know your character's opinions and feelings and learn to write the story with their point of view in mind.

Important traits of a main character include:

- Having a problem that needs to be solved or a need that needs to be met.
- Having the ability to solve a problem whether or not they know they can.
- Usually having a flaw to overcome before they can solve a problem.

If you already have a plot in mind when thinking of a character, consider the following:

- What type of character needs this plot?
- What type of character would have a need the plot's reward would fulfill?
- What type of character would grow by overcoming the obstacle or obstacles?

Begin by deciding whether your character is male or female, their approximate age, and their ethnicity. The reader or the viewer will often make an assumption about your character based on just these three traits. For example, readers might assume that an older character is wise and a young person naïve or reckless, or that someone who drives a convertible sports car is rich or cool. Keep in mind that these assumptions do not have to be actually true for your character. As you begin to consider what your character will look like, draw several sketches, much like brainstorming. Figure 40 shows an example.

Next, create a list of wants or goals for your character. Knowing their wants and goals will help you decide by what means your character addresses obstacles they encounter during the course of the story. This more clearly defines the character to the reader or the viewer.

Include on this list their fears, motivations, and biggest secrets. This helps create a more realistic character and defines how your character will respond as the story progresses.

Creating a list of likes and dislikes also helps you in writing for your character and helping them to become more believable. It is important to keep the list balanced. Think through this list and do not simply create a list of random things just to create a list of likes and dislikes. For example, if you like to stay up late, you most likely do not like to get up early in the morning. An attribute list helps you make decisions for your character as they progress through the story; it may not actually become a part of the story.

A list of quirks or habits, both good and bad, could be added to this list to help create a more interesting character. For example, think of the Kramer character on Seinfeld and how he enters a room. When creating these lists, consider people around you. People you know can inspire mannerisms and features for the characters you develop.

Finally, create a past, or backstory, for your character that may not necessarily be explained within the story you are telling. This is valuable for you as an author to know what the character's past is. Having already thought this out will help you develop interaction between characters, or to further the plot if a moment in the story needs the past to be explained.

Figure 40 *Creating a character*

QUICK TIP

When developing your character, consider the clothes, objects, and props you can use to bring life to your character.

Choosing a Name and Physical Traits for a Character

A character's name can provide a mental picture to the reader or viewer. A name gives clues to not only a character's gender, but their nationality. For example, using the name Miguel instead of Mike may tell us the character is of Hispanic heritage. A name may come from the character's lineage; they may be named after a parent, grandparent, or other relative that forms a character's backstory.

When deciding a character's physical description, consider asking a family member or friend what mental image they have when they only hear the character's name. Developing the character's appearance based on people's perception of the name may guide the character development process.

Consider exaggerating certain features to identify key qualities of the character. For example, if the character is strong you could show their muscles with a lot of definition.

Character exercise

In this exercise, you will create a character based on someone you know.

1. Think of the school bully when you were in elementary school.
2. On a piece of paper, write the **name** of that person.
3. Create a list of their **fears**, **strengths**, **weaknesses**, **positive traits**, and **negative traits**, as shown in Figure 41.
4. Finally, develop a **backstory** for this character.

   As you develop the backstory, also consider including information that would explain the different characteristics you have included on the list.

Figure 41 *Sample character exercise*

Fears:

What is your character's deepest, darkest secret—something he or she would never want anyone to know? How is this apparent in your character's actions or appearance?

Strengths:

What are your character's greatest strengths, and how can you show them in your illustrations or dialogue?

Positive Traits:

What are your character's positive traits, in other words, traits that could contribute to changing the course of the character's life, or contribute to some sort of plot twist in your story?

Negative Traits:

What are your character's negative traits? How will he/she overcome them, or will they result in his/her downfall?

Creating a Character Using Adobe Illustrator

Figure 42 *Sample character sketch*

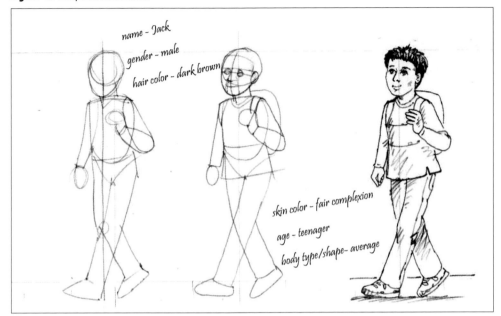

name - Jack

gender - male

hair color - dark brown

skin color - fair complexion

age - teenager

body type/shape - average

Draw a sketch of your character

You will identify physical characteristics and sketch your character.

1. Create a list of characteristics for your character that will help you when you begin sketching, such as gender, hair color, skin color, age, height, body type/shape.

2. Using drawing paper, draw a **sketch** of your character, then compare your sketch to the sample shown in Figure 42.

   You will want to draw multiple sketches to fine-tune your character.

3. Draw **items** that describe the character's backstory.

Review Drawing TIPS

What You'll Do

 In this lesson, you will review some drawing tips.

Drawing a Character Using Different Methods

If you are new to drawing, there are some simple methods you can use to create characters. Keep in mind as you review these methods that you will be able to apply these same methods to other elements in your drawing as well.

One method is to draw from shapes. By starting with simple shapes such as rectangles and ovals, you can work from those shapes to form your character, as shown in Figure 43.

Figure 43 *Example of drawing from shapes*

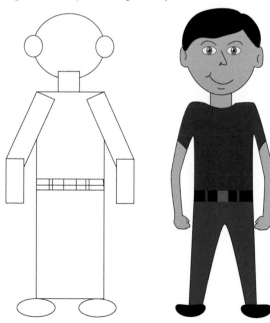

Creating a Character Using Adobe Illustrator

This can be done by adjusting the shape by adding rounded edges with the Convert Anchor Point tool, merging shapes using the Pathfinder panel, or by bending or distorting the shape with the Direct Selection tool.

Another method is drawing a stick figure. As shown in Figure 44, you can add more detail to a stick figure with clothes and props. If you are new to drawing, this is a great way to start, since drawing hands, feet, and body limbs can be difficult. As you become comfortable drawing stick figures, you can begin by adding features to the face and creating different expressions. Once you feel comfortable drawing faces and as you become more skilled, you can build out your stick figure to include limbs. This can be done using tracing paper

Figure 44 *Example stick figure character*

and identifying joints such as knees and elbows. You can then break the body down into rectangles, circles, cylinders, and triangles, as shown in Figure 45.

A third method to try is to draw from a photograph. This can be done by using tracing paper, with drawing paper and a light box, or directly in Illustrator, as shown in the building in Figure 46. This method

Figure 45 *Building out a stick figure*

Figure 46 *Tracing a building from a photograph*

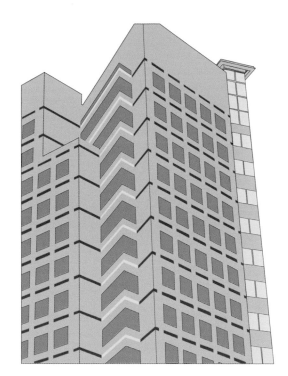

Creating a Character Using Adobe Illustrator

can also be used on people, as shown in Figure 47.

Creating a Character Sheet

Once you are happy with the way your character looks, you need to draw a character sheet. A character sheet is the final step in the character development process. A character sheet can also be referred to as a character board, a model sheet, or a character study.

A character sheet helps the illustrator maintain continuity when drawing his or her characters and should be developed for each character.

Your character sheet will provide you with picture references for your character as your character goes through the story. Therefore,

Figure 47 *Tracing a person from a photograph*

when creating your character sheet, it is a good idea to draw your character from all sides, in different action poses, and detailed close-ups of your character's face. A character sheet should provide enough detail about the character's structure and proportion so that other people can draw it. Figure 48 is an example of a character sheet for Jack from the Jack and the Beanstalk story you are working with in this

Figure 48 *Example character sheet*

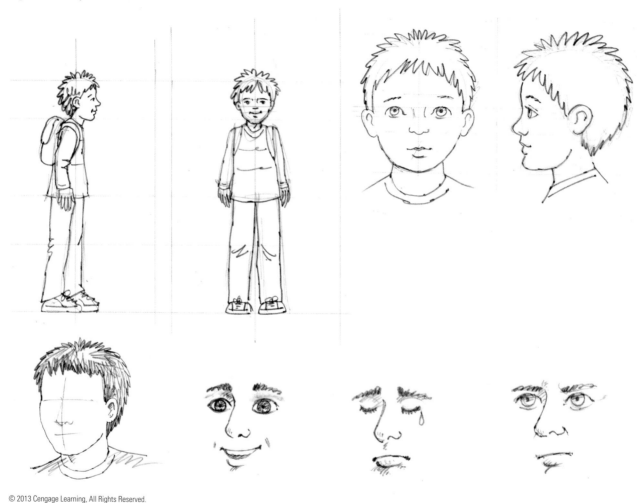

Creating a Character Using Adobe Illustrator

book. Figure 49 shows the character in a variety of poses and from different angles.

Creating a detailed character sheet is analogous to writing a backstory and characteristics for your character during character development.

Remember, the goal of the written character development process is to help you when writing dialogue and scenes for your character. This process will help you keep your character consistent in what it will say and how it will act in a variety of situations. Creating a variety of sketches on the character sheet will help you know how to draw your character as it is progressing through your story and help you to maintain consistency in their appearance in different situations.

Figure 49 *Example character sheet with various poses*

Tracing Scanned IMAGES

What You'll Do

 In this lesson, you will trace a scanned image.

Creating an Original Work

In this example, you are going to use the story of Jack and the Beanstalk to create a new original work, as shown in Figure 50. This story is in the public domain, which means anyone can reuse the story and characters legally. If it was not in the public domain, it would be protected by copyright, and you would need to get permission from the copyright holder to create a derivative work.

Figure 50 *Jack close-up*

A **derivative work** is based on one or more existing works (and previously published). **Public domain** refers to a work that is no longer protected by copyright, or whose intellectual property rights have expired. You will modernize the story by updating the storyline.

Placing the Scanned Image in Illustrator

The Place command, found on the File menu, allows you to import an image in a document. You can select placement options, color, and the maximum level of support for a variety of file formats.

You can choose to create a link to the file or to embed the file into the Illustrator document. Choosing to link a file will keep your file size smaller and allow you to make changes to the original document, which can then be quickly updated using the Link panel. A linked file can be resized and rotated, but individual components of the artwork cannot be edited. Embedding artwork will place the image at full resolution and increase the size of the Illustrator document.

You will use a variety of drawing tools to trace a scanned image in Illustrator. When you use the Place command, found on the File menu, be sure to select the Template check box in

---

Understanding Common Copyright Terms

Copyright terms include copyright, derivative works, and the fair use doctrine. **Intellectual property** refers to creations of the mind and may include copyrights, trademarks, patents, industrial design rights, and trade secrets. **Copyright** is a category of intellectual property law providing protection to the authors of "original works of authorship," including literary, dramatic, musical, artistic, and certain other intellectual works. This protection is available to both published and unpublished works.

The **fair use doctrine** allows copyrighted work to be reproduced for a variety of reasons, including news reporting, teaching, parody, and research. Four factors need to be considered together when determining if the use is fair, and fair use is only determined by the courts. These factors are:

- The purpose and character of the use, including whether such use is of a commercial nature or is for nonprofit educational purposes.
- The nature of the copyrighted work: Is the original primarily factual or fiction published or unpublished?
- The amount and substantiality of the portion used in relation to the copyrighted work as a whole.
- The effect of the use upon the potential market for, or value of, the copyrighted work.

It is important to note that simply recognizing the source of the copyrighted information is not a substitute for getting permission, and except in cases of fair use, you must obtain permission for all protected material you want to use. For additional information about citing sources, visit the Library of Congress website at www.loc.gov, type *citing primary sources* in the search field, and then click GO.

the Place dialog box, as shown in Figure 51. The image is placed on its own layer and appears dimmed and locked, Illustrator automatically creates a new layer where you can draw or trace. (*Note*: You will learn more about layers in Chapter 2.) The template layer will not print.

Tracing the Image with the Pen Tool

You use the Pen skills you practiced earlier to trace a line art drawing that has already been scanned into the computer. The Pen tool allows you to trace the image with precise lines and curves. Keep in mind, though, that it is easier to trace an image if you set a stroke color but no fill.

As you work through your tracing, it is important for you to remember to close paths as you work so that you can easily apply your fill color later. Keep in mind you will be able to fine-tune your traced image with the Direct Selection tool and the Convert Anchor Point tool when you are done. You may find it is easier to go back and fine-tune your image after your initial trace, rather than trying to trace the artwork perfectly the first time.

QUICK TIP

To improve the quality of a scan, trace the sketch with a drawing pen or a fine-tip black marker and erase any stray pencil marks before scanning.

Figure 51 *Place dialog box*

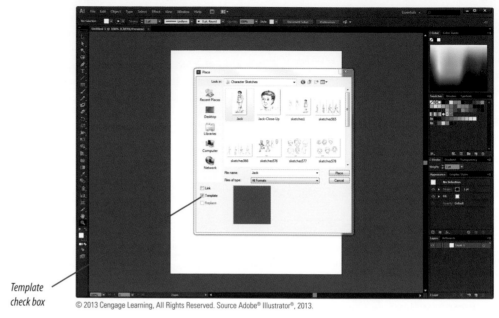

Template check box

Scanning an Image

Place your image on the scanner in the position you want it to appear in your document, then scan the image using the Black & White mode with the resolution set to 300 dpi. Rotating the image in the application after scanning can reduce the quality of the scan. Preview the image and select the area of the line art before scanning to remove any excess white space. Finally, save the scan as a TIF file to the desired folder.

Figure 52 *Settings for New Document dialog box*

Name set to Jack

Size set to Letter

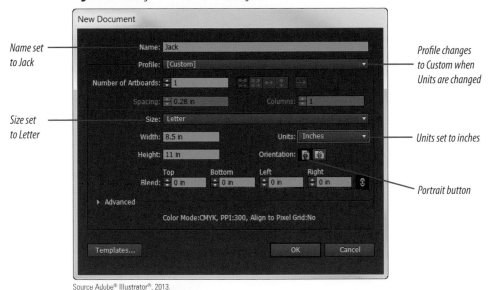

Profile changes to Custom when Units are changed

Units set to inches

Portrait button

Figure 53 *Image placed in document*

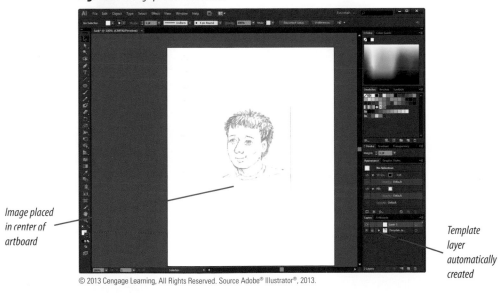

Image placed in center of artboard

Template layer automatically created

Place a scanned image in Illustrator

In this exercise, you will place a scanned image into Illustrator.

1. Click **File** on the Menu bar, then click **New**.

   The New Document dialog box opens.

2. Type **Jack** in the Name text box, click the **Units list arrow**, then click **Inches**.

3. Select **Print** from the Profile menu.

4. Click the **Size list arrow**, click **Letter**, click the **Portrait button**, then compare your screen to Figure 52.

5. Click **OK** to close the New Document dialog box.

6. Click **File** on the Menu bar, then click **Place**.

   The Place dialog box opens.

7. Click the **Template check box**.

8. Navigate to where you store your Data Files, click **Jack.tif**, then click **Place** and deselect Jack.

   The scanned image is centered in the document, as shown in Figure 53.

9. Save your work.

(continued)

Trace a scanned image with the Pen tool

In this exercise, you will trace a scanned image with the Pen tool.

1. Open the Color panel, click the **Fill box** on the Tools panel, click the **None button** on the Colors panel, click the **Stroke box** on the Tools panel, then click **black**.

2. Click the **Pen tool**, then trace **Jack**.

TIP Be sure and close the paths for each feature you traced.

3. When you have completed your tracing, select each closed path and choose a fill color of your choice to color Jack, as shown in the sample in Figure 54.

TIP You may need to rearrange your paths when you add a fill color, right-click on the path and choose Arrange.

4. Save and close your work, then exit Illustrator.

Figure 54 *Sample traced image*

Creating a Character Using Adobe Illustrator

Now that you have learned how to use drawing tools in Illustrator you will have the opportunity to create your own character.

Using what you have learned in this chapter, create the following illustration.

1. Create a new Illustrator document named **Character Practice SB1**.
2. Use at least one of the suggested drawing methods from Lesson 5 to create your own character.
3. Compare your character to the sample shown in Figure 55. (*Hint*: The sample was created by tracing a photo.)
4. Save and close your work.

Figure 55 *Sample Completed Skill Builder 1*

Creating a Character Using Adobe Illustrator

Using the skills you learned in this chapter, place an image and then trace the drawing in a new document.

1. Create a new Illustrator document titled **Jack SB2**.
2. Place the file 2D1-SB2.tif in the document as a template. (*Hint*: Remember to select Template in the Place dialog box.)
3. Trace Jack, creating layers as you work. Compare your drawing to the sample shown in Figure 56. (*Hint*: You will be able to use this drawing later in the comic book.)
4. Add color to complete your illustration.
5. Save and close your work.

Figure 56 *Sample Completed Skill Builder 2*

Choose a story in the public domain on which to create your own original work.

1. Visit the World of Tales website for story ideas at *http://worldoftales.com*.
2. Write a character analysis named **Portfolio Project-Character Analysis** for each of the main characters, as shown in the sample in Figure 57, and sketch your characters.
3. Create cover art for your story.

Figure 57 *Sample Completed Portfolio Project*

Jack and the Beanstalk

Jack

- Teenage boy who carries a backpack.
- Dark hair and big eyes.
- Has a baseball players build.
- He is a positive/optimistic person who always thinks things are going to work out.
- His Dad died about a year ago and his Mom has been taking it very hard. It's just him and his Mom; they have no other family that he is aware of. He tries to stay positive for his Mom.

Jack's Mom

- Women in her early 30s.
- Her eyes look tired and weary.
- Dark hair.
- Thin, clothes look a little bit like she has lost weight.
- Her husband died of cancer about a year ago. She has a lot of bills to pay and is working two jobs.
- She has a teenage son who is 15 and looks like his father when they met.
- She married Jack's Dad when they were both 17, against the approval of Jack's parents. Jack's parents were rich and her parents were poor. His parents disowned Jack's father because they wanted never wanted them to get married. Her parents died when Jack was a baby in a tragic car accident.

Con Man

- The con man is really a mystic or "truth slayer".
- Tall, bald, dark glasses.
- He keeps Jack from going to the pawn shop to sell his mother's ring.
- He helps Jack learn the story of his rich grandfather by giving him some "magic beans" in exchange for his mother's wedding ring.

Jack's Grandfather

- Man in his mid-50s with some gray in his hair.
- Looks like an older version of Jack's father.
- Sadness in his eyes.
- Dresses in expensive looking suits and shoes.

CHAPTER **2** CREATING A COMIC BOOK USING
ADOBE ILLUSTRATOR

1. Develop a story
2. Work with artboards and layers
3. Advanced drawing techniques
4. Work with text

CHAPTER **2**

CREATING A COMIC BOOK USING
ADOBE ILLUSTRATOR

Now that you have reviewed and practiced character development, it is time for you to work on developing your story.

In this chapter, you will work with Illustrator tools to create vector drawings and trace scanned images, but first you will begin by developing your story and making a storyboard. You will also practice working with layers, multiple artboards, the painting tools, symbols, and text to develop your own comic book.

You will also work on a story based on the story of Jack and the Beanstalk. The story and drawings for Jack and the Beanstalk have been modernized to present day.

QUICK **TIP**

If you are not familiar with Jack and the Beanstalk, review the story on the Internet.

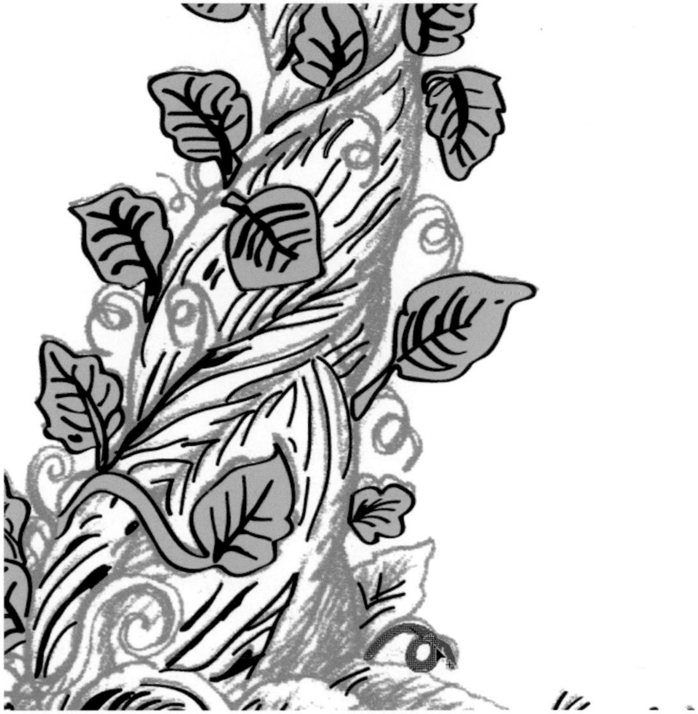

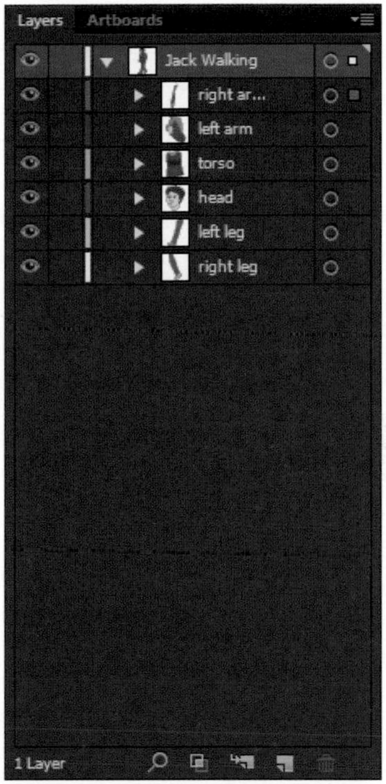

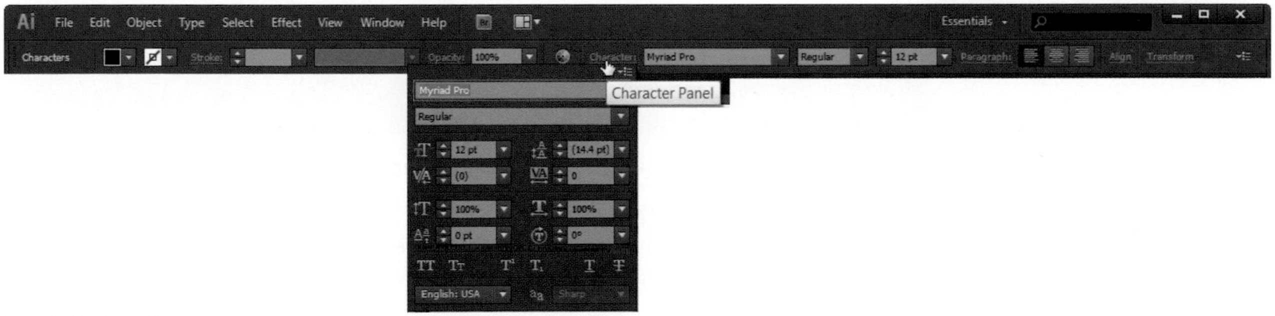

Develop
A STORY

What You'll Do

Jack and the Beanstalk - Story Development

Panel #	Panel Description	Camera Angle	Dialogue
1.	Jack's Mom is sitting at the dining room table going through a stack of bills that seem to be never ending. Panel inset – desk with papers	Long-Shot Inset – close-up	none
2.	She picks up a picture of her dead husband.	Over-the-shoulder	none
3.	Jack comes home from school to find his mother sitting at the dining room table with a stack of bills and looking at a picture of his dead father.	Long-Shot	none
4.	Jack walks over to his mom and asks if everything is alright.	Two-shot	Jack – Mom, what's wrong? Are you all-right?
5.	His mom tells him things are getting pretty bad and it looks like they are going to lose their home.	Close-up	Mom – We have so many bills. I can't get caught up with the payments. I think we are going to lose our home.
6.	His mom than looks at the ring on her finger and tells Jack she needs him to go to the Pawn Shop and sell her wedding band. She explains that it is platinum and he should be able to get a couple of thousand dollars for it.	Close-up	Mom – Jack, you need to go to the Pawn Shop and sell my ring. You should be able to get a couple of thousand dollars for it.
7.	Jack takes the ring and we see him walking down the street to the Pawn Shop.	Long-shot	none
8.	Near the Pawn Shop is a man standing with a table in front of him. He is selling some sort of items.	Medium-shot	none
9.	The man calls Jack over and tells him the Pawn Shop is closed and won't be open until tomorrow. He can help him.	Close-up	Con-Man – Hey son, the Pawn Shop is closed. Can I help you?
10.	Jack explains that he has his mother's ring and needs to sell it for a least a couple of thousand dollars.	Two-shot	Jack – I need to sell my Mom's ring and get at least a couple of thousand dollars for it.
11.	The man tells him he has something worth far more than that. He holds up a cloth bag and offers him a trade.	Medium-shot	Con-Man – This is worth a lot more than a couple of

© 2013 Cengage Learning, All Rights Reserved.

 In this lesson, you will learn the process of developing a story.

Developing a Story

When you develop a story, it is important to consider that a good story should have a reason to be told. It is set up well at the beginning and flows nicely into a resolution. When developing your own story, remember that the reader, or viewer if it is an animation, may not be acquainted with your character. If your character is original, be sure to familiarize readers with the character so they will become invested in wanting to hear the character's story. If you are using an established character, you can jump right into the story. Because Jack of Jack and the Beanstalk is an established character for most people, you will only need to provide a short backstory to modernize it.

Every story needs to have a beginning, middle, and an end. The beginning of the story, also referred to as the **set-up**, should introduce the following elements:

- Character's goal or goals
- Settings
- Situation or conflict

The **middle** of the story shows the development of the story through a sequence of obstacles, which ultimately lead to a climax. The end of the story is comprised of the climax and the resolution. The **climax** involves the final conflict that addresses your character's goals. The **resolution** ties up any loose ends of your story and usually ends the story quickly. It will be difficult to keep the reader's attention after the climax has occurred because the tension,

Consider Simplifying Your Story

When writing a story, consider simplifying it to make it easier for a reader to follow and for you to draw.

- Plan the time, action, and place
- Reduce characters to the bare minimum needed to tell the story
- Keep settings to the absolute minimum needed to make the story work
- Eliminate all subplots

which was developed during the middle of your story, disappears quickly.

You can track a story by introducing several timelines. One timeline shows the readers what they will see in the story and should include the essential actions and character development. You should also create a timeline for you to use as a backstory for each character. A backstory provides details about where their life has been and where it will be going, making it easier to write what the character will do in certain circumstances. (*Note*: Backstories help you to write a more realistic story.)

You begin by dividing a blank page into panels for your story, as shown in Figure 1. Using your timelines as a guide, fill in the panels with descriptions or sketches of the action that should be visible, the dialogue to be displayed in the panel, and the camera angles you intend to use. (*Note*: Try not to place too many words into a single panel.) The drawings, direction, and dialogue are called a **storyboard**, which is a series of pictures used to show a story in a sequence. You should always use storyboards when making movies, cartoons, and picture books. A comic strip or comic book is very similar to a storyboard, but will include more detailed drawings than you may use in a storyboard.

In this chapter, you will write a comic book. Writing your own comic book is a good way to learn the necessary skills to write an effective storyboard, as well as practice the art of storytelling. You can see the same basic elements used in composing a storyboard in the panels of a comic book. One basic element is the **camera angle**, the way the panel's layout is composed. You use a camera angle to change the composition of the panel to display different views: close-up, medium shot, long shot, two shot, over-the-shoulder shot, and a birds-eye view. See Table 1 for

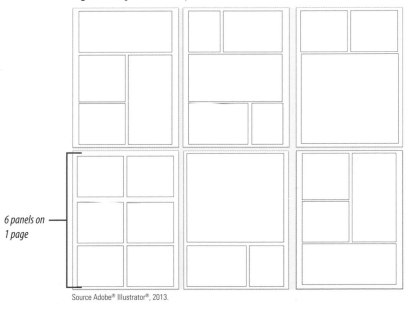

Figure 1 *Pages divided into panels*

6 panels on 1 page

Source Adobe® Illustrator®, 2013.

TABLE 1 CAMERA ANGLES	
Type of Shot	**Description**
Close-up	The subject of the panel takes up the whole frame
Medium shot	Part of the subject is shown in more detail while giving the impression of the whole scene
Long shot	An entire scene is shown; the subject is shown in a setting
Two shot	The panel displays two people
Over-the-shoulder	Looking from behind a person at the subject
Birds-eye view	The panel is shown from above

explanations of these terms. Using different camera angles conveys the illusion of action, since there is no actual movement in a comic. In addition, using different camera angles can keep a panel fresh and inviting. The sample pages from a comic book in Figure 2 display some examples of different camera angles.

Figure 2 *Examples of camera angles*

Medium shot

Over-the-shoulder

Long shot

Medium shot

Two shot close-up

© 2013 Cengage Learning, All Rights Reserved.

Figure 3 *Sample story timeline*

Jack and the Beanstalk – Story Development

- Jack's Mom is sitting at the dining room table going through a stack of bills that seem to be never ending.
- Panel inset – desk with papers.
- She picks up a picture of her dead husband.
- Jack comes home from school to find his mother sitting at the dining room table with a stack of bills and looking at a picture of his dead father.
- Jack walks over to his mom and asks if everything is alright.
- His mom tells him things are getting pretty bad and it looks like they are going to lose their home.
- His mom then looks at the ring on her finger and tells Jack she needs him to go to the Pawn Shop and sell her wedding band. She explains that it is platinum and he should be able to get a couple of thousand dollars for it.
- Jack takes the ring and we see him walking down the street to the Pawn Shop.
- Near the Pawn Shop is a man standing with a table in front of him. He is selling all sorts of items.
- The man calls Jack over and tells him the Pawn Shop is closed and won't be open until tomorrow. He can help him.
- Jack explains that he has his mother's ring and needs to sell it for a least a couple thousand dollars.
- The man tells him he has something worth far more than that. He holds up a cloth bag and offers him a trade.
- Close-up of Jack looking skeptical.
- We see Jack looking at the Pawn Shop with a closed sign on it, gone for the day.
- He trades the ring for the cloth bag and begins to walk away. Close-up of hands trading items.
- He glances back over his shoulder to look at the man and he and the table are gone.
- (Same backdrop as Panel #7, only difference is that Jack is looking over his shoulder/)
- He gets home and finds his mom in the kitchen and tells his mom the pawn shop was closed but a man traded him this cloth bag for the ring. It is supposed to be more valuable than the ring.
- His mother takes the cloth bag and pours the contents out on the table.
- We see a close up of the bag and its poured contents, several beans.
- His mother takes the beans and throws them out the kitchen window.
- Close-up on Jack who has a sad expression on his face and a tear coming out of his left eye.
- The next morning, Jack gets up and goes in the kitchen to find a note, his mom will be back by lunch.

Develop a story idea

In these steps, you will begin to develop ideas for your own story by answering some questions.

1. Open a word processor or use the Text tool in Illustrator to open a new file and save it as **Story Idea**.
2. Who is your main character and what is he or she like?
3. What challenge or problem will your character solve?
4. What is motivating your character to solve the challenge?
5. Where and when does the story take place?

   This is referred to as the setting.
6. What obstacles stand in their way?
7. How do they finally solve the challenge?

   The most interesting or intense part of the story is known as the climax.
8. What is the outcome of the story?
9. Create a timeline for the story, as shown in Figure 3.

   The timeline outlines what the readers will see in the story, including the action that must occur, and character development.
10. Create a timeline for each character.

    The timeline should outline the life of the character and how his or her background influences where he or she is going in the story.
11. Save and close your work.

Outline the story idea

In these steps, you will begin to outline your story in panels, describing the panel, camera angle, and dialogue.

1. Open a word processor or use the Text tool in Illustrator to open a new file and save it as **Story Outline**.

2. Use the timelines as guides to break down your story into components.

3. Using Figure 4 as a guide, create a table, numbering each component of your story as it will appear in the panels.

   Each number corresponds to a panel in the next set of steps.

4. In the Panel Description column, describe the action.

   The description includes characters, conversation, and setting.

5. Identify the camera angles that will be used in the Camera Angle column.

6. Type or write the dialogue for the speaker in the Dialogue column.

7. Save and close your work.

Draw the story in panels

In these steps, you will draw the story into panels.

1. On a piece of paper, divide the page into panels.

   You can draw each panel on a separate sheet of paper, or create panels that mimic comic book panels.

2. Use the outline as a guide to draw each of the panels, as shown in Figure 5.

(continued)

Creating a Comic Book Using Adobe Illustrator

Figure 4 *Sample story outline*

Jack and the Beanstalk - Story Development

Panel #	Panel Description	Camera Angle	Dialogue
1.	Jack's Mom is sitting at the dining room table going through a stack of bills that seem to be never ending. Panel inset – desk with papers	Long shot Inset – close-up	none
2.	She picks up a picture of her dead husband.	Over-the-shoulder	none
3.	Jack comes home from school to find his mother sitting at the dining room table with a stack of bills and looking at a picture of his dead father.	Long shot	none
4.	Jack walks over to his mom and asks if everything is alright.	Two shot	**Jack** – Mom, what's wrong? Are you all right?
5.	His mom tells him things are getting pretty bad and it looks like they are going to lose their home.	Close-up	**Mom** – We have so many bills. I can't get caught up with the payments. I think we are going to lose our home.
6.	His mom than looks at the ring on her finger and tells Jack she needs him to go to the Pawn Shop and sell her wedding band. She explains that it is platinum and he should be able to get a couple of thousand dollars for it.	Close-up	**Mom** – Jack, you need to go to the Pawn Shop and sell my ring. You should be able to get a couple of thousand dollars for it.
7.	Jack takes the ring and we see him walking down the street to the Pawn Shop.	Long shot	none
8.	Near the Pawn Shop is a man standing with a table in front of him. He is selling some sort of items.	Medium shot	none
9.	The man calls Jack over and tells him the Pawn Shop is closed and won't be open until tomorrow. He can help him.	Close-up	**Con-Man** – Hey son, the Pawn Shop is closed. Can I help you?
10.	Jack explains that he has his mother's ring and needs to sell it for a least a couple of thousand dollars.	Two shot	**Jack** – I need to sell my Mom's ring and get at least a couple of thousand dollars for it.
11.	The man tells him he has something worth far more than that. He holds up a cloth bag and offers him a trade.	Medium shot	**Con-Man** – This is worth a lot more than a couple of thousand dollars. Want to trade?

Figure 5 *Sample panel drawings*

Figure 6 *Photoshop scan using WIA dialog box*

3. Write dialogue off to the side.

   Keeping the dialogue in a separate area makes it easier to trace the scanned images. You can add the dialogue in a later lesson.

4. Scan the panel drawings as a grayscale drawing with the PNG file format.

   The drawings are ready to trace into an Illustrator document. (*Note:* You can use the drawings in the Portfolio Project at the end of the chapter.)

TIP You may want to ink your drawings before scanning to create a better image of your drawing.

Scanning an Image

You can scan images using Photoshop by selecting the WIA Support command on the File, Import menu. When scanning an image, it is important to consider the options available so that you can select the best settings for your intended use. The Scan using WIA dialog box includes options for adjusting the resolution, color mode, and size of the scanned image, as shown in Figure 6. When scanning line art that you will trace in Illustrator, selecting either the grayscale picture, black-and-white picture, or text option will give you a better scan of the drawing.

The scanned image opens directly in Photoshop as a bitmap image. After you have finished scanning the drawing, you will need to save it so that you can place the file in Illustrator for tracing. The PNG file format is a good saving option, as it provides good quality without creating a large file size.

(*Note*: If you are using a Mac, you will need to add WIA support. An optional plug-in is available for download from www.adobe.com. Adobe recommends that you install and use the optional plug-in with the Rosetta OS. Alternatively, you can use the software provided with your scanner or another scanning application, and then save the image to the PNG file format.)

Work with Artboards
AND LAYERS

What You'll Do

 In this lesson, you will work with layers and artboards.

Working with Template Layers

When placing a file, you can create a template layer by selecting the Template check box in the Place dialog box, as shown in Figure 7. When you place the image, the new Template layer is automatically dimmed to 50% and locked on the Layers panel. The dimmed image makes it easier to see the new paths when you trace over the template. You can hide the Template layer while you are working.

Figure 7 *Place dialog box*

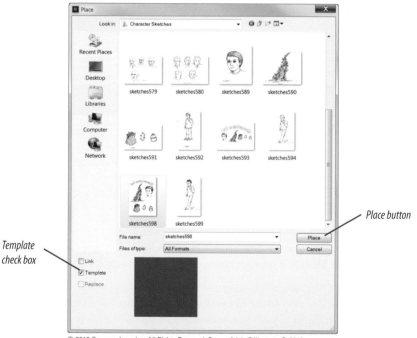

Creating a Comic Book Using Adobe Illustrator

You can convert a layer to a template after you place an image by double-clicking the layer, and then clicking the Template check box in the Layer Options dialog box, or by clicking the Panel menu button, and then clicking Template.

Working with Layers

You probably found it challenging to trace Jack's face in Chapter 1. In this lesson, you will learn to work with layers to make your work easier. You can hide or lock layers while you work, making it easier to trace and color the artwork you are working on. It is a good idea to separate components of your artwork onto separate layers. You can rearrange your layout much more easily to improve the design and copy elements of your artwork for use in other panels instead of having to retrace them.

By default, each new Illustrator document has a single layer, named Layer 1. When you draw on a layer, a series of sublayers is created that make up your drawing. To view sublayers, click the expansion triangle on a layer to expand the layer. (*Note:* You can create a new layer by clicking the New Layer icon located at the bottom of the Layers panel.)

The order of layers and sublayers, on the Layers panel determines the arrangement of items on the artboard, known as the **stacking order**. Items at the top of the stacking order appear in front of other objects on the artboard, and those at the bottom of the stacking order appear in the back. You can change the stacking order by dragging a layer to a new location in the Layers panel.

If you want to rearrange sublayers, you can also drag layers to reorder them or you can use an Arrange command. You will need to first select the object before you can apply the arrange command. You can then access Arrange commands by either right-clicking the object or clicking Object on the Menu bar, pointing to Arrange, and then clicking a command.

Separating the components of your drawing onto separate layers has many advantages, such as making it easy to rearrange the stacking order or changing the layout of your image to improve its composition. For example, in Figure 8, two variations of the

Figure 8 *Layers panel*

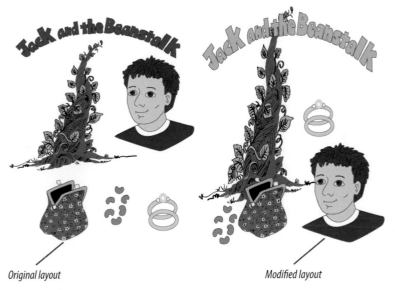

Original layout   *Modified layout*

cover for Jack and the Beanstalk are displayed. Since each object is placed on its own layer, it is much easier to select each object individually and modify the layout. If you want to change the layout, click the target icon to select all the objects on the layer, and then move the selection using the Selection tool. The **target icon** is the hollow circle to the right of the layer's name.

You can separate your artwork onto different layers after you have drawn the image, or you can choose to create new layers as you work. Either way is fine.

When you create layers as you draw, it is a good practice to lock the layers you are not working on. Locking the other layers will keep you from accidentally selecting an item on a different layer. You can lock a layer by clicking the Toggles Lock icon in the Edit column of the Layers panel, shown in Figure 9.

To move different components of the artwork to a new layer, select the objects you want to move, create a new layer, then drag the objects to the new layer.

The colored square in the selection column of the Layers panel is referred to as the **selected art indicator**. This indicates whether any items are selected on the layer. (*Note*: The

selection column is to the right of the target icon.) To move an object from one layer to another, click the selected art indicator and then drag it to the new layer.

The color of the layer on the Layers panel determines the color of the anchor points, paths, bounding boxes, and selected art when an item is selected, as shown in

Figure 9 *Viewing locked layers*

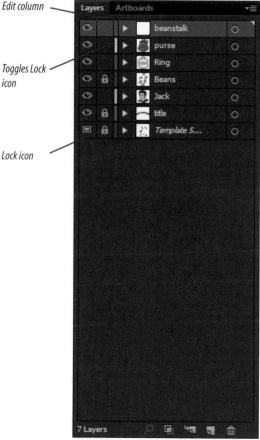

Figure 10. (*Note*: You can change the color of a selected art indicator in the Layers Options dialog box.)

Organizing Layers

Because the Layers panel displays all the layers in an Illustrator document, it can become confusing when working with many characters and multiple artboards. Unlike other Adobe programs, Illustrator does not have the option to organize layers into folders, but you can organize layers using other features: Collect in New Layer, Group, or Merge Selected. The Collect in New Layer command works much differently than the Group command or the Merge Selected command. You need to be aware of how each works so that you select the appropriate command.

Figure 10 *Color of selections*

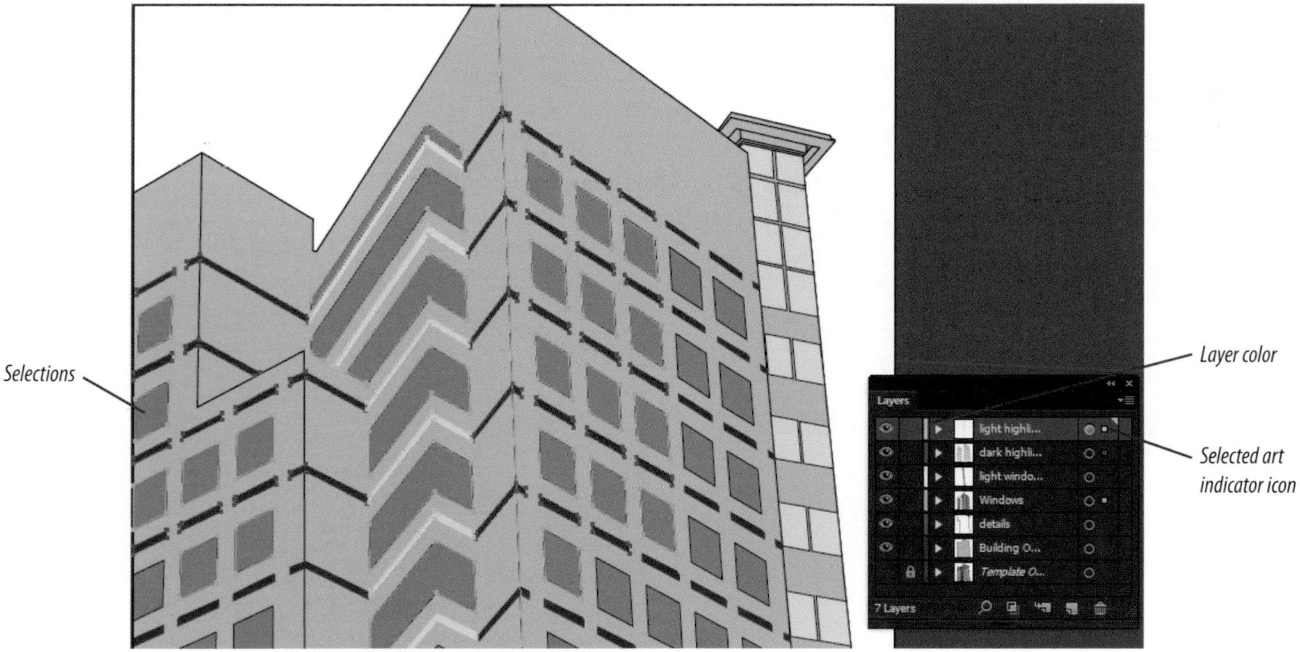

Selections

Layer color

Selected art indicator icon

© 2013 Cengage Learning, All Rights Reserved. Source Adobe® Illustrator®, 2013.

You can collect multiple layers into a single layer by selecting the desired layers, and then clicking the Collect in New Layer command on the Layers panel menu. The layers and sublayers appear intact as part of the new layer, as shown in Figure 11. You then will only need to name the new layer.

The Group command, found on the Object menu, moves all of the objects to the uppermost layer in the selection, maintaining the name of that layer. The now empty layers, from which the objects were moved, still appear on the Layers panel, as shown in Figure 12.

The Merge Selected command, found on the Layers panel menu, merges the contents of selected layers or sublayers to the last layer you clicked when you selected the layers to merge. The name of the last selected layer is retained, while the other selected layer names

Figure 11 *Results of the Collect in New Layer command*

New layer created by the Collect in New Layer command

Layers collected into new layer

Figure 12 *Results of applying the Group command*

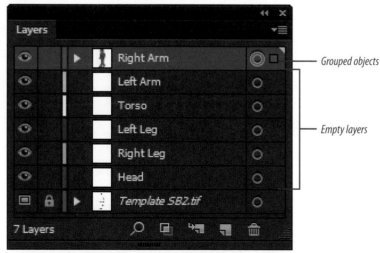

Grouped objects

Empty layers

Creating a Comic Book Using Adobe Illustrator

are removed. The objects in the other selected layers become sublayers in the merged layer, as shown in Figure 13.

Working with Multiple Artboards

An artboard displays the printable artwork. Working with multiple artboards allows you to create all of the pages of your comic book in one document, helping to speed up your workflow, and making it easier to print your comic book. You can create up to 100 artboards of various sizes.

You can designate the number of artboards in the New Document dialog box when you first create a document, or you can add additional artboards later by using the Document Setup dialog box. When you create an Illustrator document with multiple artboards, it is important to keep in mind that the size and any advanced options you may select will be applied to all the artboards. (*Note*: You can modify the size and placement of the artboards while you work on the document.)

You can specify the arrangement and spacing of multiple artboards in your document. You can choose to set up your artboards so they flow left-to-right, which you may find appropriate when writing a storyboard. You could also choose to arrange the artboards so they are stacked vertically, which may be more appropriate for a storybook layout. See Table 2 for more information on these options.

Figure 13 *Results of applying the Merge Selected command*

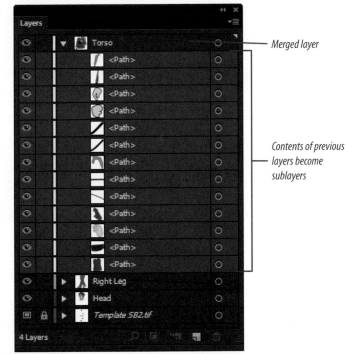

Merged layer

Contents of previous layers become sublayers

	TABLE 2 ARTBOARD LAYOUT OPTIONS	
Icon	**Option**	**Description**
	Grid By Row	Artboards arranged by the number of rows indicated
	Grid By Column	Artboards arranged by the number of columns indicated
	Arrange By Row	Artboards arranged in a single row so they flow from left-to-right
	Arrange By Column	Artboards arranged in a single column so they flow vertically
	Change To Right-To-Left Layout	Displays the artboards from right-to-left in the arrangement that has already been selected from the above options

Managing Artboards

You can use the Artboards panel to rearrange, add, and delete artboards. The Artboards panel is located in the same panel group with the Layers panel, as shown in Figure 14, or you can open it by selecting Artboards on the Window menu.

You can use the up and down arrows at the bottom of the panel to rearrange the order of artboards in the Layers panel. However, to change the layout order of the artboards, you must switch to Edit Artboards mode. To add or delete an artboard, click the New Artboard button or the Delete Artboard button, respectively. Keep in mind that changing the order of the artboards on the Layers panel does not change the order of the artboards in the document window.

Customizing the name of an artboard is another way to help you to organize your document. You can rename an artboard either in Edit Artboard mode or in the Artboards Options dialog box.

Figure 14 *Artboards panel*

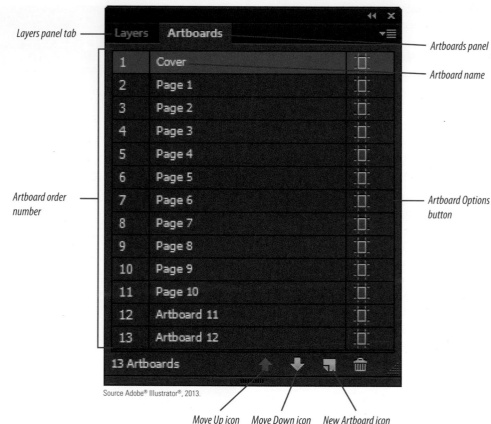

Layers panel tab

Artboards panel

Artboard name

Artboard order number

Artboard Options button

Source Adobe® Illustrator®, 2013.

Move Up icon   Move Down icon   New Artboard icon

You can enter Edit Artboard mode by clicking the Edit Artboards button in the Document Setup dialog box, or by clicking the Artboard tool on the Tools panel. (*Note*: You can open the Document Setup dialog box by clicking the Document Setup button on the Control Panel or by selecting Document Setup on the File menu.) You can then change the name of the artboards in the Name text box on the Control panel, as shown in Figure 15.

Figure 15 *Changing the name of an artboard on the Control panel*

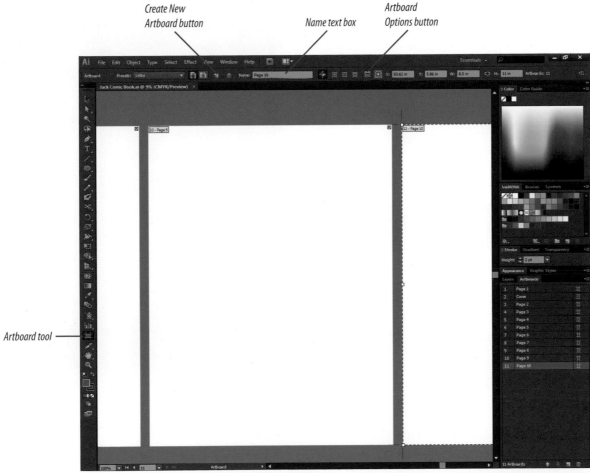

Create New Artboard button

Name text box

Artboard Options button

Artboard tool

© 2013 Cengage Learning, All Rights Reserved. Source Adobe® Illustrator®, 2013.

You can open the Artboard Options dialog box, shown in Figure 16, by clicking Artboard Options on the Artboard panel menu, or by clicking the Artboard Options button on the Control panel when the Artboards tool is active. You can change the name of the artboard in the Name text box. (*Note:* When the Artboard Options dialog box is open, the workspace changes to Edit Artboard mode.)

To navigate between artboards in the document, use the controls at the bottom of the workspace window. Figure 17 shows the navigation tools. The Page list arrow allows you to move between artboards, while the Back, Next, First, and Last arrows move you sequentially through the document.

Figure 16 *Artboard Options dialog box*

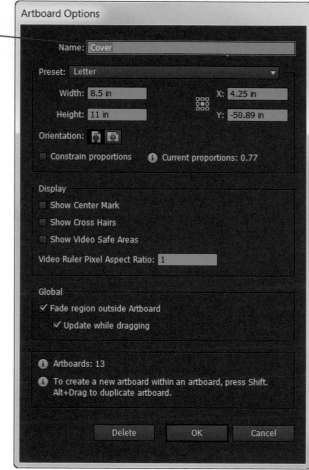

Source Adobe® Illustrator®, 2013.

Figure 17 *Artboard navigation controls*

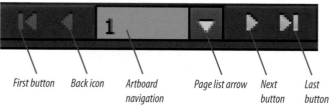

First button   *Back icon*   *Artboard navigation*   *Page list arrow*   *Next button*   *Last button*

Source Adobe® Illustrator®, 2013.

Figure 18 *Changing the name of a layer*

Layers Options
dialog box

Type layer name
here

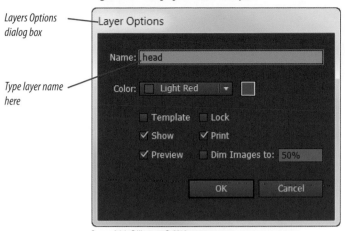

Figure 19 *Renamed layers*

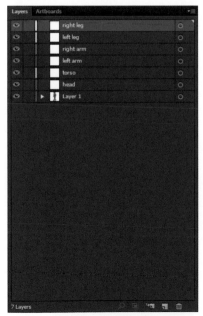

Create and name layers

In these steps, you will create and name layers in a drawing of Jack and then separate Jack onto different layers.

1. Open 2D 2-1.ai, then save it as **Jack Comic Book.ai**.

   A sample drawing of Jack appears on the artboard.

2. Open the Layers panel, then click the **Create New Layer icon** .

3. On the Layers panel, double-click **Layer 2**.

   The Layers Options dialog box opens.

4. Type **head** in the Name text box, as shown in Figure 18, then click **OK**.

   The layer is renamed.

5. Repeat steps 2–4, renaming Layer 3 **torso**, Layer 4 **left arm**, Layer 5 **right arm**, Layer 6 **left leg**, and Layer 7 **right leg**, as shown in Figure 19.

TIP You can also rename a layer by double-clicking the layer name in the Layers panel.

(continued)

6. Click the **Selection tool** , then drag a
   selection around the paths that comprise Jack's
   head, as shown in Figure 20.

TIP Press and hold [Shift] to add or subtract from your
   selection as needed.

7. Click the **Selected art indicator icon** ▢, then
   drag the **icon** to the **head layer**, as shown in
   Figure 21.

   The paths that make up Jack's head are now
   located on the head layer.

   (continued)

Figure 20 *Selecting Jack's head*

*Dragging a selection
with the Selection tool*

Selected paths

Figure 21 *Moving the Selected art indicator*

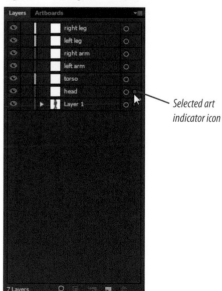

*Selected art
indicator icon*

Creating a Comic Book Using Adobe Illustrator

Figure 22 *Jack separated onto different layers*

8. Repeat steps 6–7 to move the appropriate paths for the remaining layers, **torso**, **left arm**, **right arm**, **left leg**, and **right leg**, as shown in Figure 22.

   Include the backpack and left strap with the left arm and the right strap with the right arm.

9. Save your work.

Adjust the stacking order of layers

In these steps, you will adjust the stacking order of the layers to correct the image of Jack.

1. Verify that Jack Comic Book.ai is open.

2. Drag the **right leg layer** to the bottom of the stacking order, as shown in Figure 23.

   Moving the right leg to the bottom of the stacking order places the leg behind the torso.

(continued)

Figure 23 *Moving the right leg layer in the stacking order*

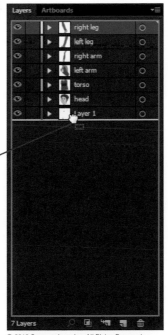

Dragging the right leg layer to the bottom of the stacking order

3. Drag the **left leg layer** above the right leg layer, then compare your screen to Figure 24.

4. Save your work.

Figure 24 *Final stacking order*

Final stacking order

Creating a Comic Book Using Adobe Illustrator

Figure 25 *Selecting the contents of a layer*

Objects
selected on
layer

Selected
Target icon

Figure 26 *Collecting layers onto a new layer*

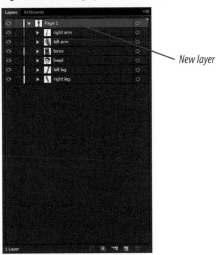

New layer

Group contents

In these steps, you will group the contents of each layer and collect the layers into a new layer.

1. Verify that Jack Comic Book L2.ai is open.

2. On the Layers panel, click the **Target icon** ◎ on the head layer to select the entire contents of the layer, as shown in Figure 25.

   The paths of the head object are selected.

   TIP When a layer is selected, the target icon has a double-ring border ◉.

3. Click **Object** on the Menu bar, then click **Group**.

   The paths of the head layer are grouped.

4. Repeat steps 2–3 to group the contents of the **torso**, **left arm**, **right arm**, **left leg**, and **right leg layers**.

   TIP You can also press [Ctrl][G] (Win) or ⌘ [G] (Mac) to create a group.

5. Click **Layer 1**, click the **Delete Selection icon** 🗑, then click **Yes** to delete the layer.

6. Click the **right arm layer**, press and hold **[Shift]**, then click the **right leg layer**.

   All the layers on the Layers panel are selected.

7. Click the **Panel menu button** ▾≣, then click **Collect in New Layer**.

   This content from all the layers is placed on a new layer, Layer 7.

8. Rename Layer 7 **Page 1**, expand the layer if necessary, then compare your Layers panel to Figure 26.

9. Save your work.

Create and name artboards

In these steps, you will create and name artboards.

1. Verify that Jack Comic Book.ai is open.

2. Open the **Artboards panel**, then click the **Artboard tool**  to enter artboard editing mode.

   You will create and adjust artboards in artboard editing mode.

3. Click the **Name text box** on the Control panel, select the **text**, then type Page 1, as shown in Figure 27.

   The artboard is renamed.

4. Click the **Select Preset menu** on the Control panel, then click **Letter**.

   The Page 1 artboard was larger than a letter size piece of paper so you have corrected the size of the paper. (*Note:* You will correct the size of Jack to fit in a panel on Page 1 in a later lesson.)

5. Drag the **bottom scroll bar** to the left to move the artboard to the right side of the workspace to make room to add a new artboard.

TIP You may want to zoom out so have room to create a new artboard.

(continued)

Figure 27 *Renamed artboard on the Control Panel*

New artboard name

Size of artboard

Artboard tool

Artboards panel

© 2013 Cengage Learning, All Rights Reserved. Source Adobe® Illustrator®, 2013.

Figure 28 *Placing a new artboard*

New Artboard button

Placing a new artboard

© 2013 Cengage Learning, All Rights Reserved. Source Adobe® Illustrator®, 2013.

6. Click the **New Artboard button** on the Control panel, place the **pointer** to the left of the Page 1 artboard, as shown in Figure 28, then click the **mouse**.

   A new artboard, Artboard 2, appears next to the Page 1 artboard.

7. Click the **Name text box** on the Control panel, select the **Artboard 2 text**, then type **Cover**.

8. Drag the **bottom scroll bar** to the right to move the artboard to the left side of the workspace to make room to add a new artboard.

   You will continue adding additional artboards for each page of the story to the right of Page 1.

   (continued)

9. Repeat steps 6–8, rename the next artboard **Page 2**, continue creating artboards until you create **Page 10**, then compare your screen to Figure 29.

TIP It is important not to overlap your artboards, the position of an artboard can be adjusted after it has been created by clicking and dragging on the artboard while in artboard editing mode.

10. Click the **Selection tool** .

Selecting another tool on the Tools panel exits artboard editing mode.

11. Save your work.

Rearrange artboards

In these steps, you will reorder and rearrange the artboards.

1. Verify that Jack Comic Book.ai is open.

2. Open the **Artboards panel** if necessary, click **Cover**, then click the **Move Up icon** .

The artboard order in the Artboards panel now matches the layout of the artboards.

3. Click the **Panel menu button** on the Artboards panel, then click **Rearrange Artboards**.

The Rearrange Artboards dialog box opens, as shown in Figure 30.

(continued)

Figure 29 *Newly created artboards*

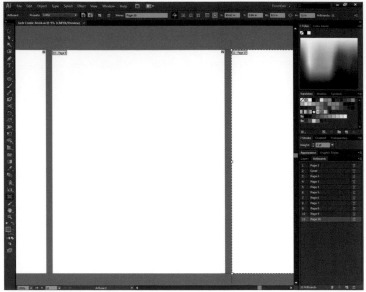

Source Adobe® Illustrator®, 2013.

Figure 30 *Rearrange Artboards dialog box*

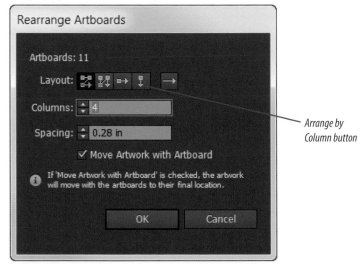

Arrange by Column button

Source Adobe® Illustrator®, 2013.

Creating a Comic Book Using Adobe Illustrator

Figure 31 *Artboards arranged in a single column*

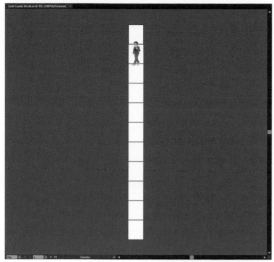

Figure 32 *Using the artboard navigation tools*

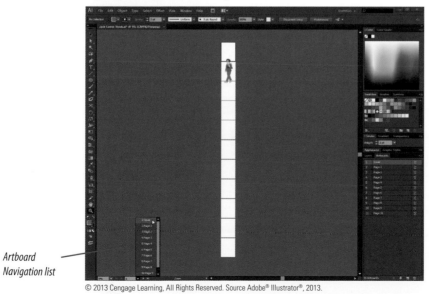

Artboard
Navigation list

4. Click the **Arrange by Column button** ⬇, then click **OK**.

   The artboards are aligned into a vertical column, as shown in Figure 31.

5. Click the **Artboard Navigation list arrow** at the bottom of the document window, as shown in Figure 32, then click **1 Cover** to open the Cover artboard in the workspace.

6. Double-click the **Hand tool** 🖐 on the Tools panel.

   The artboard is resized to fit the screen.

7. Save and close your work.

Advanced Drawing
TECHNIQUES

What You'll Do

 In this lesson, you will work with painting tools, symbols, and shading techniques in Illustrator.

Modifying Path Styles

When you draw paths with any of the drawing tools, the default styles are applied to the paths. If you want to customize a path's width or stroke, you can do so by selecting the path with the Selection tool. The style of a path includes the Variable Width Profile and the Brush Definition.

The **Variable Width Profile** changes the shape of the stroke. When you create a path, the uniform width is applied to all paths by default, but you can change the Variable Width Profile by selecting a menu option on the Control panel, as shown in Figure 33, or on the Stroke panel.

The **Brush Definition** applies a unique stroke to a path using one of five types of brushes: calligraphic, scatter, art, bristle, or pattern. Table 3 describes these brushes in more detail. When you create a path, the basic brush is applied to all strokes by default. You can access brush definitions and additional libraries by clicking the Brush Definition list on the Control panel, and then clicking the

Figure 33 *Variable Width Profile options on the Control panel*

Variable Width Profile menu

Source Adobe® Illustrator®, 2013.

TABLE 3 TYPES OF BRUSHES

Name	Example	Description
Calligraphic	© 2013 Cengage Learning.	Stroke has the style of a calligraphic pen
Scatter	© 2013 Cengage Learning.	Draws copies of a single object along a path
Art	© 2013 Cengage Learning.	Stroke has the style of different drawing tools such as pencils, crayons, charcoal, and oil
Bristle	© 2013 Cengage Learning.	Stroke has the style of a natural bristle brush
Pattern	© 2013 Cengage Learning.	Draws copies of one or more objects along a path; if creating a custom brush, add the objects to the Swatches panel

Panel menu button, as shown in Figure 34, or by the clicking the Panel menu button on the Brushes panel. You can customize an existing brush by double-clicking a brush thumbnail, or create a custom brush by clicking New Brush on the Brush panel menu.

Working with Painting Tools

Illustrator has a variety of painting tools available that customize and improve the quality of your artwork. Some of these tools are explained in Table 4. In this chapter, you will use painting tools to continue to develop the Jack and the Beanstalk comic book and a comic book of your own creation. The painting tools will allow you to enhance your artwork and make it appear more professional.

QUICK TIP

To learn more about Illustrator painting tools, type keywords in the Search for Help text box on the Menu bar, or click Illustrator Help from the Help menu.

Working with the Paintbrush Tool

You can select styles for the Paintbrush tool on the Control panel. Regardless of the style you select, you will see a dotted line as you draw until you release the mouse. You can create an open path by simply drawing a path and then releasing the mouse. If you want to draw a closed path, draw a path, then press and hold [Alt] (Win) or [option] (Mac) before releasing the mouse—the path closes automatically from the last position of the pointer on the artboard.

You can modify the shape of a path created with the Paintbrush tool using the Direct Selection tool. You learned to modify paths with the Direct Selection tool in Chapter 1. You can also use the Paintbrush tool to extend a path or modify a path's shape when the path is selected.

TABLE 4 PAINTING TOOLS		
Name	**Tool**	**Description**
Paintbrush tool		Uses the stroke color to draw paths; can select style to be applied as you draw
Blob Brush tool		Uses the stroke color to draw paths; can merge or erase paths of the same color while you draw
Gradient tool		Applies, creates, or modifies a gradient
Eyedropper tool		Samples and applies color, stroke styles, type, and appearance attributes from an object to the selected object

© 2013 Cengage Learning, All Rights Reserved. Icons: Source Adobe® Illustrator®, 2013.

Figure 34 *Brush Definition options on the Control panel*

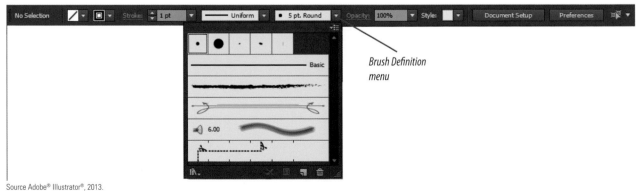

Brush Definition menu

Source Adobe® Illustrator®, 2013.

Working with the Width Tool

You can use the Width tool to create variable widths on lines quickly and precisely. Changing the width adds dimension, and improves the quality of your image, as shown in Figure 35. You can use this tool on any line as long as it has a basic stroke definition applied to it. It is important to note that by default, lines drawn with the Pen tool and the Pencil tool are drawn with the basic stroke. However, when you draw a line with the Brush tool, you need to convert the stroke definition to the basic stroke style before you can use the Width tool to adjust that stroke.

To widen a stroke, click and drag the line. Additional anchor points are added automatically, which you can use to adjust the width of the line, as shown in Figure 36.

Figure 35 *Example of creating variable widths*

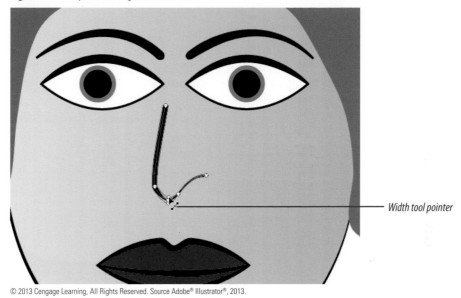

Width tool pointer

Figure 36 *Using the Width tool to widen a stroke*

Original image

Image with variable widths applied

You can also adjust a width point using options in the Width Point Edit dialog box, shown in Figure 37. To open the Width Point Edit dialog box, double-click the end point of a line, then adjust the values of the sides and total width.

You can save a modified width as a custom variable width profile by clicking the Variable Width Profile list arrow on the Control panel or on the Stroke panel, and then clicking the Add to Profiles button.

Illustrator provides a variety of shaping tools to enhance your artwork further. Table 5 explains some of these tools in more detail. You can learn more about the shaping tools in Help.

Expanding Objects

When you draw a path with the Brush tool, the stroke is applied to the path. By taking advantage of either the Expand or Expand Appearance commands you can create an outline of your path, as shown in Figure 38. Both of these commands can be found on the Object menu.

Figure 37 *Width Point Edit options dialog box*

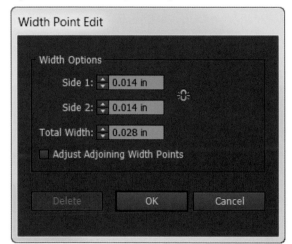

Figure 38 *Applying the Expand Appearance command*

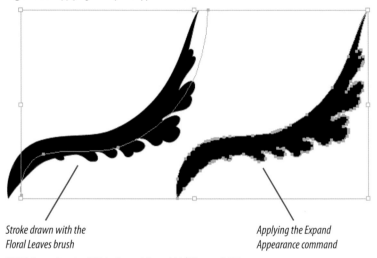

Stroke drawn with the Floral Leaves brush

Applying the Expand Appearance command

TABLE 5 SHAPING TOOLS		
Name	**Tool**	**Description**
Free Transform tool		Scales, rotates, or skews the selected object
Width tool		Modifies the stroke on a path to create a variable width
Warp tool		Molds objects similar to molding clay; located in the Liquify tool group
Wrinkle tool		Adds wrinkle-like details to the path of an object; located in the Liquify tool group
Shape Builder tool		Merges selected shapes to create a single object

Creating a Comic Book Using Adobe Illustrator

Depending on the complexity of your brush, you may be able to ungroup the outline you just created to have even greater control over customizing your artwork, including adding a stroke to your new outline.

If you want to expand a path created with the Pen tool, you will need to apply the Expand command, located on the Object menu. When you apply the Expand command the Expand dialog box opens. This is because when you draw with the Pen tool, both a stroke and fill color are applied, whereas when drawing with the Brush tool, only a stroke is applied. The two options you will need to be concerned with at this time are Fill and Stroke. The fill option expands the fill and the stroke option expands the stroke. You will not notice a difference in the fill being an outline, but selecting this option separates the fill from the stroke, allowing you to still modify the fill and stroke colors easily. You can also add strokes to the outline of your stroke and the outline of your fill.

Working with Symbols

You can access various symbol libraries on the Symbols panel. Click the Panel menu button, point to Open Symbol Library, then select a library. To use a symbol, drag it to the artboard, then modify its size or rotation. When you drag a symbol to the artboard, it is known as an **instance** of the symbol. You

can edit a symbol by clicking the Edit Symbol button on the Control panel. The edits you make affect the appearance of the instance on the artboard and permanently affect the symbol in the library. Additional instances

you drag to the artboard reflect these changes. To modify just the instance on the artboard, select the instance, then click the Break Link button on the Control panel, as shown in Figure 39.

Figure 39 *The Symbol Control panel*

The Edit Symbol button edits the symbol and all instances

The Break Link button edits just the instance

Figure 40 compares an instance in editing mode to a symbol. In editing mode, you can modify an instance's paths using the Direct Selection tool and tools in the Liquify tool group (the Width tool is the default tool).

You can create your own symbols and symbol libraries from any object on the artboard. Select the object with the Selection tool, then drag it to the Symbols panel. (*Note:* You cannot create a symbol by dragging an object to a Symbol Library panel.) In the Symbol Options dialog box, you must give the symbol a unique name and set the symbol type to either Movie Clip or Graphic. If you plan to use the symbols in Flash, set the symbol type to Movie Clip. (*Note:* Movie clip is the default symbol type in Flash and Illustrator.)

Figure 40 *Editing an instance of a symbol*

Instance in editing mode after clicking the Break Link button while hovering with the Direct Selection tool

Original symbol instance

Using the Drawing Modes

There are three different drawing modes available when drawing in Illustrator: Draw Normal, Draw Behind, and Draw Inside. **Draw Normal** is the default drawing mode. **Draw Behind** allows you to draw behind all artwork on a selected layer, if no selections are made. Using this drawing mode will save you from having to use an arrange command after you have drawn your object. The **Draw Inside** mode allows you to draw inside a selected object. This mode eliminates having to create a clipping mask or change the stacking order. To switch between drawing modes, click the Drawing Modes panel located below the Color Selector tools on the Tools panel, as shown in Figure 41.

Figure 41 *Drawing Modes panel*

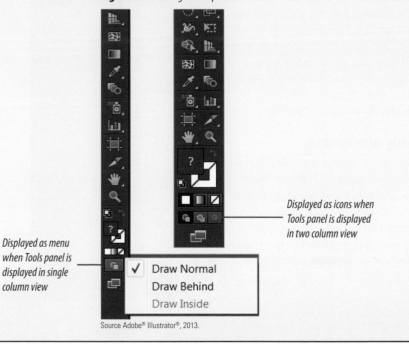

Displayed as menu when Tools panel is displayed in single column view

Displayed as icons when Tools panel is displayed in two column view

✓ Draw Normal
Draw Behind
Draw Inside

Creating a Clipping Mask

If you want to hide part of an image or change the shape of an image using another object, you can use a clipping mask. A **clipping mask** hides everything outside the shape used to create the mask. A **clipping set** includes the clipping mask and the objects that are included in the mask. You can add additional elements to your clipping mask by dragging a layer into the clipping set.

You can create a clipping mask in any shape, as shown in Figure 42. First, you create a new layer and draw the shape you would like to be your clipping mask. Next, select that layer, open the Layers panel menu, click Make Clipping Mask, then drag the layers containing the objects you want masked on top of the clipping mask layer to create the clipping set.

Figure 42 *Applying a clipping mask*

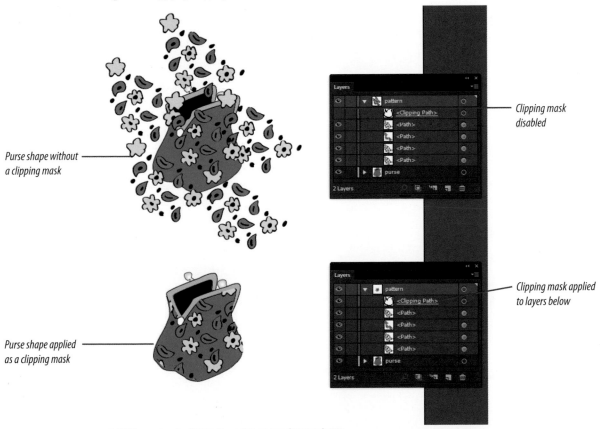

Purse shape without a clipping mask

Purse shape applied as a clipping mask

Clipping mask disabled

Clipping mask applied to layers below

Customize the styles on paths

In these steps, you will customize the paths on Jack on Page 1 of the comic book to improve the composition.

1. Open Jack Comic Book.ai.

2. Click the **Artboard Navigation list arrow** at the bottom of the document window, then click **2 Page 1** to open the Page 1 artboard in the workspace.

3. Double-click the **Hand tool**  on the Tools panel.

   The artboard is resized to fit the screen.

4. Click the **Selection tool** .

   TIP You can also press [V] to activate the Selection tool.

5. Open the Layers panel if necessary, then click the **Target icon** on the Page 1 layer to select the entire contents of the layer.

6. Press and hold **[Shift]**, hover the mouse over the **top-right sizing handle**, then drag the **pointer** down to resize Jack to approximately ¼ in size, as shown in Figure 43.

   TIP You may need to scroll up so that you can see the sizing handle.

7. Click the **Zoom tool** , then zoom in on Jack's face.

   You will vary the stroke width on the features of his face.

   (continued)

Figure 43 *Resizing Jack*

Jack resized

Figure 44 *Using the Width tool*

Width tool ——

Drag the
pointer to
modify the
width of the
eyebrow

Figure 45 *Example of adjusting facial features with Width tool*

Lesson 3   Advanced Drawing Techniques

8. Click the **Width tool** , place the **pointer** over the right end of Jack's right eyebrow, as shown in Figure 44, click the **white dot** on the bottom edge of the dark line, drag the **pointer** to increase the width of the line at that point, then adjust the width of the line to your liking.

   You may need to drag out from the line before you can drag towards the path to narrow the path.

9. Repeat steps 3–4 to adjust the remaining lines for Jack's facial features, then compare your figure to Figure 45.

TIP You may need to lock or unlock layers as you work.

10. Save your work.

Work with the Paintbrush tool

In these steps, you will draw with the Paintbrush tool to create the leaves on the beanstalk for the Jack Cover.

1. Verify that Jack Comic Book.ai is open.

2. Click the **Cover Artboard**, resize it to fit the screen, then lock the **Page 1 layer**.

3. Create a new layer named **Cover** above the Page 1 layer.

   You will draw the leaves on the beanstalk.

4. Click **File** on the Menu bar, then click **Place**.

5. In the Place dialog box, click the **Template check box**.

6. Navigate to where you store your Data Files, click **Jack-Cover.tif**, click **Place**, then deselect the picture.

   A template layer is created below the Cover layer.

7. Zoom in on the beanstalk.

   You will trace the leaves on the beanstalk.

TIP You may find it easier to work with the Brush tool if you have a graphic tablet.

8. Click the **Paintbrush tool**, set the Stroke Color to **black**, the Variable Width Profile to **Width Profile 5**, the Brush Definition to **3 pt. Oval**, the Stroke Weight to **0.5 pt**, then trace the **outline** of the leaves, as shown in Figure 46.

   Be sure to close the paths so you can add a fill color later.

   For long lines, you can stop drawing, select the end anchor point, then continue with the Brush tool.

(continued)

Figure 46 *Drawing with the Paintbrush tool*

Stroke weight set to 0.5 pt

Variable Width Profile set to Width Profile 5

Brush Definition set to 3 pt. Oval

Paintbrush tool

Drawing with the Paintbrush tool

Figure 47 *Example of traced beanstalk*

*Vines will be traced in
the next set of steps*

9. Click the **Blob Brush tool** , adjust the Stroke Color to **black**, then trace the veins.

   Adjust the size of the Blob Brush by clicking the Right Bracket ( ]) to increase the size of the brush or by clicking the Left Square Bracket ([ ) to decrease the size of the brush.

10. Use the **Paintbrush tool** , to add additional lines to the beanstalk, adjusting the stroke weight as you work.

TIP You can use the Direct Selection tool to adjust the shape of your path or use the Selection tool to select the path and modify the brush stroke settings after you have drawn your path.

11. Fill the leaf paths with a **light green**, then compare your artboard to Figure 47.

12. Save your work.

Work with the Shape Builder tool

In these steps, you will trace the vines with the Paintbrush tool and then work with the Shape Builder tool.

1. Verify that Jack Comic Book.ai is open.

2. Click the **Paintbrush tool** [icon], set the Stroke Color to **dark green**, the Variable Width Profile to **Width Profile 5**, the Brush Definition to **3 pt. Oval**, the Stroke Weight to **1.5 pt**, then trace the **vines**, as shown in Figure 48.

   The vines are not closed paths.

3. Click the **Selection tool** [icon], then select the **vine** you just traced.

(continued)

Figure 48 *Tracing the vines with the Paintbrush tool*

Stroke weight set to 1 pt

Variable Width Profile set to Width Profile 5

Brush Definition set to 3 pt. Oval

A traced vine

Creating a Comic Book Using Adobe Illustrator

Figure 49 *Applying the Expand Appearance command*

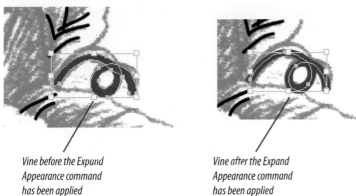

Vine before the Expand
Appearance command
has been applied

Vine after the Expand
Appearance command
has been applied

Figure 50 *Combining paths with the Shape Builder tool*

Drag the cursor to highlight
part of the vine

Figure 51 *Example of vines traced on beanstalk*

4. Click **Object** on the Menu bar, then click **Expand Appearance**.

   An outline of the path is created, as shown in Figure 49.

5. With the vine still selected, click the **Shape Builder tool** , then drag the **pointer** to highlight the path, as shown in Figure 50.

   You want the vine to look like it is a spiral.

6. Click the **Selection tool** , select the vine you just modified, then set the stroke color to **black** and the stroke weight to **0.75 pt**.

7. Repeat steps 2–6 for the remaining vines, then compare your work to Figure 51.

8. Save your work.

Open a custom symbol library

In these steps, you will open a custom symbol library of symbols that has been created for you to use on the Jack cover.

1. Verify that Jack Comic Book.ai is open.

2. Open the Symbols panel, click the **Panel menu button** 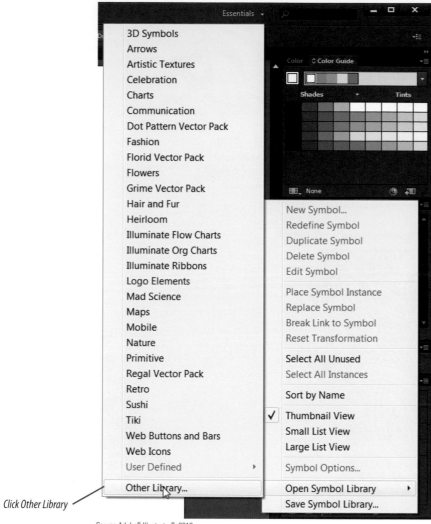, point to **Open Symbol Library**, then click **Other Library**, as shown in Figure 52.

   The Select a Library to open dialog box opens.

   (continued)

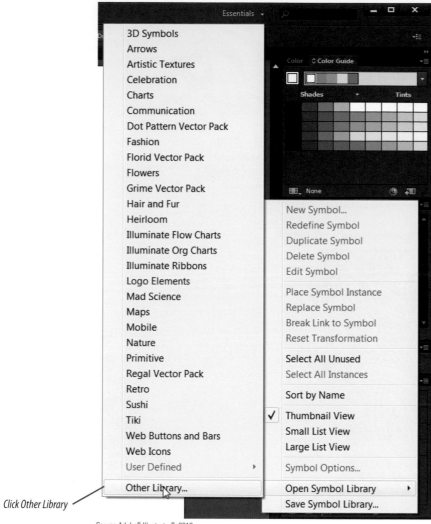

Figure 52 *Opening an external symbol library*

Click Other Library

Source Adobe® Illustrator®, 2013.

Creating a Comic Book Using Adobe Illustrator

Figure 53 *Opening the Jack Symbols library*

Select a library to open dialog box

Select Jack Symbols

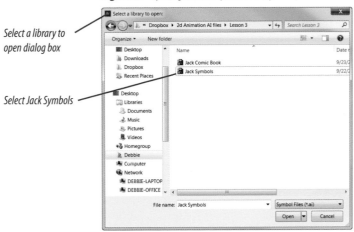

Figure 54 *Jack Symbols library opens as a floating panel*

Jack Symbols library

3. Navigate to where you store your Data Files, click **Jack Symbols.ai**, as shown in Figure 53, click **Open**, then compare your screen to Figure 54.

   The Jack Symbols library opens as a floating panel.

4. Click the **Selection tool** , drag the **beanstalk symbol** from the Jack Symbols library to the artboard, then position the **beanstalk** over the sketch.

   (continued)

5. With the beanstalk still selected, click **Object** on the Menu bar, point to **Arrange**, click **Send to Back**, then compare your work to Figure 55.

   The beanstalk is moved behind the leaves and vines.

Create a custom symbol library

In these steps, you will create a custom symbol library of speech bubbles.

1. Create a new document, type **speech bubbles** in the Name text box, set the New Document Profile to **Print**, the size to **Letter**, the orientation to **Portrait**, then click **OK** to close the New Document dialog box.

2. Click **File** on the Menu bar, then click **Place**.

   The Place dialog box opens.

3. Click the **Template check box**, click **speech_bubbles.tif** from where you store your Data Files, deselect the Link check box if necessary, then click **Place**.

   A graphic containing several speech bubbles appears on the artboard.

4. Click the **Paintbrush tool** , then set the Stroke Color to **black**, the Stroke Weight to **.75 pt**, the Variable Width Profile to **Uniform**, and the Brush Definition to **3 pt. Oval**.

5. Trace each **speech bubble** on the artboard in one motion.

6. Open the **Symbols panel**.

7. Click the **Selection tool** , then click the first **speech bubble** in the top-left corner of the image, as shown in Figure 56.

(continued)

Figure 55 *Example of beanstalk*

Figure 56 *Selected speech bubble*

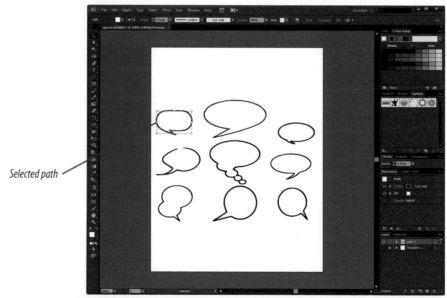

Selected path

Creating a Comic Book Using Adobe Illustrator

Figure 57 *Symbol Options dialog box*

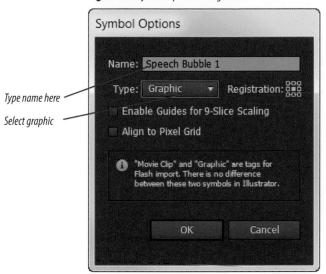

Type name here

Select graphic

Figure 58 *Making a custom brush*

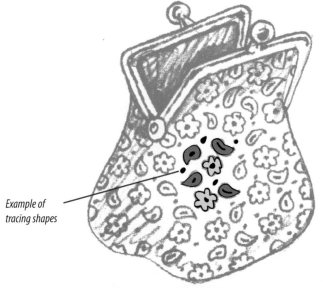

Example of tracing shapes

8. Drag the **selection** to the Symbols panel. The Symbol Options dialog box opens.

9. Type **Speech Bubble 1** in the Name text box, select **Graphic** from the Type menu, compare your screen to Figure 57, then click **OK**.

10. Repeat steps 7–9 for each of the speech bubbles, renaming the symbols until you create **Speech Bubble 9**.

11. Click the **Panel menu button** in the Symbols panel, then click **Save Symbol Library**.

    The Save Symbols as Library dialog box opens.

12. Click **Save**.

    The speech bubbles library is saved to the Illustrator Symbols folder.

    If you are unable to save to this folder because of lab restrictions, save it to the same location where you save your Data Files, and the library can be opened as you did in the previous set of steps.

13. Save and close your work.

    You can open the new library by pointing to User Defined from the Open Symbol Library.

Create a custom brush

In these steps, you will create a custom brush to design the purse found on the Jack and the Beanstalk cover.

1. Verify that Jack Comic Book.ai is open.

2. Open the Layers panel if necessary, then zoom in on the purse.

3. Using the tools of your choice, trace and fill a cluster of flowers and petals on the purse, as shown in Figure 58.

(continued)

4. Open the Brushes panel.

5. Click the **Selection tool** 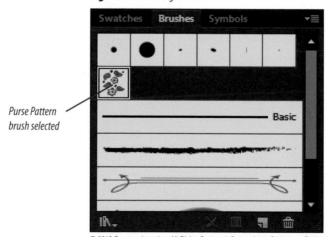, then draw a **selection** around the cluster of flowers and petals.

6. Drag the **selection** to the Brushes panel.

   The New Brush dialog box opens, as shown in Figure 59.

7. Click **OK**.

   The Scatter Brush dialog box opens.

8. Type **Purse Pattern** in the Name text box, then click **OK**.

9. Delete your selection from the artboard.

10. Save your work.

Draw with a custom brush

In these steps, you will draw with a custom brush to design the purse found on the Jack and the Beanstalk cover.

1. Verify that Jack Comic Book.ai and the Brush panel are open.

2. Click the **Paintbrush tool** 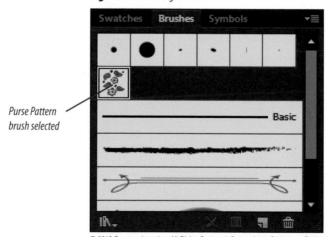, then select the **Purse Pattern brush** on the Brushes panel, as shown in Figure 60.

   (continued)

Figure 59 *New Brush dialog box*

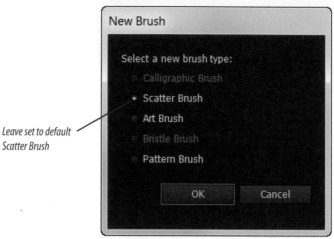

Leave set to default
Scatter Brush

Figure 60 *Selecting a custom brush*

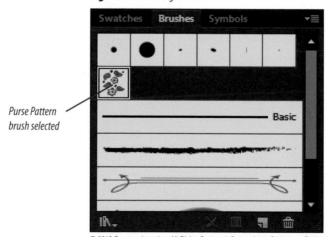

Purse Pattern
brush selected

Creating a Comic Book Using Adobe Illustrator

Figure 61 *Drawing with a custom brush*

*Don't worry about going
outside the lines*

3. Click **several times** over the purse to draw with your custom brush, as shown in Figure 61.

   Clicking gives you more control over the placement of your flowers; do not worry about going outside the boundaries of the purse in the sketch.

4. Click the **Selection tool** , then draw a selection around what you have just drawn.

5. Click **Object** on the Menu bar, then click **Group**.

6. Open the Layers panel, then expand the **Cover layer**.

   You will create a mask for the purse and brush stroke. First, you will create a new layer.

7. Click the **Group layer** at the top of the stack, click the **Create New Layer button** , then rename the sublayer **purse mask**.

   A new sublayer appears below the Cover layer.

   (continued)

8. Drag the **Purse symbol** from the Jack Symbol library, placing it over the sketch.

9. Click the **Break Link button** on the Control panel.

   The symbol is no longer linked, so you can edit it.

10. Deselect the **selection**, click the **Selection tool** 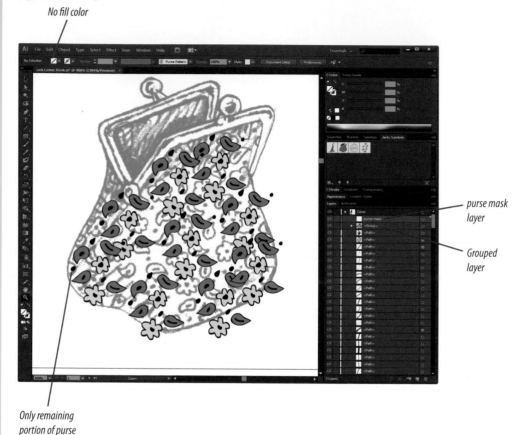, then delete all the components of the purse except the light purple portion of the bag.

    You may need to expand the purse layer in the Layers panel to verify you have only the light purple portion remaining.

11. Select the **light purple portion**, remove the **fill color**, as shown in Figure 62, but keep the purse selected.

    (continued)

Figure 62 *Creating a mask*

No fill color

purse mask layer

Grouped layer

Only remaining portion of purse

Figure 63 *Moving a layer to join a clipping path*

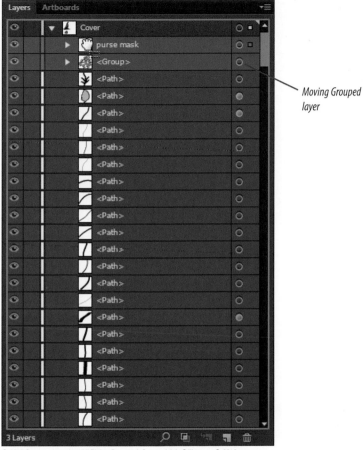

Moving Grouped layer

12. Click the **Panel menu button** ![icon], then click **Make Clipping Mask**.

   The effect is not visible until you move the Group layer.

13. Select the **Group layer**, then drag it on the **purse mask sublayer**, as shown in Figure 63.

   (continued)

14. Expand the **purse mask layer**, then move the **Group sublayer** below the Clipping Path sublayer.

The brush strokes are clipped to the shape of the purse, as shown in Figure 64.

(continued)

Figure 64 *A clipping mask applied*

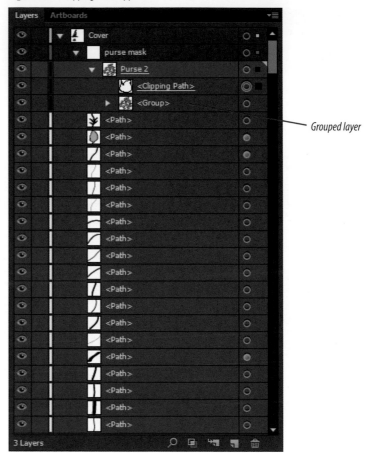

Grouped layer

Creating a Comic Book Using Adobe Illustrator

Figure 65 *Purse final image*

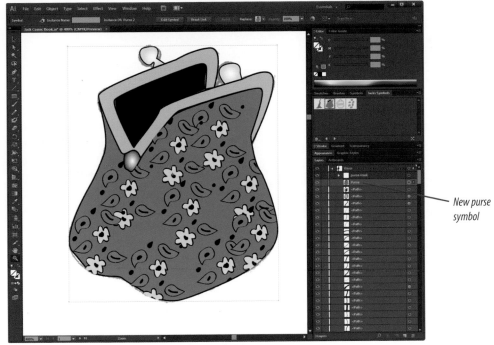

New purse symbol

15. With the Cover layer selected, drag another **instance** of the **purse symbol** to the artboard, right-click the instance, point to **Arrange**, click **Send Backward**, then compare your screen to Figure 65.

The brush strokes appear on top of the purple bag.

16. Save and close your work.

Work with
TEXT

What You'll Do

 In this lesson, you will work with the Illustrator type tools.

Working with the Type Tools

You use the Type tools to add text to your artwork. Adding text in Illustrator is much like working in any word processing application—you can add a single line of text, place text on or in a shape, type in paragraph format, or import text from a Microsoft® Word document or a Notepad file. Table 6 describes some of the Type tools.

You can modify the font, font style, font size, fill, and stroke colors on the Control panel, as shown in Figure 66. You can adjust additional text attributes such as kerning, horizontal and vertical scale, and leading on the Character panel. To open the Character panel, click Character on the Control panel or click Character on the Window, Type menu. Options available on the Character panel vary

Figure 66 *Type options on the Control panel*

Character panel link   *Formatting options*

TABLE 6 TYPE TOOLS		
Name	**Tool**	**Description**
Type tool	T	Enters text on the artboard at the location of the flashing cursor
Area Type tool	T	Enters paragraphs of text inside the area of an already drawn object or shape
Type on a Path tool		Enters text on a path; this can be a line or shape

depending on where you open it. Figure 67 shows the Character panel as it appears on the Control panel, where you can adjust many options. Figure 68 shows the Character panel when you open it from a panel group, where only the most commonly used options appear. To expand the available options, click the Panel menu button, then click Show Options. (*Note*: Many panels have additional options that are hidden and can be expanded by selecting this command.)

Creating Outlines of Text

You can convert text into compound paths, or outlines, that you can manipulate like any other graphic object. You can then customize the text using the Direct Selection tool, the

Figure 67 *Viewing the Character panel on the Control panel*

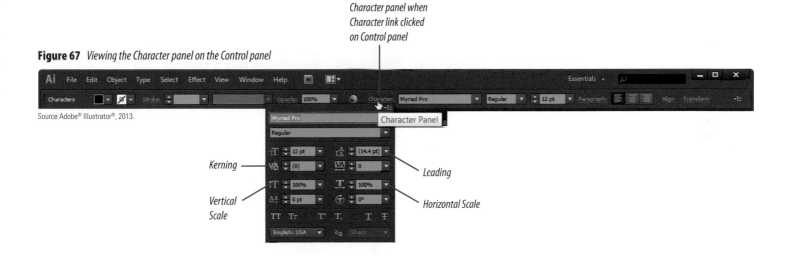

Character panel when Character link clicked on Control panel

Character Panel

Kerning

Vertical Scale

Leading

Horizontal Scale

Source Adobe® Illustrator®, 2013.

Figure 68 *Character panel in panel groups*

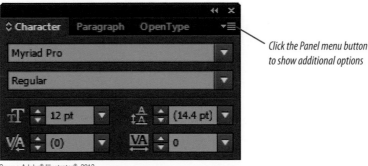

Click the Panel menu button to show additional options

Source Adobe® Illustrator®, 2013.

shaping tools, or apply gradient fill colors, as shown in Figure 69. It is important to realize that once you convert your text to outlines; it will no longer be editable, meaning you will not be able to change the style of font or any of the text. To make text into an outline, click Type on the Menu bar and then click Create Outlines.

Figure 69 *Create Outlines command applied to type*

Original type

Modified type

Attaching Type to a Path

You can attach text to the edge of any open or closed path by clicking the path with the Type tool, the Type on Path tool, or their vertical counterparts. If you have a closed shape, such as a circle, the Type tool will place the text inside the circle. (*Note:* Any style attributes applied to the path will be removed once text is attached.) The text flows in the same direction that the anchor points were created on the path. The characters of horizontal text are parallel to the baseline of the path. The characters of vertical text are perpendicular to the baseline of the path. Figure 70 shows examples of text on a path.

Figure 70 *Example of placing text on a path*

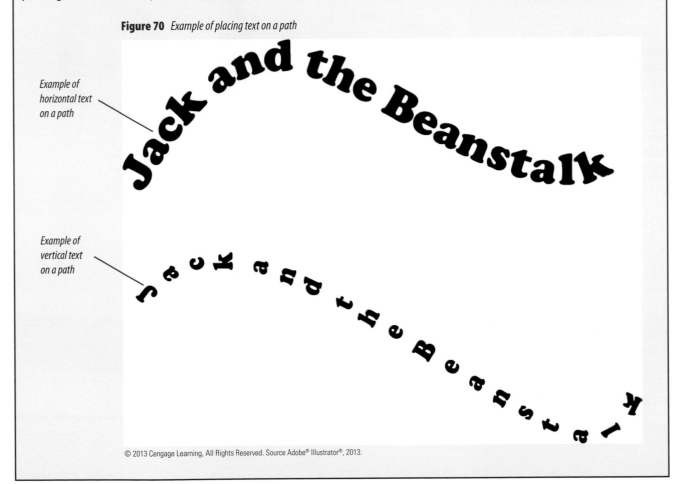

Example of horizontal text on a path

Example of vertical text on a path

Add a title to the comic book cover

In these steps, you will add a title to the cover.

1. Open Jack Comic Book.ai.
2. Click the **Cover layer** on the Layers panel.
3. Click the **Type tool** T , click the **artboard** above Jack's head, then type **Jack and the Beanstalk**.
4. Click the **Selection tool** ▶ , then drag the **bottom-right corner sizing handle** of the bounding box to increase the type to the size shown in Figure 71.
5. With the text still selected, click the **Stroke Color list arrow** on the Control panel, click **Black**, click the **Stroke Weight list arrow**, click **3 pt**, click the **Font list arrow**, click **Comic Sans MS**, click the **Font Style list arrow**, then click **Bold**.
6. Click **Type** on the Menu bar, then click **Create Outlines**.

   The text is converted to a compound path.
7. Click **Object** on the Menu bar, then click **Ungroup**.

TIP The letters are ungrouped, which allows you to select one letter at a time. First, you apply a gradient swatch to the text.

8. Open the **Swatches panel**, click the **Panel menu button** ▾≣ , point to **Open Swatch Library**, point to **Gradients**, then click **Foliage**.

   The Foliage swatch library opens.

(continued)

Figure 71 *Resizing text*

Your font type and color may vary

Bounding box

Resizing pointer

Figure 72 *Modified outlined text*

Resized individual letters

Gradient applied to text

Foliage Library panel

© 2013 Cengage Learning, All Rights Reserved. Source Adobe® Illustrator®, 2013.

9. Verify that the text is still selected, then click **Foliage 1** in the Foliage swatch library.

   The Foliage 1 gradient is applied to the title.

10. Click **Select** on the Menu bar, then click **Deselect**.

    The title is deselected.

11. Click the **J**, then click and drag the **top-middle handle** up to make the letter taller.

12. Click the **B**, click and drag the **bottom-middle handle** down to make the letter taller, then compare your artboard to Figure 72.

13. Deselect the letter **B**.

(continued)

14. Click the **Wrinkle tool** [icon], then drag the **pointer** –⁞– along the **Jack and the Beanstalk letters** to "wrinkle" the edges, as shown in Figure 73.

TIP You may need to lock the other layers so the Wrinkle tool does not change the clouds.

15. Move the **title text** so that it is centered towards the top of the page.

16. Save and close your work, then exit Illustrator.

Figure 73 *Wrinkle tool applied to title text*

Wrinkles on stroke of letters

Creating a Comic Book Using Adobe Illustrator

You'll continue working with the Jack Comic Book you created in this chapter to place the scanned images on separate layers.

1. Open **Jack Comic Book.ai**, then save the file as **Jack Comic Book SB1**.
2. Trace the images for each page onto separate layers.
3. Using the skills learned in this chapter, collect the layers that comprise a single page into a layer and name it after the page it represents. (*Hint:* Create symbols when you will be reusing a drawing so you don't need to trace it again.)
4. Compare your screen to the sample shown in Figure 74.
5. Save and close your work.

Figure 74 *Sample Completed Skill Builder 1*

You'll continue working with the Jack Comic Book, using the dialogue bubbles symbol library you created earlier in this chapter. You'll add the dialogue to the panels of the comic book.

1. Open **Jack Comic Book SB1.ai**, then save it as **Jack Comic Book SB2**.
2. Add dialogue bubbles and dialogue to the panels of the comic book, then compare your screen to the sample shown in Figure 75.
3. Save and close your work.

Figure 75 *Sample Completed Skill Builder 2*

Creating a Comic Book Using Adobe Illustrator

You'll create your own comic book based on the character analysis and sketches of your characters you created in from Chapter 1.

1. Open a new Illustrator document, then save it as **Portfolio Project—Comic**.
2. Create the number of artboards necessary to match the number of pages in your comic book.
3. Place the scanned images of your sketches on a template layer. (*Hint:* You will need to keep the layer unlocked until you have completed placing all of your sketches.)
4. Trace your artwork, creating and naming layers as you work.
5. Add color to complete your illustrations, then compare your screen to the sample shown in Figure 76.
6. Save and close your work, then exit Illustrator.

Figure 76 *Sample Completed Portfolio Project*

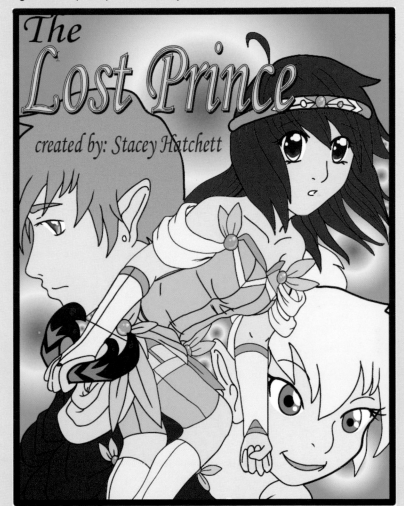

Courtesy of Stacey Hatchett.

CHAPTER **3**

CREATING ANIMATIONS USING
ADOBE PHOTOSHOP

1. Review Photoshop workspace and tools.
2. Animate the walk cycle.
3. Animate a bouncing ball.

CHAPTER 3

CREATING ANIMATIONS USING
ADOBE PHOTOSHOP

In this chapter, you will continue to improve your skills with character and story development to create different styles of animation.

Adobe Photoshop CS6 is well known as a professional image-editing program. You can also use Photoshop to create and edit animations. You will work with timeline animations, flip-style animations, and stop-motion animations.

Before you begin creating your own animations, you first need to review some basic animation concepts.

In their book, *Illusion of Life*, first published in 1981, the ideas and history behind Disney animations were explained by Frank Thomas and Ollie Johnston. These two men were members of the team of animators referred to as Disney's Nine Old Men. Disney's Nine Old Men were the group of core animators who began working at the Walt Disney Company between 1927 and 1935. By 1973, when *Robin Hood* was released, only four were

still at Disney. Two retired in 1976 and the last two in 1978. They influenced numerous Disney animations including *Snow White*, *The Jungle Book*, *Alice in Wonderland*, *Lady and the Tramp*, and *Winnie the Pooh*, among countless others.

In *Illusion of Life*, Thomas and Johnston developed and explained 12 basic principles of animation: squash and stretch, anticipation, staging, straight ahead action and pose-to-pose, follow through and overlapping action, slow in and slow out, arc, secondary action, timing, exaggeration, solid drawing, and appeal. These 12 principles have become widely accepted as the techniques an animator should use to create realistic characters. They apply not only to the basic laws of physics, but also to comedic and emotional timing. Keep in mind you do not need to apply all 12 principles to create a realistic animation; simply use these as a framework as you begin to develop your own animations in your own style.

Source Adobe® Illustrator®, 2013.

Source Adobe® Illustrator®, 2013.

Source Adobe® Illustrator®, 2013.

Review Photoshop workspace
AND TOOLS

What You'll Do

 In this lesson, you will review the Photoshop workspace and work with the drawing and painting tools.

Exploring the Photoshop Workspace

You should already have some familiarity with Photoshop before beginning this chapter, but first you will briefly review some of the key elements of the Photoshop workspace. (*Note*: You will see some similarity with the Illustrator workspace.)

When you first open the application without an open document, you see the **application window**, which is the main window comprised of various panels. The arrangement of panels in the application window is known as the **workspace**. Photoshop offers several preformatted workspaces that are designed for specific tasks. Photoshop opens with the default workspace, called **Essentials**. The Essentials workspace, as its name implies, displays the essential panels needed to create a document. In these exercises, you will be working primarily with the Painting and the Motion workspaces. The Motion workspace displays the Timeline panel, as shown in Figure 1.

In Photoshop, you work with individual panels and panel groups just as you did in Illustrator. When you drag a panel, it is removed from the dock and you can place it anywhere on the screen or in a different panel group. When moving a panel to another panel group, a blue highlighted area appears, called a **drop zone**, indicating where the panel will be placed when you release the mouse, as shown in Figure 2. If you open or move panels while you work, you can reset the workspace or save a new configuration as a custom workspace.

If you want to reset the workspace, you can do so by selecting Window, Workspace on the Menu bar and then clicking Reset *Workspace*

Figure 1 *Photoshop Motion workspace (Windows)*

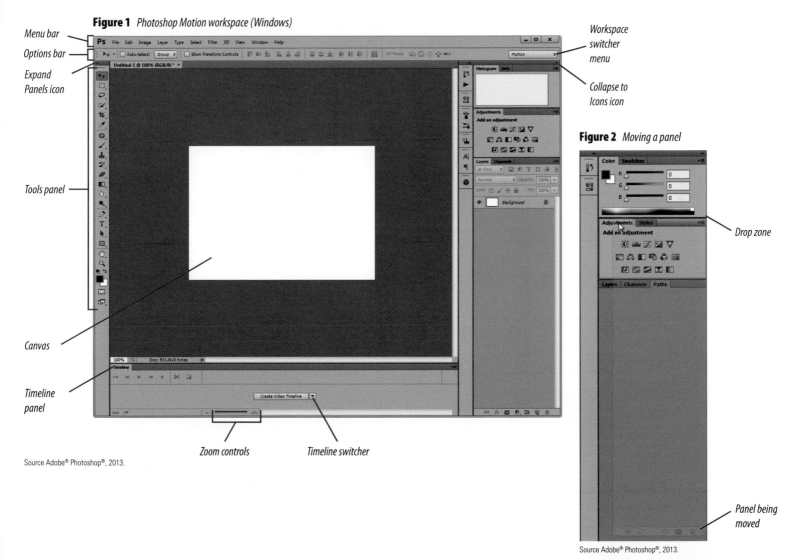

Menu bar

Options bar

Expand
Panels icon

Tools panel

Canvas

Timeline
panel

Zoom controls

Timeline switcher

Workspace
switcher
menu

Collapse to
Icons icon

Figure 2 *Moving a panel*

Drop zone

Panel being
moved

Name, or by clicking the Workspace switcher menu. (*Note*: The name of the workspace appearing next to the word "Reset" changes based on the current workspace you are using.) The Photoshop Workspace switcher is available in two formats: buttons and a drop-down menu, as shown in Figure 3. You can adjust the number of buttons to show one or all of the different workspaces.

If you want to save a custom workspace, you can do so by clicking the New Workspace command on the Window, Workspace menu, or the Workspace switcher menu on the Menu bar.

Understanding the New Dialog Box

When you create a new document, the New dialog box opens. The New dialog box is where you specify the settings for a Photoshop document, as shown in Figure 4.

In Photoshop, you can select a predefined setting from the Preset menu. The list of categories is defined based on the final output of your document. **Final output** is how you intend to use the document when you are finished. You should decide on the final output

Figure 4 *New dialog box*

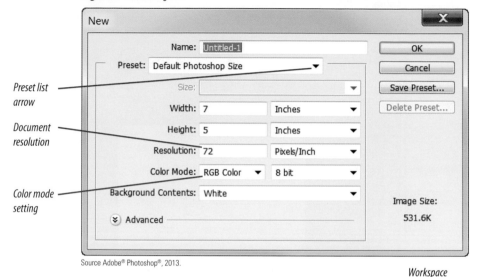

Source Adobe® Photoshop®, 2013.

Figure 3 *Workspace switcher*

Source Adobe® Photoshop®, 2013.

Creating Animations Using Adobe Photoshop

before beginning your project: Is the design for print, video, or the web? The presets designed for print will automatically be set to a resolution of 300 ppi, and those that will be viewed on a screen will be set to a resolution of 72 ppi. The options available under the Size menu will change based on the selection you make from the Preset menu. The measurements for the presets designed for print display in inches and those for a screen display in pixels.

When you have created a document, the **canvas**, the white area in the center of the workspace, appears in the application window. The canvas is the printable or publishable region of the document.

Working with the Selection Tools

You should already have experience making selections from your previous work with Photoshop. Making selections is probably one of the most important skills you can have when working in Photoshop. Selection tools allow you to highlight specific areas of an image, to which you may then apply special effects or filters. You can also cut, copy, or paste a selection. Table 1 provides a review of the Photoshop selection tools.

You have probably found that when working with the selection tools that some tools work better than others do in certain circumstances. For example, you can quickly isolate pixels in images that have high contrast with either the Quick Selection tool or the Magic Wand tool, shown in Figure 5. In images that do not have a great deal of contrast, you may have

Figure 5 *Selection in a high contrast image made with the Quick Selection tool*

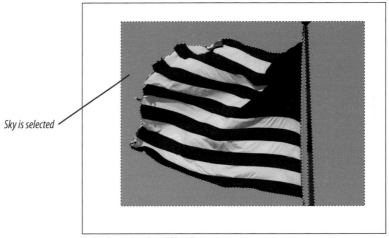

Sky is selected

TABLE 1 PHOTOSHOP SELECTION TOOLS			
Name	**Tool**	**Description**	**Location**
Move tool		Moves selections, layers, and guides	Default tool on the Tools panel
Marquee tools		Makes a rectangular, elliptical, or 1-pixel row or column selection	Rectangular Marquee tool is the default tool in this tool group
Lasso tools		Makes freeform-shaped selections, straight-edged selections, or selections against a highly contrasted background	Lasso tool is the default tool in this tool group
Quick Selection tool		Creates a selection with a round brush that automatically finds a distinct edge in an image	Quick Selection tool is the default tool in this tool group
Magic Wand tool		Creates a selection based on a color range	Located under the Quick Selection tool

found that working with a Lasso tool is more effective, as shown in Figure 6.

QUICK TIP

You can fill a selection that was created with any of the selection tools with a fill color, a stroke color, or both.

Using Photoshop Drawing and Painting Tools

Drawing tools include the Pen tool and shape tools; painting tools include the Brush and Pencil tools. The drawing tools work much like those in Illustrator, so you will review these tools briefly in this chapter and make note of their differences. See Table 2.

You create vector graphics when you draw with the Pen tools or with any of the shape

Figure 6 *Selection in a low contrast image made with the Polygonal Lasso tool*

Selected area

TABLE 2 PHOTOSHOP DRAWING AND PAINTING TOOLS		
Name	**Default Tool**	**Description**
Pen tools		Works like the Pen tool in Illustrator but also includes the Freeform Pen tool, which behaves like drawing with a pencil on paper
Shape tools		Draws a variety of shapes including rectangle, rounded rectangle, ellipse, and polygon; available options for the specific shape tool are available in the options bar
Line tool		Draws straight lines
Custom Shape tool		A variety of custom shape libraries are available to draw with this tool
Brush tool		Draws (paints) brush strokes; a variety of brushes are available including round, flat, and spatter with a variety of bristle settings
Pencil tool		Draws hard line strokes much like a real pencil

tools, but when you draw with the painting tools you create a bitmap or raster image. In this chapter, you will create characters and backgrounds for use in your various animations. Therefore, it is important to become proficient in using these tools before you can bring your character to life in Photoshop.

You can select three **drawing modes** when drawing with shapes in Photoshop: shape layers, paths, and fill pixels. You need to select the drawing mode on the options bar before you begin drawing with any of the shape tools. When you work in the **shape layers mode**, a shape is created on a separate layer, as shown in Figure 7. If you want to change the color of a shape after drawing the shape

Figure 7 *Drawing in shape layers mode*

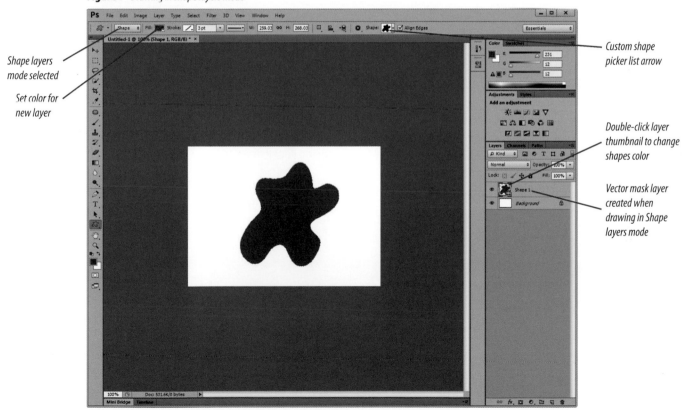

Shape layers mode selected

Set color for new layer

Custom shape picker list arrow

Double-click layer thumbnail to change shapes color

Vector mask layer created when drawing in Shape layers mode

using the shape layers mode, double-click the layer's thumbnail on the Layers panel to open the Pick a solid color dialog box, or select the Fill or Stroke color from the options bar. When working in **paths mode**, you create a work path that is created on the current layer.

A **work path** is temporary and you can use it to create a mask, fill and/or stroke, or to make a selection, as shown in Figure 8. When using

Figure 8 *Drawing in paths mode*

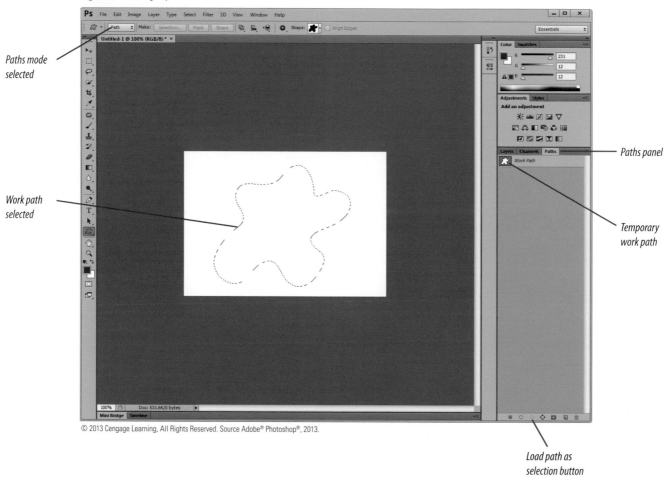

Paths mode selected

Work path selected

Paths panel

Temporary work path

Load path as selection button

fill pixels mode, you create the shape on the selected layer, as shown in Figure 9.

QUICK TIP

If you want to create a vector image when drawing, you will need to use shape layers mode; The other two drawing modes create bitmap images. (*Note*: Vector masks can be created with the path drawing mode.)

The painting tools work in the same way as their traditional counterparts for which they are named, applying color to strokes. When you draw with the painting tools, the color of the stroke is determined by the foreground color and you must first select the size and style of the brush tip in the options bar, as shown in Figure 10.

Figure 9 *Drawing in fill pixels mode*

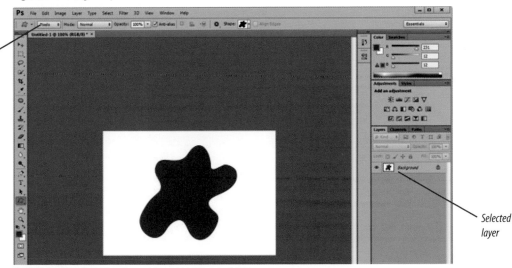

Fill pixels mode selected

Selected layer

Figure 10 *Brush tool options panel*

Toggle the Brush panel button

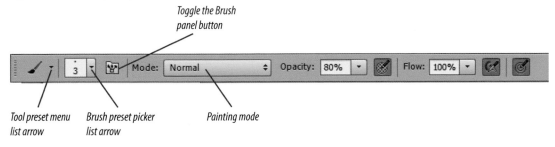

Tool preset menu list arrow

Brush preset picker list arrow

Painting mode

Lesson 1   Review Photoshop workspace and tools

Understanding the Path Operations Menu

When Shape layer mode or Path mode is selected, a new layer is created each time you draw a new shape with either a Shape tool or the Pen tool. The Path operations menu gives you the ability to draw on a single layer and is explained in Table 3.

The Path Selection tool and the Direct Selection tool can be used to modify shapes and paths that have been drawn on a single layer using the various options on the Path operations menu. The Path Selection tool works in a similar manner to the Selection tool in Illustrator, allowing you to move a path or shape. The Direct Selection tool is very similar to the Direct Selection tool in Illustrator, allowing you to select anchor points to modify the path or shape. Keep in mind when drawing in Photoshop with these options, all of your shapes and paths will be the same color. Therefore, this method of drawing would be good for creating silhouettes or anything that you would use as a solid color.

TABLE 3 PATH OPERATIONS MENU		
Name	**Icon**	**Description**
New Layer		Default option; a new layer is created when a shape or path is drawn
Combine Shapes		Adds an additional area to the existing path or shape
Subtract Front Shape		Removes any overlapping area when you continue to draw a path or shape
Intersect Shape Areas		Leaves only the intersecting area visible when drawing a path or shape
Exclude Overlapping Shape Areas		Removes the overlapping area when drawing a path or shape

Figure 11 *New dialog box*

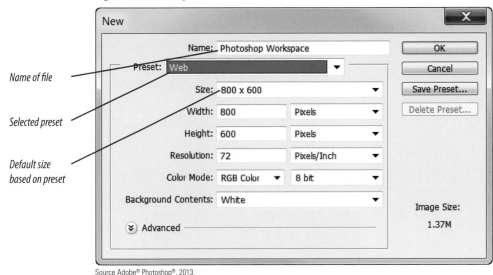

Name of file

Selected preset

Default size
based on preset

Source Adobe® Photoshop®, 2013.

Start Photoshop, create a new document, and explore the workspace

In this exercise, you will explore the Photoshop workspace.

1. Click the **Start button** 🌐 on the taskbar, point to **All Programs**, then click **Adobe Photoshop CS6** (Win), or open the **Finder** from the dock, then click **Applications** from the sidebar, select the **Adobe Applications folder**, then click **Adobe Photoshop CS6** (Mac).

   You may need to look in a subfolder if you have installed the Creative Suite.

2. Click **File** on the Menu bar, then click **New**.
   The New dialog box opens.

   Tip To restore default preference settings while starting Photoshop, press and hold [Alt][Ctrl][Shift] (Win) or [option]⌘[Shift] (Mac).

3. Type **Photoshop Workspace** in the Name text box, click the **Preset menu list arrow**, click **Web**, then compare your dialog box to Figure 11.

   While you can name the document here, the document will not be created until you click OK.

4. Click **OK** to close the New dialog box.

5. Click **Window** on the Menu bar, point to **Workspace**, then click **Motion**.
   The Motion workspace appears in its original configuration.

   Tip If a workspace is already selected, you can click the Workspace switcher, then click Reset to set that workspace to its original configuration.

6. Click the **Collapse to Icons icon** ▶▶ at the top of the panel dock.
   The panel dock collapses to icon view from panel view.

   (continued)

7. Click the **Expand panels icon** 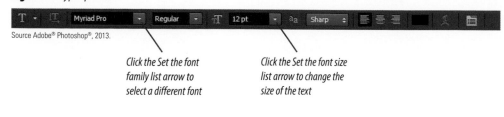 at the top of the Tools panel.

The Tools panel changes from a single column to a double column.

8. Click the **Horizontal Type tool** on the Tools panel.

The options bar appears with options associated with the selected tool, as shown in Figure 12.

9. Position the **pointer** near the middle of the canvas, click the **mouse**, then type **your name**.

10. Highlight the **text**.

11. On the options bar, click the **Set the font family list arrow**, then click a different font.

TIP The font type, style, and size can be selected on the options bar before you begin typing.

12. Click the **Set the font size list arrow**, then click a larger size.

13. Click the **Move tool** on the Tools panel, then drag the **name block** to the top of the canvas.

14. Click **File** on the Menu bar, then click **Save**.

The Save As dialog box opens, where you can select where to save the file.

15. Click **Save**.

16. Click **File** on the Menu bar, then click **Close**.

Use the Photoshop drawing tools

In this exercise, you will familiarize yourself with the drawing tools.

1. Create a new document named **Photoshop Drawing Practice**, click **Web** from the Preset menu, then click **OK**.

2. Set the workspace to **Essentials**.

3. Click and hold the **Rectangle tool**, compare your screen to Figure 13, then click the **Custom Shape tool**.

(continued)

Figure 12 *Type options bar*

Source Adobe® Photoshop®, 2013.

Click the Set the font family list arrow to select a different font

Click the Set the font size list arrow to change the size of the text

Figure 13 *Selecting the Custom Shape tool*

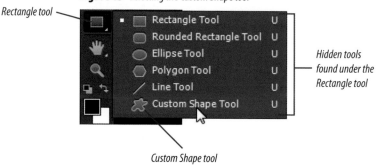

Rectangle tool

Hidden tools found under the Rectangle tool

Custom Shape tool

Source Adobe® Photoshop®, 2013.

Understanding the Photoshop Format Options dialog box

The Photoshop Format Options dialog box activates the Maximize Compatibility option by default making the file compatible with other versions of Photoshop. You will see this dialog box the first time you save a file. It is a good idea to leave Maximize Compatibility active and simply click OK.

Figure 14 *Custom Shape tool options bar*

Pick tool mode   Set shape fill   Set shape stroke   Arrow 7 selected   Custom Shape
arrow   type button   type button   Picker list
                                                                                                   arrow

Figure 15 *Creating a shape with a vector mask layer*

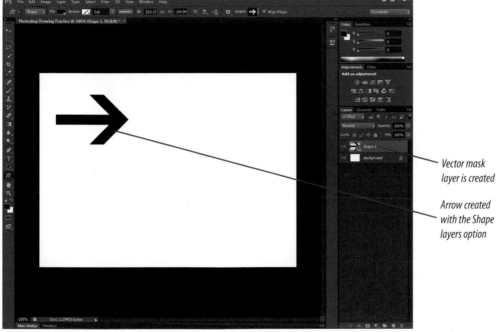

Vector mask
layer is created

Arrow created
with the Shape
layers option

4. If necessary, click the **Pick tool mode arrow** on the options bar, as shown in Figure 14, then click **Shape**.

5. Click the **Click to open custom Shape Picker list arrow**, then click **Arrow 7**, the second arrow in the first row.

6. Drag the **pointer** ─┼─ to draw an **arrow** in the upper-left corner of the canvas, as shown in Figure 15.

   A vector mask layer named Shape 1 is created on the Layers panel. Vector masks are created when a pen or shape tool is used in the shape drawing mode.

7. Click the **Pick tool mode arrow** on the options bar, click **Path**, then draw an **arrow** in the upper-right corner of the canvas.

   A work path is created on the Shape 1 layer.

8. Click the **Create a new layer button** on the Layers panel.

9. Open the **Paths panel**, then click the **Load path as selection button**.

   The outline of the arrow is selected.

TIP The Paths panel is in the same panel group as the Layers panel; click the Paths panel tab to open the panel.

(continued)

10. Click **Edit** on the Menu bar, then click **Stroke**.
    The Stroke dialog box opens.

11. Type **5 px** in the Width text box, click the
    Center Location radio button if necessary,
    then click **OK**.

    The path arrow has a black stroke.

12. Click **Select** on the Menu bar, then click
    Deselect, as shown in Figure 16.

    The arrow is deselected.

TIP You can also press [Ctrl][D] (Win) or ⌘[D] (Mac) to
remove the selection.

(continued)

Figure 16 *Creating a shape with the Paths option selected*

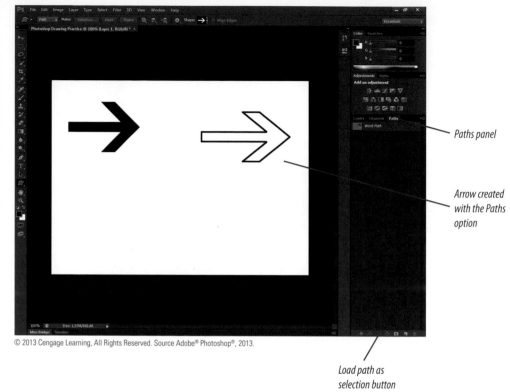

Paths panel

Arrow created
with the Paths
option

© 2013 Cengage Learning, All Rights Reserved. Source Adobe® Photoshop®, 2013.

Load path as
selection button

Figure 17 *Completed arrows*

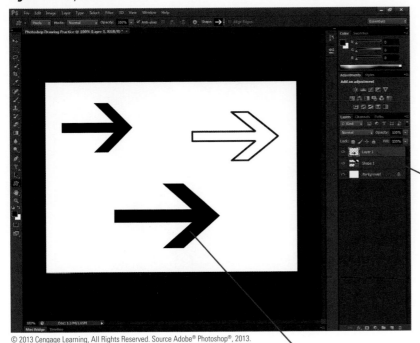

Layer with arrow created with paths and pixels options

Arrow drawn with Pixels option

13. Open the **Layers panel**.

14. Click the **Pick tool mode arrow** on the options bar, click **Pixels**, draw an **arrow** in the lower-middle area of the canvas, then compare your document to Figure 17.

    The arrow is drawn on the Layer 1 layer.

15. Save and close your work.

Use the Photoshop painting tools

In this exercise, you will familiarize yourself with the various painting tools by painting a flower in a watercolor style.

1. Open 2D 3-1.psd, then save it as **Photoshop Painting Practice**.

   If necessary, reset the workspace to Essentials.

2. Click the **Set foreground color icon** ▣ on the Tools panel to open the Color Picker, click a **light orange color** in the Color Picker box, then click **OK**.

   The color used in the example is R: 234, G: 66, B: 50.

   TIP You can also use the Eyedropper tool to sample a shade of orange from the flower.

3. Click the **Brush tool** ✎ , then using the orange flower as a guide, paint the **petals** of the orange flower, varying the brush size as you work.

   Your brush strokes appear on the existing brush layer, as shown in Figure 18. Next, you will create additional layers to paint other elements of the flower.

   TIP To vary the brush size, click the left bracket [to decrease the brush size or the right bracket] to increase the brush size.

4. Click the **Create a new layer button** ◰ on the Layers panel, then name the layer **mixer brush**.

   (continued)

Figure 18 *Painting with the Brush tool with a picture as a guide*

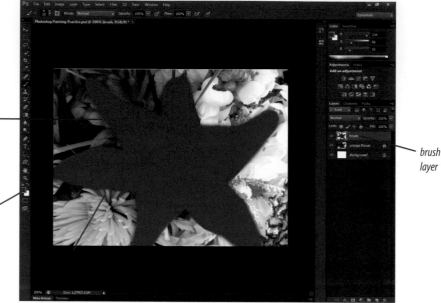

Flower painted with light orange color

Foreground color

brush layer

Figure 19 *Brush Preset Picker dialog box*

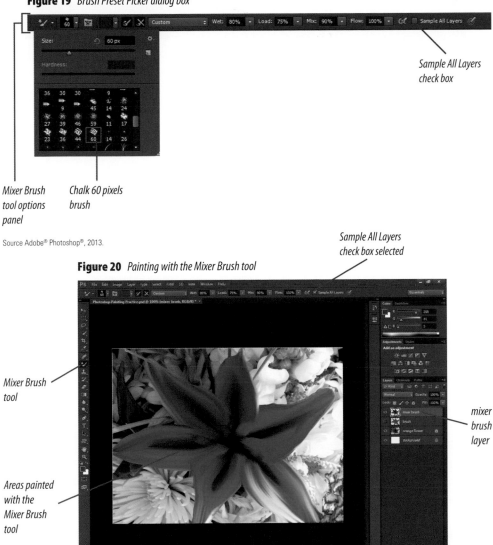

Sample All Layers check box

Mixer Brush tool options panel

Chalk 60 pixels brush

Source Adobe® Photoshop®, 2013.

Figure 20 *Painting with the Mixer Brush tool*

Sample All Layers check box selected

Mixer Brush tool

Areas painted with the Mixer Brush tool

mixer brush layer

© 2013 Cengage Learning, All Rights Reserved. Source Adobe® Photoshop®, 2013.

Lesson 1   Review Photoshop workspace and tools

5. Click the **Set foreground color icon** on the Tools panel, click a **dark orange color** in the Color Picker dialog box, then click **OK**.

   The color used in the example is R: 208, G: 41, B: 5.

6. Click the **Layer visibility icon** on the brush layer on the Layers panel to hide the layer.

   The orange flower layer is visible. You will use it as a guide to paint over the darker areas of the petals.

7. Click the **Mixer Brush tool**, click the **Brush Preset menu list arrow** on the options bar, click **Chalk 60 pixels**, as shown in Figure 19, then click the **Sample All Layers check box** on the options bar.

   TIP The Mixer Brush tool is in the Brush tool group.

8. Drag the **brush** from the center of the flower to the end of a petal, then vary the direction on the other petals to paint over the **darker areas** of the flower's petals, as shown in Figure 20.

   The brush paints by blending the colors from the layers below with the foreground color.

9. Click the **Layer visibility icon** on the mixer brush layer on the Layers panel to hide the layer.

   The orange flower layer is visible.

(continued)

10. Create a new layer named **spatter brush** on the Layers panel.

11. Click the **Default Foreground and Background Colors icon** 🔳 on the Tools panel.

    The foreground color is reset to black.

12. Click the **Brush tool** 🖌, click the **Brush Preset Picker list arrow** on the options bar, then click **Spatter 24 pixels**, as shown in Figure 21.

    (continued)

Figure 21 *Selecting the Spatter 24 pixels preset*

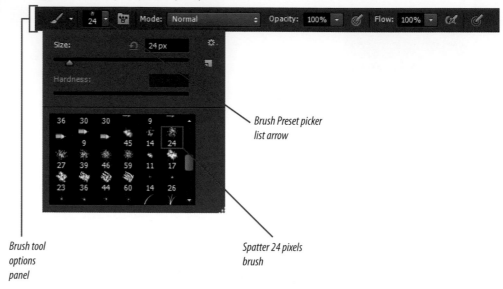

Brush Preset picker
list arrow

Brush tool
options
panel

Spatter 24 pixels
brush

Source Adobe® Photoshop®, 2013.

Figure 22 *Flower painted with Photoshop painting tools*

Spatter brush layer with the black specs of the flower painted

Mixer brush layer with the darker orange areas of the flower painted

Orange flower layer hidden

Brush layer with the lighter orange areas of the flower painted

13. Using the orange flower image as a guide, paint over the **black specs**.

14. Click the **Layer visibility icon** on the mixer brush and brush layers to show them, click on the orange flower layer to hide it, then compare your screen to Figure 22.

    Only the layers you painted are visible.

15. Save and close your work.

Animate the Walk CYCLE

What You'll Do

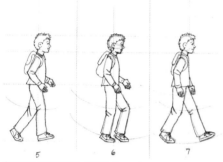

In this lesson, you will create a flip-style animation to the walk cycle.

Understanding Flip-Style Animations and the Walk Cycle

Flip-style animation is a style of hand-drawn animation and is the first animation to use a linear sequence of images. Images are drawn on the pages of a book, known as a **flip book** or **flick book**, with each image differing slightly so that when you flip the pages, the image appears to move across the page. The first flip book was patented in 1868 by John Barnes Linnett under the name **kineograph**. By the end of the 19th century, a new style of flip book was made with photographs; these flip books were called **Living Pictures** or **Living Photograph**, and are analogous to stop motion animation, which you will learn about in Lesson 5.

QUICK TIP

If you want to learn more about flip books, and see examples of them visit *www.flipbook.info/index_en.php.*

The walk cycle is a good place to begin drawing flip-style animations. The **walk cycle**, drawing a character walking, is a foundation concept in animation. Notice by changing the position of the right and left leg, you can repeat your drawings to create the walk cycle, as shown in Figure 23. You can draw a basic walk cycle showing a full stride in as few as eight frames and then repeat them to extend the length of the walk. After you have mastered a basic cycle, you can make variations to create a more interesting walk by adding a bounce, a slouch, or a shuffle to your character's steps. Becoming proficient in the walk cycle helps you develop your skills in applying the principles of overlapping action and anticipation. If you take the time to become proficient at drawing a walk cycle, you will be able to animate almost anything.

Drawing the walk cycle uses the drawing principle called straight ahead. The **straight ahead** drawing method draws the scene from the beginning to the end. In this case, you draw each frame of the walk cycle and if done correctly, you will not need to add additional frames between any of the frames to improve the quality of the walk cycle.

Early Forms of Animation

Some early forms of animation included the thaumatrope, the phenakistoscope, and the zoetrope. The **thaumatrope** is from the Victorian era and blends two images that were on opposite sides of a spinning disc. Using the phenomenon known as persistence of vision, the two images appear to merge into one image. The first thaumatrope showed a bird on one side and a bird cage on the other.

Figure 23 *Example of a walk cycle*

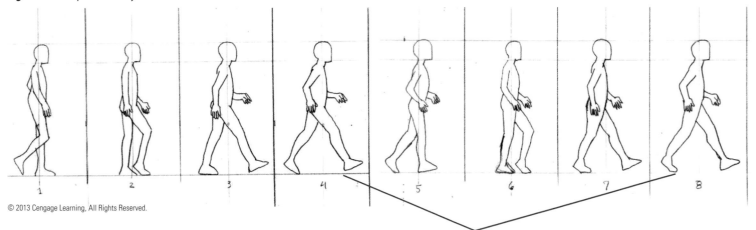

Body is in the same position but the right and left leg have changed positions

When the thaumatrope was spun, the bird appeared inside the cage. Figure 24 shows an early example of a thaumatrope; the illusion displays flowers in a vase.

The **phenakistoscope** also used a disc; however, the disk was kept flat, attached to a handle, and a series of drawings depicting an animation was drawn on the disk with equally spaced slits placed in the disk. Using a mirror, the user would look through a slit while spinning the disc and the image appeared to be a single moving image. Figure 25 shows an early example from 1893 of a couple waltzing. This technology could only be used by one individual at a time and was quickly replaced with versions that would allow more than one person to view the animation at a time. One example was the **zoetrope**, which produced the illusion of motion by using a cylinder on which a series of static pictures were placed; spinning the zoetrope made the image appear to move, as shown in Figure 26. These techniques were early forms of what would later become stop-motion animation.

Figure 24 *Example of a thaumatrope*

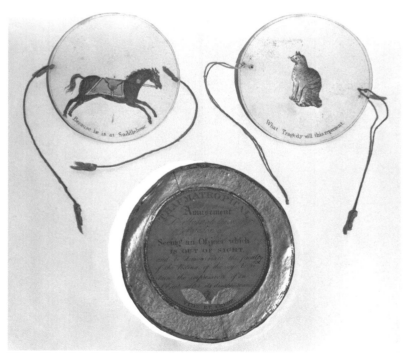

Figure 25 *Example of a phenakistoscope*

Creating Animations Using Adobe Photoshop

Early stop-motion animation evolved into the process of using film cameras by stopping the camera during filming, making a change to something on the set, and then starting the camera again. This was a simple way to create the illusion of making something appear or disappear. Techniques improved and illusions became more complicated. A chalk artist, J. Stuart Blackton, made what may have been the first animation film called *Humorous Phases of Funny Faces* in 1906, as shown in Figure 27. (*Note*: If you would like to view this cartoon, search the Library of Congress website, *www.loc.gov*.) Using stop-motion animation techniques, he drew lines on a chalkboard and at intervals took pictures with a movie camera. From this example of stop-animation, frame animation was then developed.

Early frame animation began by tracing separate drawings on cards with each card showing the next position in movement, after which all of the cards were photographed with a movie camera. (*Note*: This was similar to how a video camera captures movement, except all the drawings were made before filming began.) Frame animation evolved from drawing on cards to drawing on a cel.

A **cel** is a transparent celluloid sheet that contains a drawing and is then overlapped with other celluloid sheets. Using transparent sheets reduced the number of times some images needed to be redrawn. This type of animation was widely used in Disney animated films during the 20th century; it was referred to as **cel animation** or hand-drawn animation. Cel animations were first drawn on paper and then transferred to a cel. Each cel was used to make one frame in an

Figure 26 *Example of a zoetrope*

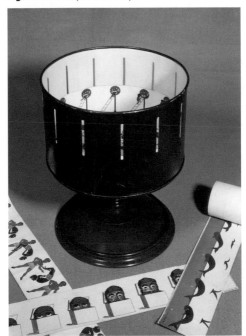

Courtesy of SSPL/National Media Museum/Art Resource, NY

Figure 27 *A 1906 silent cartoon by J. Stuart Blackton*

Courtesy Library of Congress

animation to create characters, backgrounds, and foregrounds, each on their own cels. If you watch animations created with this method, you see that backgrounds were often left in one position and only the characters changed to create a continuity of movement. It was much easier to align and draw characters in different positions when working from a transparent sheet. The cels were photographed onto motion picture film against a painted background. Cel animations led the way for computer animation, eliminating the necessity of having to first draw on paper.

Disney's first attempt at going paperless in an animation was the short-animation starring Goofy named *How To Hook Up Your Home Theater* in 2007.

QUICK TIP

To familiarize yourself with techniques for drawing basic characters and drawing characters in motion, visit *www.animationresources.org*. This website has made parts of Preston Blair's book, *Cartoon Animation*, available online for students; just look on the instructions page.

Working with the Timeline Panel in Frame Mode

You can create a flip-style animation on a computer using frames. A frame on the computer would be equivalent to one page in a flip book. The Motion workspace in Photoshop displays the animation on the Timeline panel. You can choose to display the timeline in Frame mode or in Video mode. The Frame mode option allows you to create flip-style animations, which are referred to as **frame-by-frame animations** when drawn on a computer.

When you change the workspace to Motion, the Timeline panel opens. Click Create Frame Animation from the drop-down menu on the Timeline panel, as shown in Figure 28, then click the Create Frame Animation button. The Timeline panel is displayed in Frame mode, as shown in Figure 29. (*Note*: In this lesson, you will work in Frame mode.)

Figure 28 *Converting Timeline panel to Frame Animation*

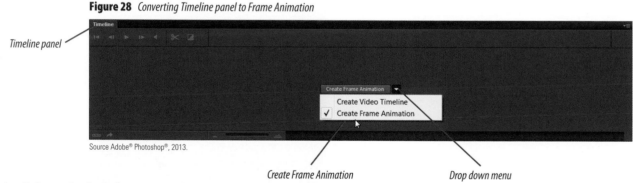

Timeline panel

Create Frame Animation

Drop down menu

Source Adobe® Photoshop®, 2013.

Figure 29 *Timeline panel displayed in frame animation mode*

Button toggles between Convert to video timeline (shown) and Convert to frame animation

Source Adobe® Photoshop®, 2013.

Each frame in the Timeline panel displays the layers that are visible on the Layers panel. If you plan to animate several objects, you should create each object on its own layer for that frame. You can edit the selected frame by turning the visibility of the layers on or off; moving the objects on a layer; redrawing the object; or changing the layer's opacity, blend mode, or layer style. Each frame is displayed for the length of time indicated on the Delay value menu, located just below the frame; each frame's delay is set independently.

You can save an animation either as an animated GIF or as a QuickTime movie. To save a file as an animated GIF, you need to select the Save for Web command, found on the File menu. In the Save for Web dialog box, choose one of the GIF file options from the Preset menu, as shown in Figure 30.

Figure 30 *Save for Web dialog box*

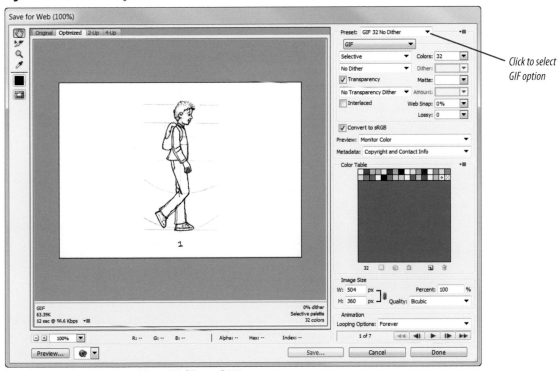

© 2013 Cengage Learning, All Rights Reserved. Source Adobe® Photoshop®, 2013.

If you would like to save the file as a QuickTime video, select the Render Video command from File, Export menu. The Render Video dialog box allows you to set file options for your video, as shown in Figure 31.

QUICK TIP

Be sure to also save the animation as a PSD file so you can work on the animation again.

Figure 31 *Render Video dialog box*

Name your video file here

Selected video format

Click the Render button to save the file as a video

Source Adobe® Photoshop®, 2013.

Figure 32 *Scanned walk cycle images*

walk-cycle 1   walk-cycle 2   walk-cycle 3   walk-cycle 4

walk-cycle 5   walk-cycle 6   walk-cycle 7   walk-cycle 8

Hand-drawing a walk cycle exercise

In this exercise, you will hand-draw a character in the walk cycle.

1. Cut two pieces of **8½″ × 11″ paper** into four equal pieces.

   You have eight pieces of paper, each measuring 4¼″ × 5½″.

2. On each piece of paper, draw **one** of the eight frames of a walk cycle.

TIP Using tracing paper allows you to overlap your images, making it easier to draw a walk cycle.

3. Stack the **paper** while you draw so you can flip between pages to see your progress.

4. Scan your **images** into separate files so you can use them for the next exercise.

5. Name the scanned images **walk-cycle 1**, **walk-cycle 2**, **walk-cycle 3**, and so on, as shown in Figure 32.

Create a walk cycle in Photoshop

In this exercise, you will use Frame Animation mode to create a flip-style animation.

1. Create a new Photoshop document named **Walk Cycle**, set the Preset to **Web**, the Width to **306 pixels**, the Height to **396 pixels**, then click **OK** to close the New dialog box.

   The Preset changes to Custom after you modify the width and height.

2. Set the workspace to **Motion**, click the **Create list arrow** on the Timeline panel, click **Create Frame Animation** if necessary, then click the **Create Frame Animation button** on the Timeline panel.

   The Animation panel changes to Frame Animation mode.

3. Click **File** on the Menu bar, then click **Place**.

   The Place dialog box opens.

4. Navigate to the **walk-cycle 1** file you created earlier, as shown in Figure 33, then click **Place**.

   (continued)

Figure 33 *Place dialog box*

walk-cycle 1 file selected; your view may differ

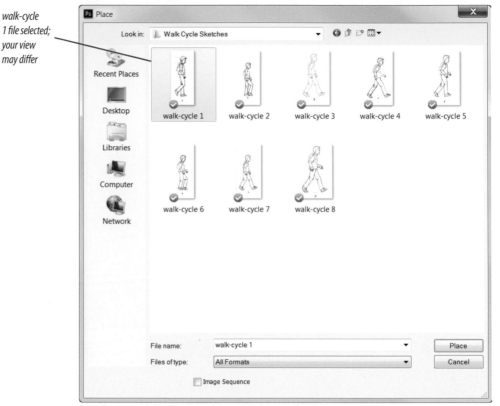

Figure 34 *Layers panel after placing scanned images*

Figure 35 *Layers converted to frames*

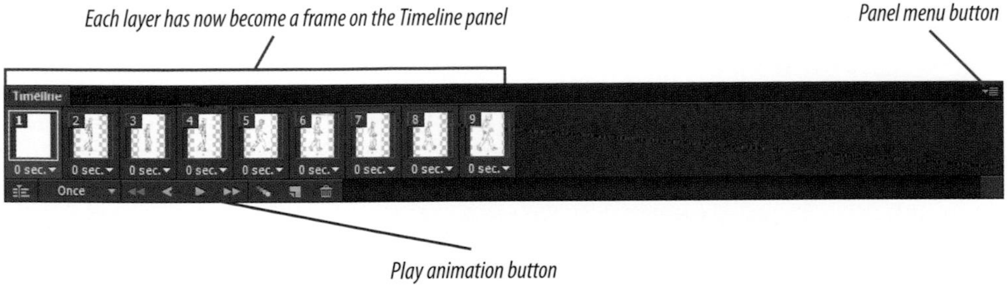

Each layer has now become a frame on the Timeline panel

Panel menu button

Play animation button

Figure 36 *Layers panel for frame 1*

New layer named walk 1

5. Press **Enter** (Win) or **return** (Mac) to commit the changes.

6. Repeat steps 3–4 for each of the remaining scans, then compare your Layers panel to Figure 34.

7. Click the **Panel menu button** ◥≡ on the Timeline panel, then click **Make Frames From Layers**.

   Each layer on the Layers panel is placed in its own frame, as shown in Figure 35.

8. Make sure frame 1 is selected, click the **Panel menu button** ◥≡ on the Timeline panel, click **Delete Frame**, then click **Yes** when prompted to delete the frame.

   The background layer frame is deleted.

9. Click the **Plays animation button** ▶ on the Timeline panel to preview the animation.

   The animation plays, beginning from the selected frame to the last frame on the Timeline panel.

10. Click **frame 1** on the Timeline panel if necessary, click the **walk-cycle 1 layer** on the Layers panel, then create a new layer above it named **walk 1**.

11. Click the **Layer visibility icon** ▣ on the Background layer to show it.

    The walk 1, walk-cycle 1, and Background layers are visible, as shown in Figure 36.

    (continued)

12. Make sure the walk 1 layer is selected, then use the tools of your choice to trace the figure.

Show and hide the layer below as you work to check your progress.

13. Click the **Layer visibility icon** ▣ on the **walk-cycle 1 layer** to hide the layer.

14. Click **frame 2** on the Timeline panel, duplicate the **walk 1 layer** on the Layers panel, move it above the walk-cycle 2 layer, then rename it **walk 2**.

The figures are aligned on top of one another so the only changes that can be seen are those parts of the image that should be moving.

TIP Use the Move tool to adjust the image so it lines up with the scanned image.

15. Make sure the walk 2 layer is selected, click the **Eraser tool** ✐, erase the **portions of the figure** that have changed on the walk-cycle 2 layer, then trace those **parts** of the figure, as indicated in Figure 37.

Duplicating the previous layer and re-using some of the figure will help you to keep the figure aligned and looking the same from frame to frame.

(continued)

Figure 37 *Re-using drawing from previous layer*

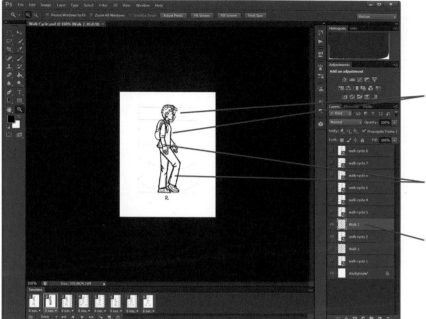

The head and torso should remain in the same position

Erase the arms and legs and trace using the walk-cycle 2 layer as your reference

Duplicated layer renamed walk 2

Figure 38 *Save for Web dialog box*

Click to select GIF 32 No Dither from the Preset menu

16. Repeat steps 11–15 for each of the remaining frames, naming the layers **walk 3**, **walk 4**, **walk 5**, and so on.

17. Click the **Plays animation button** ▶ on the Timeline panel to preview the animation.

18. Click **File** on the Menu bar, then click **Save for Web**.

    The Save for Web dialog box opens.

19. In the Save for Web dialog box, click the **Preset list arrow**, click **GIF 32 No Dither** as shown in Figure 38, then click **Save**.

    The Save Optimized As dialog box opens.

20. Click **Save** in the Save Optimized As dialog box.

21. Save and close your work.

Animate a Bouncing BALL

What You'll Do

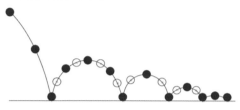

In this lesson, you will create an animation of a bouncing ball.

Creating a Bouncing Ball

Now that you have worked on the technique to create a walk cycle, it is time to animate a bouncing ball. Animating a bouncing ball is one of the basic skills and classic exercises in animation and is often one of the first assignments in any animation class. Creating a bouncing ball will help you to develop skills in the animation principles described below: arc, timing, squash and stretch, and volume.

- The **arc principle** shows how the ball should fall in an elliptical arc through space over a period of time.
- The **timing principle** is affected by gravity and causes the ball to accelerate as the ball moves in a downward path or slows down as the ball moves in an upward path. The speed of the ball continues to change over time.
- The **squash and stretch principle** causes the ball to change shape as it hits the ground and again when it bounces off the ground. As the ball bounces over time, the shape changes less and less.
- The **volume principle** indicates the mass of the ball should not change when the ball squashes or stretches.

As with drawing any animation, it is important that you first storyboard your ideas on paper. You have already reviewed some of the animation principles that should apply to an animation of a bouncing ball. With these ideas in mind, consider what a bouncing ball might look like. Did you consider the arc that it created? What type of ball was it? Did it change shape as it hit the ground? Did the ball increase speed at some point? Did it slow down?

Drawing a bouncing ball animation uses the drawing principle called pose-to-pose. The **pose-to-pose** drawing method draws only the main poses in the animation. In this case, you would draw the ball as it follows the arc, changes direction on the arc, or when it changes shape, as shown in Figure 39. (*Note*: You will draw a rubber bouncing ball in Flash later in this book.)

Creating a frame-by-frame animation of a bouncing ball would take a long time. Fortunately, Photoshop can create a tween between two objects. This means you can draw a ball bouncing with fewer frames. When you apply a tween to two frames, the computer determines what should happen between those two frames in a process called **tweening**.

To create a tween between two frames, select the two frames on the Timeline panel, click the Panel menu button, then click Tween. In the Tween dialog box, you specify how many frames to create, as shown in Figure 40. The more frames you create, the slower the object will appear to move. Fewer frames will make the object move faster. You can adjust the position, opacity, and effects parameter options in the Tween dialog box. Parameter options have the following effects:

- The position option creates a copy of the object on new frames at an equal distance between the frames adjacent on both sides. (*Note*: This option will not work if you create a tween between two differently sized or shaped objects.)
- The opacity option modifies the transparency between frames to make the object fade out and then fade back in.
- The effects option varies the layer effects between the first and last frames.

Figure 39 *Bouncing ball examples*

Path of a rubber ball   Path of a hard ball

Figure 40 *Tween dialog box*

Number of frames to add between frames

Layer properties to apply to the added frames

Tween

Tween With: Selection

Frames to Add: 3

Layers
- ● All Layers
- ○ Selected Layers

Parameters
- ☑ Position
- ☑ Opacity
- ☑ Effects

OK   Cancel

Stages of Drawing an Animation by Hand

Timeline animation terminology comes from the keyframe system developed by Disney Corporation when they created animations by hand.

An animator would draw various stages of the animation, which were called **intermediate frames** or **keyframes**. This animator was known as the **key animator** or **lead animator**. It was important when drawing these intermediate frames that they be timed in such a way that the next animator could infer what needed to be drawn between those frames.

The in-between frames were then drawn by a different animator, called the **inbetweener** or the **in-between animator**. The in-between frames would show the transition from one keyframe to the next keyframe and were called **inbetweening** or **tweening**.

Drawing a bouncing ball animation

In this exercise, you will sketch the path of a hard bouncing ball on two sheets of tracing paper.

1. On a sheet of tracing paper, draw a **path** for a bouncing ball that contains at least **5 arcs**.

2. Draw an **X** on the path to indicate the position of the ball as it travels along each arc.

3. Place a second sheet of tracing paper on top of the arc path, then draw a **circle** around each X to indicate the ball's location, as shown in Figure 41.

4. Scan the **image** so you have it available for the next exercise.

5. Name the scanned image **hard bouncing ball scan**.

Creating a bouncing ball animation

In this exercise, you will create a bouncing ball animation in Photoshop.

1. Start Photoshop, create a new document named **hard bouncing ball**, set the Preset to **Web**, set the size to **640 × 480**, then click **OK** to close the New dialog box.

2. If necessary, select the **Motion** workspace, then set the Timeline panel to **Frame mode**.

3. Click **File** on the Menu bar, then click **Place**. The Place dialog box opens.

4. Select the **hard bouncing ball scan** file you created in the previous exercise, then click **Place**.

5. Press **Enter** (Win) or **return** (Mac) to commit changes.

6. Create a new layer named **ball 1** above the hard bouncing ball layer on the Layers panel.

(continued)

Figure 41 *Hard bouncing ball with five arcs*

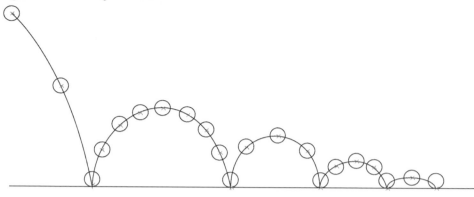

Creating Animations Using Adobe Photoshop

Figure 42 *Example of drawing balls for tween animation*

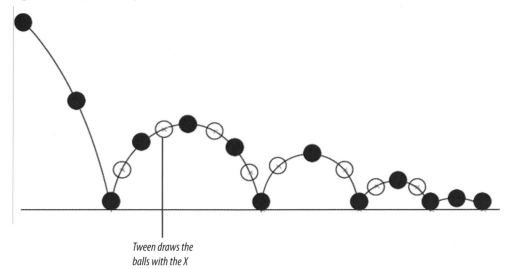

Tween draws the
balls with the X

7. Select a **foreground color** of your choice on the Tools panel, click the **Ellipse tool** , click **Shape** on the options bar, then draw a **circle** over the first circle on the arc path.

8. Duplicate the **ball 1 layer**, rename the layer **ball 2**, then adjust the location of the ball on the arc.

TIP To duplicate a layer quickly, right-click a layer, click Duplicate Layer, then rename the layer in the Duplicate Layer dialog box.

9. Repeat step 8 for the remaining balls.

   Keep in mind you will be making tweens between frames, so you do not need to draw every ball, you need to draw only the balls that will help the computer make an accurate tween, as shown in Figure 42.

10. Delete the **hard bouncing ball scan layer** on the Layers panel.

11. Click the **Panel menu button** ▾≡ on the Timeline panel, then click **Make Frames From Layers**.

12. Click the **Panel menu button** ▾≡ on the Timeline panel, click **Delete Frame**, then click **Yes** when prompted to delete the frame.

    The background layer frame is deleted.

TIP The Background layer on the Layers panel is not deleted.

13. Click **frame 1**, click the **Panel menu button** ▾≡, then click **Select All Frames**.

14. Click the **Layer visibility icon** on the Background layer on the Layers panel.

    The visibility of the Background layer is turned on for all frames on the Timeline panel.

15. Click **frame 1** on the Timeline panel to deselect the other frames.

(continued)

16. Click the **Plays animation button** 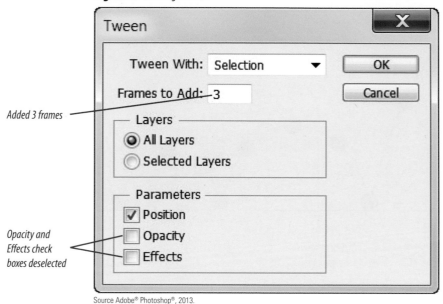 to preview the animation.

17. Click **frame 1**, press and hold **[Shift]**, click **frame 2**, click the **Panel menu button** ▾≣, then click **Tween**.

    The Tween dialog box opens.

18. Type **3** in the Frames to Add text box, click the **Opacity** and **Effects check boxes** in the Parameters section to deselect them, as shown in Figure 43, then click **OK**.

    Since the ball is going downward on the first arc, you only need to add three frames to make the ball appear to fall faster.

19. Click **frame 5**, press and hold **[Shift]**, click **frame 6**, click the **Panel menu button** ▾≣, then click **Tween**.

    Vary the number of frames based on the speed you want the ball to move.

20. Repeat step 19 for each of the remaining frames for the balls drawn in step 9.

    The frames you will be selecting will depend on your drawing and where you placed the balls in step 9.

21. Click **File** on the Menu bar, then click **Save for Web**.

    The Save for Web dialog box opens.

22. Click the **Preset list arrow**, click **GIF 32 No Dither**, then click **Save**.

    The Save Optimized As dialog box opens.

23. Click **Save** to close the Save Optimized As dialog box.

TIP Click the Preview button to preview your animation in a web browser.

24. Save and close your work, then exit Photoshop.

Figure 43 *Creating a tween*

Added 3 frames

Opacity and Effects check boxes deselected

Source Adobe® Photoshop®, 2013.

Creating Animations Using Adobe Photoshop

Applying the Twelve Principles of Animation can prove useful to understanding different movement. You'll compare techniques for different movement.

1. Visit *http://www.animationresources.org/pics/ pbanimation26-big.jpg*, then print out the Movements of the Two Legged Figure illustration.
2. Using the twelve principles of animation described in Figure 44 as a reference, write down how Preston Blair applies the Twelve Principles of Animation to differentiate a character from walking, running, running fast, sneaking, skipping, or strutting.

Figure 44 *Twelve Principles of Animation*

Principle	Explanation
1. Squash and stretch	Gives the impression of weight, volume, and flexibility as the character or object moves
2. Anticipation	Prepares the audience for an action or motion that a character is about to execute; helps the movement appear more realistic, such as a character bending his knees before jumping
3. Staging	Used in film or theatre; done with the use of camera angles and camera position, and placement of the character in the frame
4. Straight ahead action and pose-to-pose	Used to draw a scene from start to finish, frame-by-frame; the pose-to-pose method draws a scene at major intervals and adds in between details later
5. Follow through and overlapping action	Refers to what would continue to move when the character has stopped moving; overlapping action refers to how different parts of the body, clothing, or props move at different rates
6. Slow in and slow out	Provides time for an object to begin moving by increasing the speed of its movement, or to stop moving by decreasing the speed of its movement; fewer drawings increase the speed of the object, whereas more drawings slow down the speed of the object
7. Arc	Improves realism; the trajectory an object would follow while in that particular motion, such as the movement of a head or arm
8. Secondary action	Improves the quality or realism of the scene and enhances or supports the main action; consider facial expressions
9. Timing	Used to add interest to a scene; varied timing can help establish a mood
10. Exaggeration	Used to create realism or a parody of live action; this can be done through an exaggerated walk, facial expression, or a character's features
11. Solid Drawing	Gives a drawing volume and weight through the understanding of three-dimensional space and gives the illusion of three-dimensions
12. Appeal	Makes an animated character seem real; analogous to charisma in a live performer

Using the skills you have learned in this chapter, you will create a walk cycle for a track athlete running the hurdles.

1. Scan the figures, then place them in Photoshop.
2. Name the animation **Walk Cycle SB2**.
3. Using your skills with frame animations, including tweens, make your athlete appear to be running the hurdles, as shown in the sample in Figure 45. Add color to the figure.
4. Save and close your work.

Figure 45 *Sample Completed Skill Builder 2*

Using the animation you have created in Skill Builder 2, you will add hurdles, a track, and other features found at a track and field meet.

1. Rename Walk Cycle SB2 **Walk Cycle PP**.
2. Considering the animation principle of secondary action write down what could be animated in the scene besides the runner to add quality and realism to the animation.
3. If time allows, add additional animated elements to your animation.
4. Review the other 12 principles of animation and consider adding additional principles to improve the animation. See the sample shown in Figure 46.
5. Save and close your work, then exit Photoshop.

Figure 46 *Sample Completed Portfolio Project*

Creating Animations Using Adobe Photoshop

CHAPTER 4

ENHANCING YOUR CHARACTER USING ILLUSTRATOR AND PHOTOSHOP

1. Add realism to Illustrator artwork and create a simple animation.

2. Work with the video timeline in Photoshop.

3. Create an animatic in Photoshop.

CHAPTER 4

ENHANCING YOUR CHARACTER USING ILLUSTRATOR AND PHOTOSHOP

In this chapter, you will continue to improve your skills with Illustrator and Photoshop. There are times that you want to enhance your images to help add realism, such as adding shading or reflections. The appearance of your artwork can be improved in Illustrator to help it appear more realistic. You can also create simple animations using Illustrator and taking advantage of its blend options and export capabilities.

If you have found it easier to draw your artwork in Illustrator rather than drawing in Photoshop, you can take artwork created in Illustrator and work with it in Photoshop. You will learn some tips on how to prepare an Illustrator file so that when it is exported to the Photoshop file format (PSD) the layers and sublayers are ready to be animated in Photoshop. The video timeline is another method that can be used to create animations in Photoshop. You will also create an animatic in Photoshop, one of the steps in the animation process.

Source Adobe® Photoshop®, 2013.

Source Adobe® Photoshop®, 2013.

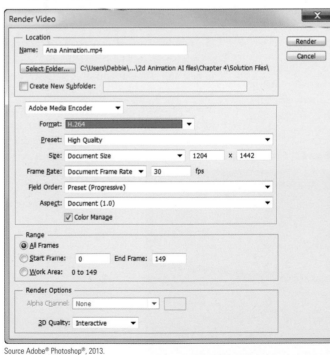

Source Adobe® Photoshop®, 2013.

Add Realism to Illustrator Artwork and CREATE A SIMPLE ANIMATION

What You'll Do

Courtesy of Sarah Galvan.

 In this lesson, you will add realism to your artwork in Illustrator and create a simple SWF animation.

Working with Gradients

Working with gradients is the simplest way to begin adding shading to your artwork. A **gradient** is a blending of colors, which is defined by a series of color stops along a gradient slider, as shown in Figure 1. A gradient can be either linear, blending along a line, or radial, blending from the center outward, as shown in Figure 2.

When working with gradients in Illustrator, you have the option to use a ready-made gradient from any of the gradient libraries found on the Swatches library, or you can create a custom gradient on the Gradients panel. A gradient can be modified on the Gradient panel or by using the Gradient tool.

QUICK TIP

The Kuler panel can be used to find and share groups of colors that are shared by an online community. The Kuler panel is found in Illustrator, Photoshop, and Flash Professional on the Extensions menu.

The Gradient panel can be used to apply a default black-and-white gradient to a selected object; the Type menu then allows you to make the gradient either linear or radial. You can then customize the gradient by adjusting color stops on the slider bar. Colors can be changed by double-clicking the stop

Figure 1 *Gradient panel*

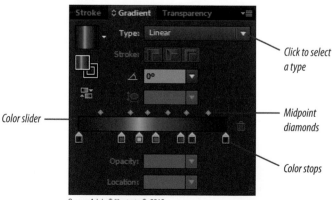

Click to select a type

Midpoint diamonds

Color slider

Color stops

Source Adobe® Illustrator®, 2013.

Enhancing your Character Using Illustrator and Photoshop

or by dragging a color from the Swatches panel to an existing color stop. You can add additional color stops to the color slider either by double-clicking the slider or by dragging a color to the slider. The midpoint diamonds are located above the slider bar and are located between two color stops; moving the midpoint diamond adjusts the shading between the two colors stops.

Using the **gradient annotator** also allows you to customize a gradient in the same way you can in the Gradient panel. In addition, you can also adjust the size and location of the gradient in relation to the object. *Note*: The size of the gradient extends past the size of the object. You may also find it much easier to adjust the angle of the gradient using the gradient annotator rather than options on the Gradient panel. To do so, hover the rotate pointer just outside the small square, then click and drag. The appearance of the gradient annotator varies slightly between a linear and radial gradient, as shown in Figure 3, but they essentially work the same. If you want to move the location of your gradient, click and drag the solid black circle. The length of the gradient can be adjusted by dragging the hollow circle. The length and width can be adjusted by dragging the solid diamond. When working with a radial gradient, you can also make these same adjustments on the dotted line circle that surrounds the gradient.

QUICK TIP

If the gradient annotator is not visible after you select the Gradient tool, click Show Gradient Annotator on the View menu.

Figure 2 *Types of gradients*

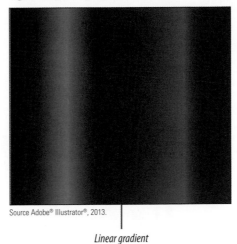

Source Adobe® Illustrator®, 2013.

Linear gradient

Radial gradient

Figure 3 *Using the gradient annotator*

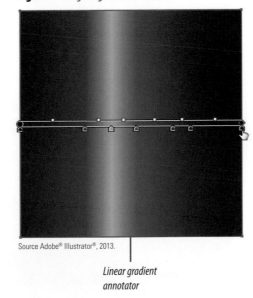

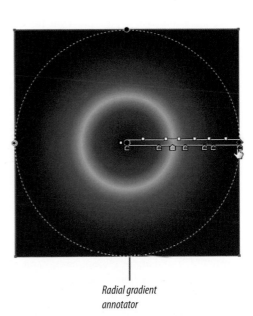

Source Adobe® Illustrator®, 2013.

Linear gradient annotator

Radial gradient annotator

Working with a Gradient Mesh

A **gradient mesh** allows you to create more complex gradients than you can with the Gradient panel or gradient annotator. You can add additional colors and change the directions of your color gradients (in more than one direction) creating curves and contours. A gradient mesh is made up of mesh lines, mesh patches, mesh points, and anchor points, as shown in Figure 4. The mesh lines create a grid. At the intersection of the mesh lines are diamond-shaped mesh points, which can have color applied to them. Anchor points are also a part of the mesh grid, are shaped like a square, and behave just as they do in any Illustrator object. A mesh patch is the area between four mesh points.

You may decide to apply a gradient to an object first and then customize it further by applying a gradient mesh. In order to do this, you first need to click the Expand command, found under the Object menu, and then select Gradient Mesh in the Expand dialog box.

You can select mesh points with the Direct Selection tool or the Lasso tool and then apply a different color to those points. The Mesh tool allows you to add mesh gridlines as well as reshape existing mesh lines to modify the contour of your colors.

A mesh can be applied either with the Create Gradient Mesh command or by using the Mesh tool. The Create Gradient Mesh command, found on the Object menu, creates a uniform grid based on the number of rows and columns you designate in the Create Gradient Mesh dialog box, shown in Figure 5.

Figure 4 *Applying a gradient mesh*

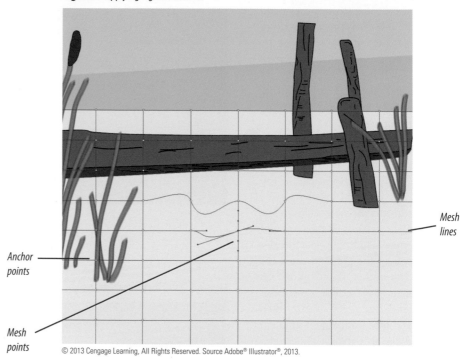

Mesh lines

Anchor points

Mesh points

Figure 5 *Create Gradient Mesh dialog box*

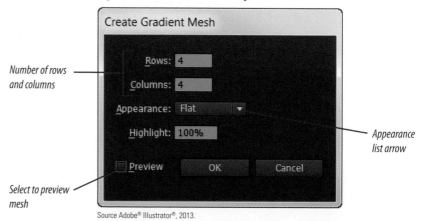

Number of rows and columns

Appearance list arrow

Select to preview mesh

Enhancing your Character Using Illustrator and Photoshop

The Appearance menu has three options: Flat, To Center, and To Edge. Flat applies the current fill color evenly across the surface without any highlights. To Center applies a highlight to the current fill color at the center of the surface. To Edge applies a highlight on the edge of the surface to the current fill color. The Mesh tool applies mesh points to your object, converting it to a mesh object with the minimum number of mesh lines needed. The currently selected fill color is applied to the mesh point as you click, allowing you to apply different fill colors, as shown in Figure 6.

Working with the Transparency Panel

The Transparency panel can be used to apply a blending mode to modify how colors interact with overlapping objects, to adjust the opacity to blend artwork on multiple layers, or to create an opacity mask to create variations in transparency.

Applying a blending mode to an object is an easy way to create shadows in your artwork to create a more realistic scene. In contrast, adjusting the opacity of a layer blends objects on other layers with each other. With this method, you can add textures to an object that has a gradient mesh applied to it. You can

use an opacity mask to add a realistic light effect to your object, which is a great way to add shine to a sphere (as shown in Figure 7), a sparkle to an eye, or reflection on water. An opacity mask works with black and white. Black areas create transparent areas, allowing what is below to bleed through; white areas do not allow anything to bleed through; and shades of gray create a range of transparency. (*Note*: Layer masks in Photoshop work in a similar way.)

Figure 6 *Working with the Gradient Mesh tool*

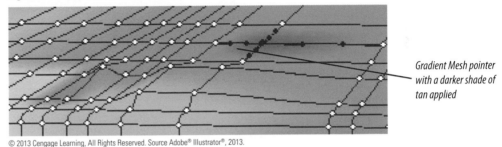

Gradient Mesh pointer with a darker shade of tan applied

© 2013 Cengage Learning, All Rights Reserved. Source Adobe® Illustrator®, 2013.

Figure 7 *Shine applied to a sphere*

© 2013 Cengage Learning, All Rights Reserved. Source Adobe® Illustrator®, 2013.

When creating an opacity mask, you first need to create a black-and-white gradient. You can use the gradient annotator to customize the gradient for your opacity mask. The mask is applied to the targeted object below the mask.

An opacity mask is created by applying the Make Opacity Mask command, located on the Transparency panel menu. The Release Opacity Mask command allows you to make any edits. You can also select the thumbnail of the opacity mask on the Transparency panel, as shown in Figure 8, and then edit the mask with the gradient annotator while you view the effects of the mask.

Figure 8 *Editing an opacity mask*

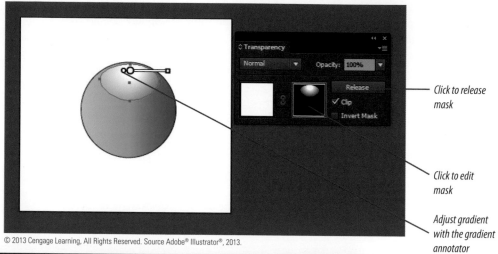

Click to release mask

Click to edit mask

Adjust gradient with the gradient annotator

Using the Reflect Command

Illustrator provides several transform commands that either transform an object or create a copy of the transformation. The Reflect command reflects your selection vertically, horizontally, or at an angle. The Reflect dialog box also allows you to either reflect the object or create a copy of the reflection, as shown in Figure 9.

Figure 9 *Reflect dialog box*

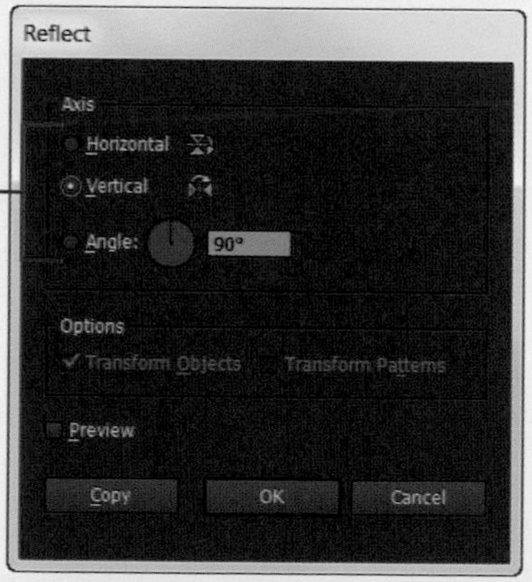

Reflection options

Enhancing your Character Using Illustrator and Photoshop

Applying Blend Options

You can use blends to quickly and easily create a series of in-between objects that can be used to make something move or, if they are different shapes, to make them morph, as shown in Figure 10. You can create blends with either the Make Blend command on the Object menu or the Blend tool.

Figure10 *Applying the Blend Mode command*

Before you can apply the Make Blend command, you need to select the two objects you want to blend. You can modify the spacing and orientation in the Blend Options dialog box, shown in Figure 11. The spacing option determines the number of steps that will be added between the two objects to create the blend. The number of steps can be controlled based on color, specified steps, or specified distance. The orientation option determines the orientation of the objects that make up the blend; they are aligned either to the page or to the path.

The Blend tool allows you to blend two objects by simply clicking on one shape and then another to create a sequential blend of shapes without rotation. You can also double-click the Blend tool to open the Blend Options dialog box. The path of the blended object can be modified with the Direct Selection tool by adjusting anchor points. You can also add additional anchor points if needed to modify the shape of your path.

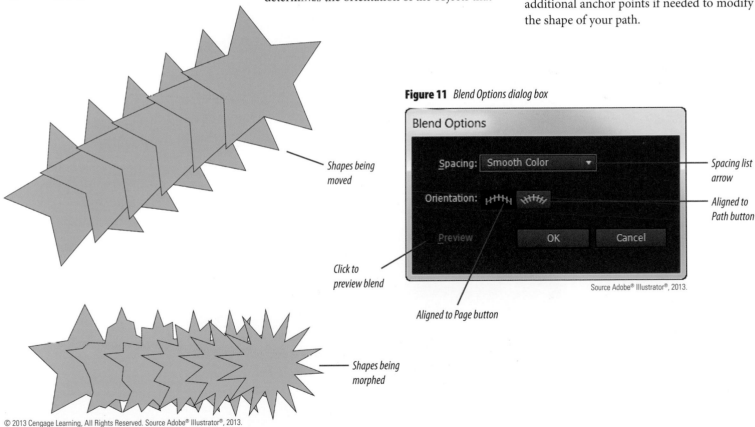

Shapes being moved

Figure 11 *Blend Options dialog box*

Spacing list arrow

Aligned to Path button

Click to preview blend

Source Adobe® Illustrator®, 2013.

Aligned to Page button

Shapes being morphed

Exporting a Document as a SWF File

One of the export options available in Illustrator is to export a document as a Flash file in the SWF format, which creates a simple animation. The SWF Options dialog box has a Basic and Advanced mode, shown in Figure 12; you will need to use both to create an animation.

Figure 12 *SWF Options dialog box in Basic mode*

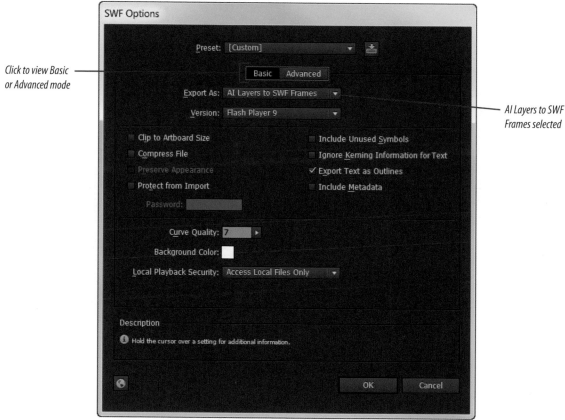

Click to view Basic or Advanced mode

AI Layers to SWF Frames selected

Source Adobe® Illustrator®, 2013.

In the Basic mode, you first need to select the option to export AI Layers to SWF Frames, then in the Advanced mode, you designate which layers will remain static, as shown in Figure 13. Keep in mind this is a very simple frame animation and can only display one layer at a time in sequential order. Click the Web preview button in the bottom-left corner to preview your animation in a web browser before exporting the file.

Figure 13 *SWF Options dialog box in Advanced mode*

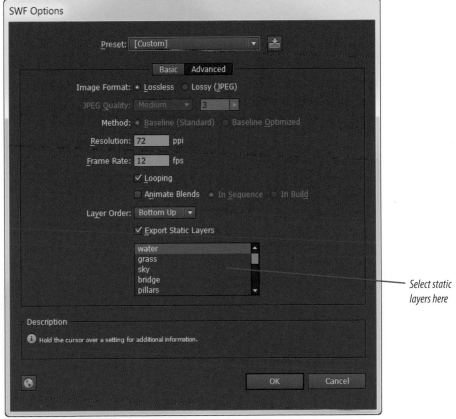

Source Adobe® Illustrator®, 2013.

Working with gradients

In this exercise, you will work with the Gradient tool to add shading to the walls in the illustration.

1. Start Illustrator, reset the Essentials workspace, open 2D 4-1.ai, then save it as **Pierre Animation**.

   An image has already been traced for you in Illustrator.

2. Click **Window** on the Menu bar, point to **Extensions**, then click **Kuler**.

   The Kuler panel opens.

3. Type **wall** in the search text box, then compare your screen to Figure 14.

   The search produces color groups you can use to shade the walls.

4. Click **the wall color group** at the bottom of the panel, click the **theme arrow** ▶, click **Add to Swatches Panel**, then close the Kuler panel.

   The color group is added to the Swatches panel, as shown in Figure 15.

   (continued)

Figure 14 *Kuler panel*

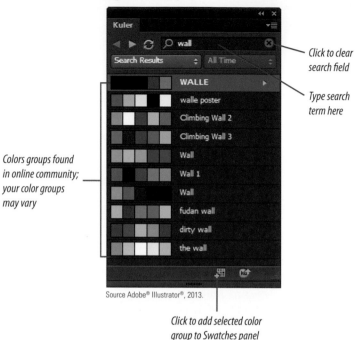

Click to clear search field

Type search term here

Colors groups found in online community; your color groups may vary

Source Adobe® Illustrator®, 2013.

Click to add selected color group to Swatches panel

Figure 15 *Color group added to Swatches panel*

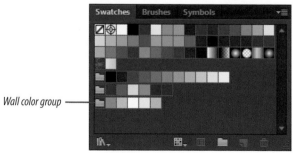

Wall color group

Source Adobe® Illustrator®, 2013.

Figure 16 *Applying a default gradient*

Black-and-white linear gradient applied to back wall

Gradient box

Courtesy of Sarah Galvan. Source Adobe® Illustrator®, 2013.

5. Open the **Gradient panel**, click the **Selection tool** on the Tools panel, then click the **back wall** on the artboard.

6. Click the **Gradient box** on the Swatches panel to apply the default black-and-white linear gradient to the back wall, as shown in Figure 16.

   Once you apply a gradient, you can edit it with the wall color group.

   (continued)

7. Double-click the **black color stop**, click the **Swatches icon** 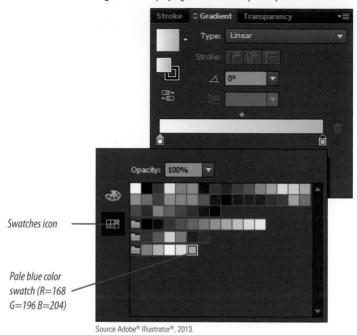 on the Gradient Stop Color panel, click the **pale blue color swatch (R=168 G=196 B=204)**, which is the last color swatch on the wall color group, as shown in Figure 17, then click away from the Gradient Stop Color panel to close it.

The color of the back wall changes to a white-to-blue linear gradient.

8. Repeat step 7 for the **white color stop**, changing the color to the **gray color swatch (R=153 G=153 B=153)**, which is the first color swatch on the wall color group.

(continued)

Figure 17 *Displaying the Gradient Stop Color panel*

Swatches icon

Pale blue color swatch (R=168 G=196 B=204)

Source Adobe® Illustrator®, 2013.

Figure 18 *Adding a color swatch to the Color slider*

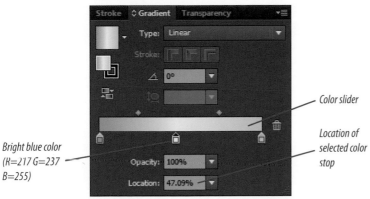

Color slider

Bright blue color (R=217 G=237 B=255)

Location of selected color stop

Source Adobe® Illustrator®, 2013.

Figure 19 *Left wall with customized gradient color*

Left wall with Appearance color applied

Appearance panel thumbnail

Courtesy of Sarah Galvan. Source Adobe® Illustrator®, 2013.

Lesson 1   Add Realism to Illustrator Artwork and Create a Simple Animation

9. Drag the **bright blue color swatch (R=217 G=237 B=255)**, the fourth color swatch on the wall color group, to the **middle** of the Color slider as shown in Figure 18, double-click the **Location text box**, then type **55.91%**.

10. Open the **Appearance panel**, click the **Selection tool** on the Tools panel, drag the **thumbnail** at the top of the Appearance panel to the **left wall**, then compare your image to Figure 19.

    The attributes of the back wall are applied to the left wall.

TIP To copy the appearance attributes, you need to have the object selected.

11. Save your work.

Apply an opacity mask

In this exercise, you will apply an opacity mask to add a reflection to the mirror.

1. Verify that Pierre Animation is open.

   You will continue working with your file from the previous set of steps.

2. Click the **Target icon** ⊙ on the **Furniture layer** on the Layers panel, then expand the layer so you can work with the sublayers.

3. Click the **Pen tool** ✐ on the Tools panel, set the fill color with a **bright blue** and the stroke to **None**, then draw an **outline** of the inside of the picture frame to create a copy of the mirror object, as shown in Figure 20.

4. Click **Edit** on the Menu bar, then click **Copy**.

5. Click **Edit** on the Menu bar, then click **Paste in Front**.

   A second copy of the mirror object appears in front of the selection. You will use this object to create a reflection.

TIP Be sure to keep the object selected before choosing the Paste in Front command so the copied object is placed as a sublayer in front of the selection.

6. With the copy of the new mirror still selected, change the fill color to **white**.

7. Click **Edit** on the Menu bar, then click **Paste in Front**.

   You will not need to apply the copy command again since you still have a copy of the original mirror on the clipboard. Three mirror object sublayers appear on the Furniture panel. The top and bottom mirror sublayers are blue; the middle sublayer is white. You will use the top object to create the mask.

   (continued)

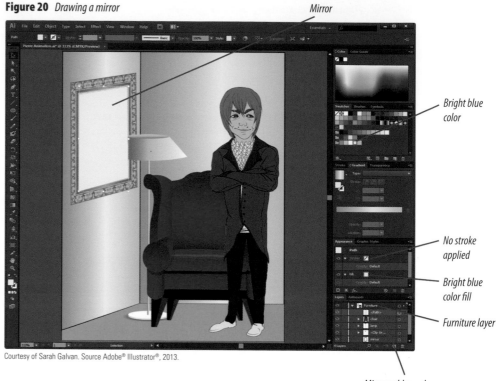

Figure 20 *Drawing a mirror*

Mirror

Bright blue color

No stroke applied

Bright blue color fill

Furniture layer

Mirror sublayer drawn with Pen tool

Courtesy of Sarah Galvan. Source Adobe® Illustrator®, 2013.

Enhancing your Character Using Illustrator and Photoshop

Figure 21 *Applying the default radial gradient*

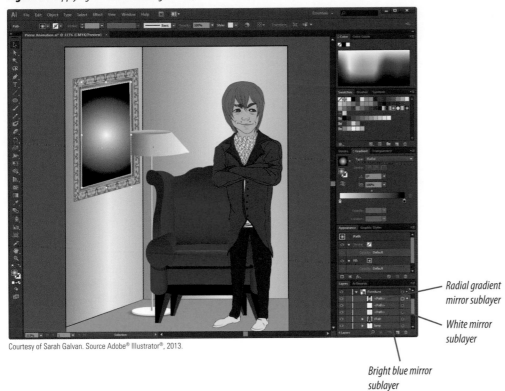

Courtesy of Sarah Galvan. Source Adobe® Illustrator®, 2013.

Radial gradient mirror sublayer

White mirror sublayer

Bright blue mirror sublayer

8. Click the **Radial Gradient swatch** on the Swatches panel, then compare your screen to Figure 21.

9. Press and hold **[Shift]**, then click the **Target icon** on the **middle <Path> sublayer**.

   The white <Path> sublayer is selected on the Layers panel.

   (continued)

10. Click the **Transparency panel tab**, click **Make Mask**, then compare your screen to Figure 22.

    The lamp is no longer visible in the mirror and part of the lamp is cut off; you will fix that in the next step.

11. Select both **<Path> sublayers** on the Layers panel, then drag them down in the stacking order until they are above the mirror layer.

    The lamp and its reflection in the mirror are visible.

12. Save your work.

Figure 22 *Applying an opacity mask*

Transparency panel

Applied mask

<Path> sublayers to be moved

Courtesy of Sarah Galvan. Source Adobe® Illustrator®, 2013.

Enhancing your Character Using Illustrator and Photoshop

Figure 23 *Editing an opacity mask*

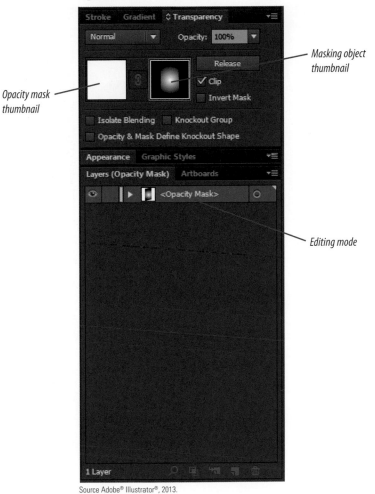

Opacity mask thumbnail

Masking object thumbnail

Editing mode

Source Adobe® Illustrator®, 2013.

Edit an opacity mask

In this exercise, you will adjust the reflection in the mirror by editing the opacity mask.

1. Verify that Pierre Animation is open.

   You will continue working with your file from the previous set of steps.

2. Click the **masking object thumbnail** on the Transparency panel to edit the mask, as shown in Figure 23.

   (continued)

3. Click the **Gradient tool**  on the Tools panel, then click the **mirror** on the artboard, as shown in Figure 24.

The gradient annotator and radial circle appear. You change the shape of the gradient to an oval.

(continued)

Figure 24 *Working with the Gradient tool*

Black circle

Gradient annotator

Gradient tool

Courtesy of Sarah Galvan. Source Adobe® Illustrator®, 2013.

Enhancing your Character Using Illustrator and Photoshop

Figure 25 *Reshaping a radial gradient*

Drag gradient
circle control down
to create oval

Courtesy of Sarah Galvan. Source Adobe® Illustrator®, 2013.

Figure 26 *Adjusting the rotation of a gradient*

Oval adjusted to be
vertical

Courtesy of Sarah Galvan. Source Adobe® Illustrator®, 2013.

4. Click and drag the **black circle** at the top of the radial gradient circle down to create an **oval**, as shown in Figure 25.

5. Hover over the **square** at the right end of the gradient annotator, when the **pointer** changes to ⟨⟩, rotate the **oval** until it is vertical, then compare your screen to Figure 26.

6. Click the **opacity mask thumbnail** on the Transparency panel to exit editing mode.

7. Save your work.

Work with the Gradient Mesh tool and the Appearance panel

In this exercise, you will work with the Gradient Mesh tool and the Appearance panel to add shading and texture to your artwork.

1. Verify that Pierre Animation is open, and there is nothing selected.

   You will continue working with your file from the previous set of steps.

2. Expand the **Room layer** on the Layers panel.

   The floor and left wall sublayers are visible.

3. Click the **Selection tool** ▷ , then click the **Target icon** ◎ on the **floor sublayer** on the Layers panel.

   The floor object is selected on the artboard.

4. Click **Edit** on the Menu bar, then click **Copy**.

5. Click **Edit** on the Menu bar, then click **Paste in Back**.

   A copy of the floor is pasted below the existing floor sublayer. You will use it in a later step.

6. Click the **Swatches panel menu button** ▼≡ , point to **Open Swatch Library**, point to **Nature**, then click **Stone and Brick**.

   The Stone and Brick swatches panel opens with colors you can use to shade the floor.

7. Click the **Mesh tool** 🔲 on the Tools panel, click the **tan color swatch (C=7 M=19 Y=50 K=10 2)**, which is the first color swatch in the first row on the Stone and Brick swatch panel, then click to the **left of the floor lamp**.

   A gradient mesh is created with a mesh point using the tan color, as shown in Figure 27.

   (continued)

Figure 27 *Working with the Mesh tool*

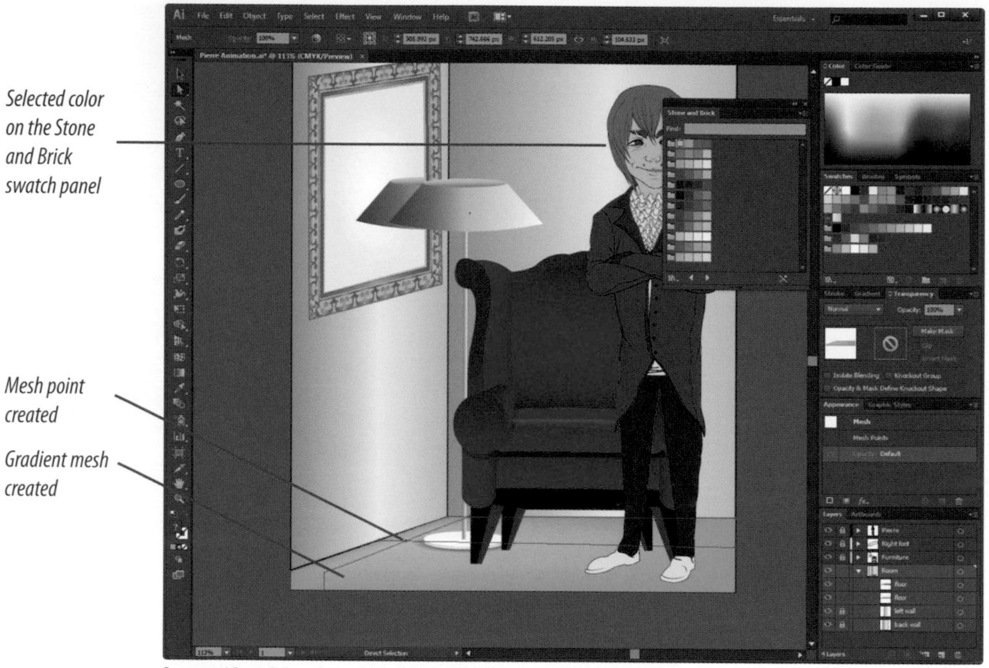

Selected color on the Stone and Brick swatch panel

Mesh point created

Gradient mesh created

Courtesy of Sarah Galvan. Source Adobe® Illustrator®, 2013.

2D ANIMATION 4-22

Enhancing your Character Using Illustrator and Photoshop

Figure 28 *Gradient mesh applied to floor layer*

Colors added to
gradient mesh; your
colors will vary

Courtesy of Sarah Galvan. Source Adobe® Illustrator®, 2013.

Figure 29 *Applying the Hatching Dense texture*

Your swatches
may vary

Hatching
Dense swatch

Hatching Dense
swatch applied
as a fill

Source Adobe® Illustrator®, 2013.

TIP You may find it easier to work with the floor by first locking the other layers.

8. Continue to select **various shades** from the first row of colors to add shading to the floor, then compare your screen to Figure 28.

 When selecting colors and shading the floor, consider where shadows would be based on the placement of the lamp.

TIP Use the Direct Selection tool ▶ to select and modify Mesh points.

9. Close the **Stone and Brick swatches panel**.

10. Click the **Swatches panel menu button** ▾☰, point to **Open Swatch Library**, point to **Patterns**, point to **Basic Graphics**, then click **Basic Graphics_Textures**.

 The Basic Graphics_Textures swatch panel opens with colors you can use to add texture to the floor.

11. Click the **Selection tool** ▶, then click the **Target icon** ◎ on the **second floor sublayer** on the Layers panel.

12. Click the **Hatching Dense swatch** on the Basic Graphics_Textures swatches panel, as shown in Figure 29.

 The texture is applied to the second floor layer; however, you cannot see the effect because of the floor layer above it.

(continued)

Lesson 1   Add Realism to Illustrator Artwork and Create a Simple Animation

13. Click the **Selection tool** , then click the **Target icon** on the **first floor sublayer** on the Layers panel.

14. Open the Transparency panel if necessary, then set the Opacity to **60%**.

15. Close the **Basic Graphics_Textures swatches panel**, deselect the **layer**, then compare your illustration to Figure 30.

16. Save your work.

Figure 30 *Floor texture applied*

Courtesy of Sarah Galvan.

Texture visible on floor

Figure 31 *Symbol Options dialog box*

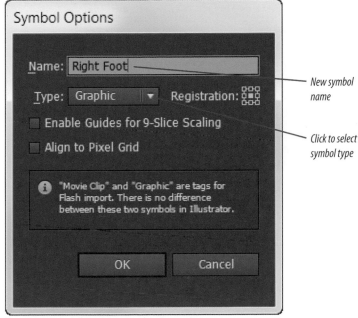

Name: Right Foot — *New symbol name*

Click to select symbol type

Figure 32 *Rotating the second right foot instance*

Second instance of foot

Apply the Blend tool

In this exercise, you will apply the Blend tool to make the foot tap.

1. Verify that Pierre Animation is open, then lock all **layers** on the Layers panel except the **Right foot layer**.

   You will continue working with your file from the previous set of steps. You will first need to convert the right foot to a symbol.

2. Click the **Selection tool** , then click the **Target icon** on the **Right foot layer** on the Layers panel.

3. Click the **Symbols panel tab**, then drag the selected **right foot** from the artboard to the Symbols panel.

   The Symbol Options dialog box opens and an outline surrounds the symbols on the Symbols panel.

4. Type **Right Foot** in the Name text box, select **Graphic** from the Type menu, compare your screen to Figure 31, then click **OK**.

   The foot symbol appears on the Symbol panel.

5. Drag a **second instance of the foot** from the Symbols panel to the artboard near the first foot, then rotate the **foot to the right**, as shown in Figure 32.

   You may need to adjust the location of the foot near the pants cuff after you rotate it.

   (continued)

6. Expand the **Right foot layer** on the Layers panel, press and hold **[Shift]**, then click the **Target icons** 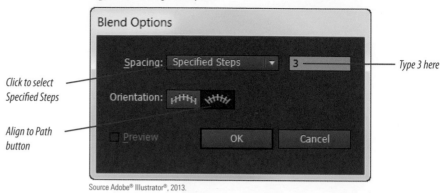 on both **Right foot sublayers**.

   You need to have both instances of the foot selected so there is something to blend when applying the Blend command.

7. Click **Object** on the Menu bar, point to **Blend,** and click **Blend Options**.

   The Blend Options dialog box opens.

8. Select **Specified Steps** from the Spacing menu, type **3** in the text box, click the **Align to Path button** , compare your screen to Figure 33, then click **OK**.

   This will create five more feet between the two existing feet.

9. Click **Object** on the Menu bar, point to **Blend**, then click **Make**.

   The blend options are applied to the selection.

10. Expand the **Blend sublayer** on the Layers panel, then compare your screen to Figure 34.

    Right foot sublayers appear on the Blend sublayer and five instances of the foot appear on the artboard.

11. Click **Object** on the Menu bar, point to **Blend**, then click **Expand**.

    The target icon on the Blend layer is selected.

12. Click **Object** on the Menu bar, then click **Ungroup**.

    The Group sublayer is deleted and the Right foot sublayers appear beneath the Right foot layer.

    (continued)

Figure 33 *Setting blend options*

Click to select
Specified Steps

Align to Path
button

Type 3 here

Source Adobe® Illustrator®, 2013.

Figure 34 *Blend command applied*

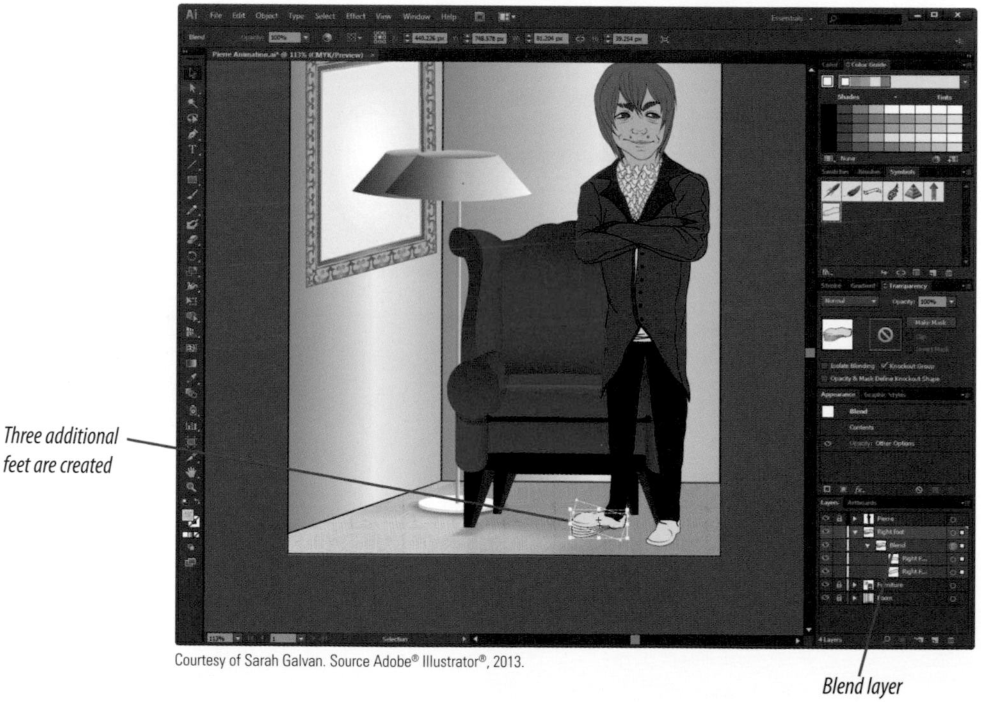

Three additional
feet are created

Blend layer

Courtesy of Sarah Galvan. Source Adobe® Illustrator®, 2013.

Enhancing your Character Using Illustrator and Photoshop

Figure 35 *Applying the Release to Layers (Sequence) command*

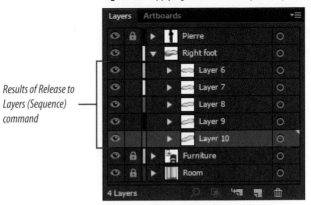

Results of Release to Layers (Sequence) command

Figure 36 *Moving new layers*

Empty Right foot layer

Figure 37 *Renamed layers*

13. Click the **Target icon** on the **Right foot layer** on the Layers panel, click the **Layers panel menu button**, then click **Release to Layers (Sequence)**.

    The instances of the foot are distributed to individual layers, as shown in Figure 35.

14. Select the **numbered sublayers** on the **Right foot layer**, drag them below the **Pierre layer**, as shown in Figure 36, then delete the **Right foot layer**.

15. Rename each of the **numbered layers** beginning from the top, **Foot 1**, **Foot 2**, **Foot 3**, **Foot 4**, and **Foot 5**, then compare your screen to Figure 37.

16. Save your work.

Lesson 1   Add Realism to Illustrator Artwork and Create a Simple Animation

Apply the Reflect command

In this exercise, you will create a reflection of Pierre in the mirror.

1. Verify that all the layers are locked except the **Pierre layer**.

2. Click the **Selection tool** on the Tools panel, then click the **Target icon** on the Pierre layer.

3. Click **Object** on the Menu bar, point to **Transform**, then click **Reflect**.

   The Reflect dialog box opens.

4. In the Reflect dialog box, click the **Vertical option button**, then click **Copy**.

   A reflection is created on each of the layers.

5. Click the **Selection tool**, then drag the **reflection of Pierre** to the mirror, as shown in Figure 38.

   (continued)

Figure 38 *Applying the Reflection command*

Reflection of Pierre

Courtesy of Sarah Galvan. Source Adobe® Illustrator®, 2013.

Reflection of Pierre in expanded Pierre layer

Enhancing your Character Using Illustrator and Photoshop

Figure 39 *Resizing Pierre to fit inside the mirror*

Resize handle

6. Press and hold **[Shift]**, then drag a **resizing handle** to make the reflection of Pierre's head and torso small enough to fit inside the mirror, as shown in Figure 39.

   Next, you move the reflected Pierre sublayer to the Clip Group on the Furniture layer.

TIP You may need to move the reflection of Pierre to place him inside the mirror after you resize him.

7. Unlock and expand the **Furniture layer** on the Layers panel.

8. Make sure the reflection of Pierre still is selected, then drag the **<Group> reflection sublayer** (Pierre's reflection) to the <Clip Group> sublayer.

(continued)

9. Expand the **<Clip Group> sublayer**, move the **<Group> reflection sublayer** beneath the Lamp sublayer to the bottom of the stacking order, then deselect your selection, as shown in Figure 40.

10. Save your work.

Figure 40 *Moving the Pierre reflection into a Clip Group*

Pierre reflection is now behind lamp reflection

Sublayer with Pierre reflection

Courtesy of Sarah Galvan. Source Adobe® Illustrator®, 2013.

Enhancing your Character Using Illustrator and Photoshop

Figure 41 *SWF Options dialog box in Basic mode*

Basic mode
button

Select AI Layers
to SWF Frames

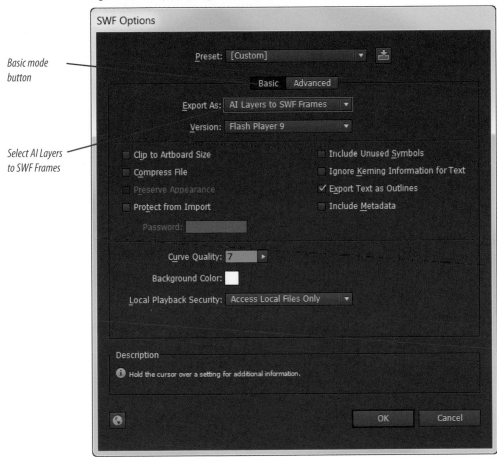

Source Adobe® Illustrator®, 2013.

Export an Illustrator document as a SWF file

In this exercise, you will export your Illustrator document as a SWF file to create an animation.

1. Verify that Pierre Animation is open.

   You will continue working with your file from the previous set of steps.

2. Click **File** on the Menu bar, then click **Export**.

   The Export dialog box opens.

3. Click the **Save as type list arrow**, click **Flash (*.SWF)**, then click **Save**.

   The SWF Options dialog box opens.

4. Verify that the **Basic mode button** is selected, click the **Export As list arrow**, then click **AI Layers to SWF Frames**, as shown in Figure 41.

   (continued)

5. Click the **Advanced mode button**, check the **Looping**, and **Export Static Layers check boxes**, select all the layers except those with foot in the name, make sure that **Bottom Up** appears as the Layer Order, then compare your screen to Figure 42.

TIP Press and hold [Ctrl] (Win) or [option]⌘ (Mac) to select multiple layers.

(continued)

Figure 42 *Setting options in the SWF Options dialog box Advanced mode*

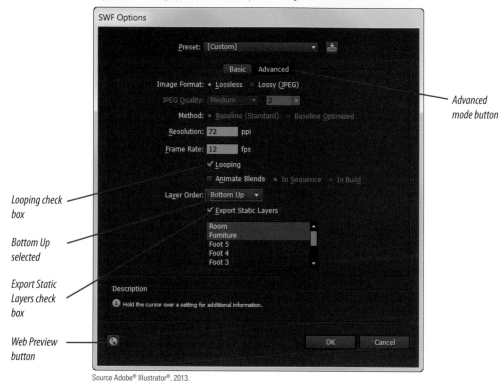

Source Adobe® Illustrator®, 2013.

Enhancing your Character Using Illustrator and Photoshop

Figure 43 *Web Preview from local file*

Temporary file name

Temporary path for file

ai13514729111.swf

file:///C:/Users/Debbie/AppData/Local/Temp/ai13514729111.tmp/ai13514729111.swf

10 cool features...   Suggested Sites   Web Slice Gallery   Imported From IE   Pin It

Courtesy of Sarah Galvan.

6. Click the **Web Preview button** ⊙ to preview your animation, compare your screen to Figure 43, then click **OK**.

Your default web browser opens, displaying your animation. A SWF file is created with the same name and in the same location as your Illustrator file.

7. Save your work and exit Illustrator.

Work with the Video Timeline
IN PHOTOSHOP

What You'll Do

 In this lesson, you will work with the video timeline in Photoshop to animate an Illustrator file.

Preparing an Illustrator File to Animate in Photoshop

A layer in Illustrator will become a Group in Photoshop and properly prepared sublayers will become separate layers in the Photoshop Group, as shown in Figure 44. Therefore, in order to be able to work with an Illustrator file in Photoshop and then animate it, you first need to complete the following steps in Illustrator:

1. Separate the parts of your illustration that you will want to animate in to their own layers.
2. Rasterize each layer.
3. Apply the Release to Layers (Sequence) command.
4. Name the layers to make it easier to work with when you work in Photoshop.
5. Export your file to Photoshop.

Figure 44 *Comparing Illustrator Layers panel to Photoshop Layers panel*

Illustrator layer

Illustrator sublayers that have been rasterized and released to layers

Photoshop group

Photoshop layers

There are several methods you can use to separate parts of an illustration; each method begins by selecting the object you want to move, and then doing one of the following:

1. Click and drag the colored box in the Selection column of the Layers panel to a new layer.
2. Select the layer on the Layers panel that you want your object to be moved to, click Object on the Menu bar, select Arrange, then click Send to Current Layer.
3. Apply the Collect in New Layers command from the Layers panel menu.

Keep in mind that when you draw in Illustrator, many sublayers are created and you need to combine all the paths into one layer. This can be done by applying the rasterize command. Rasterizing a layer converts the graphic's paths into pixels, so the vector graphic becomes a bitmap image. When preparing your Illustrator file to animate in Photoshop, it is important to rasterize each individual layer, rather than rasterizing the entire document. Rasterizing each layer keeps the objects on separate layers, whereas if you rasterize the entire document, all of the vector graphics would be flattened into one layer, making it impossible to animate.

To rasterize a layer, select the contents of the layer, click Object on the Menu bar, then select Rasterize. Be sure to select Transparent in the Rasterize dialog box so that a white background is not added to each of the layers. You will notice that each layer that has grouped contents (<Group>) is converted to an <Image> layer. Rasterizing the layer combines all the components of your object into one sublayer; converting sublayers into layers transfers to Photoshop as a layer within a Photoshop group.

As you learned in the previous lesson, the Release to Layers (Sequence) command, located on the Layers panel menu, converts the sublayers into layers.

Finally, you are ready to export your Illustrator file to Photoshop by clicking the Export command on the File menu. Select Photoshop (*.PSD) as the file type, then select options in the Photoshop Export Options dialog box that opens after you select the file type, shown in Figure 45. If you are

Figure 45 *Photoshop Export Options dialog box*

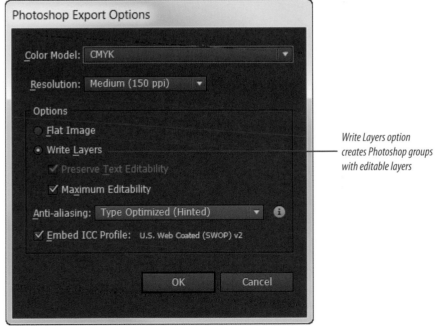

Write Layers option creates Photoshop groups with editable layers

Source Adobe® Illustrator®, 2013.

working with multiple artboards, you have the option to export each artboard, or a range of artboards, to a separate Photoshop file. Additional options are explained in Table 1.

Converting to Smart Objects in Photoshop

When a file is converted from Illustrator to Photoshop, the Illustrator layers with sublayers that have been rasterized are organized in groups. You will need to convert each sublayer to a smart object, as shown in Figure 46, so that layer properties can be modified when animating the layers on the Video Timeline. Layer properties include transform, opacity, and style. A **smart object** is a layer that contains image data from raster or vector images, such as Photoshop or Illustrator files. They preserve an image's source content with all its original characteristics and allow you to perform nondestructive editing to the layer.

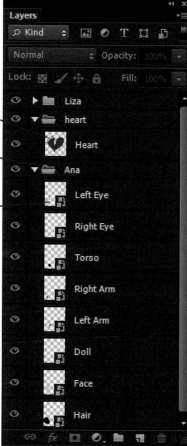

Figure 46 *Layers converted to a smart object*

Layer not a smart object

The folder represents a Photoshop group with editable layers inside the group

Layer converted to a smart object

TABLE 1: PHOTOSHOP EXPORT OPTIONS	
Option	**Explanation of Option**
Color Model	The color model of the exported file. *Note*: Changing the color model during export may affect transparency and blending modes; it is suggested that if you want to change the color model at this stage, export it as a flattened image.
Resolution	The resolution of the exported file.
Flat Image	All layers are rasterized into a single layer.
Write Layers	Groups, compound shapes, nested layers, and slices are exported as Photoshop groups with editable Photoshop layers. *Note*: Layers that are nested more than five levels deep will be merged into a single Photoshop layer.
Preserve Text Editability	Horizontal and vertical point text is exported in layers as Photoshop editable type. Text will be rasterized if this option is not selected.
Maximum Editability	Each top-level sublayer is written as a separate Photoshop layer; top-level layers become Photoshop layer sets.
Anti-Alias	The artwork is sampled to remove jagged edges when this option is selected; if not selected, the line art retains hard edges.
Embed ICC Profiles	A color management document is created.

Enhancing your Character Using Illustrator and Photoshop

You can create a smart object by using one of the following methods:

1. Use the Open As Smart Object command on the File menu.
2. Use the Place command on the File menu.
3. Copy an object in Illustrator and apply the Paste command in Photoshop. (*Note*: This can also be done by dragging an Illustrator layer into a Photoshop document.)
4. Convert a Photoshop layer by applying the Convert to Smart Object command on the Layer menu, then pointing to Smart Objects, the Layers panel menu, or by right-clicking the layer.

Working with Smart Objects

Smart objects can be used to create nondestructive transformations such as scale, rotate, skew, distort, or perspective transform. Warping a layer can also be applied without losing original image data or quality. You can also use them to:

- Work with vector artwork from Illustrator that would otherwise be rasterized in Photoshop.
- Apply nondestructive filtering effects.
- Edit one Smart Object and update all linked instances automatically.
- Apply a layer mask that can be either linked or unlinked to the Smart Object layer.

Animating on the Video Timeline

Once you have converted your layers to smart objects, you can apply changes to the layer properties in the Video Timeline to add movement. In order for a layer property to create movement, you will need to create keyframes. A **keyframe** is an instruction that tells Photoshop how you want your layer to appear at that time. When you create more

Pasting Adobe Illustrator Art into Photoshop

Instead of exporting your Illustrator document to the Photoshop file format, you can also copy art from Illustrator and paste it into a Photoshop document. First, disable the PDF and the AICB (No Transparency Support) options that are selected by default on the File Handling & Clipboard category in the Preferences dialog box. The line art automatically becomes rasterized when it is pasted in a Photoshop document. *Note*: Preferences can be accessed on the Edit menu (Win) or the Illustrator menu (Mac).

If you want to paste the line art as a smart object, a rasterized image, a path, or a shape layer, select the PDF and the AICB (No Transparency Support) options. The line art can then be copied in Illustrator with the Copy command and pasted into a Photoshop document with the Paste command.

If you choose to keep the PDF and AICB (No Transparency Support) selected, you will then need to choose how you want to paste the line art in the Paste dialog box when you paste it in Photoshop. Figure 47 shows the Paste dialog box. Pasting as a Smart Object pastes the line art on a separate layer embedding the file data and creating a Vector Smart Object, which will allow you to scale, transform, or move without degrading the line art. Pasting as Pixels pastes the line art as a rasterized image on its own layer and will also allow you to scale, transform, or move the line art. Pasting as a Path pastes the line art in the selected layer and the path can be edited with the pen tools, the Path Selection tool, or the Direct Selection tool. Pasting as a Shape Layer pastes the line art as a new shape layer, which is a layer containing a path fill with the foreground color.

Figure 47 *Photoshop Paste dialog box*

Source Adobe® Photoshop®, 2013.

than one keyframe, Photoshop determines what needs to be done to the layer to make it change from one keyframe to the next, in a process known as **interpolation**.

You first need to turn on keyframing for a layer property by clicking the triangle next to the layer name. A down-pointing triangle displays the layer's properties. You then click the stopwatch to set the first keyframe for the layer property you want to animate, as shown in Figure 48. (*Note:* Clicking the stopwatch after keyframes have already been activated will delete all the keyframes for that layer.) You can set keyframes for more than one layer property at a time if you know you want the other layer properties to change at the same time. The red line is referred to as the **current time indicator (CTI)**. You must move this line before creating additional keyframes by dragging the blue icon located at the top of the red line to the time or frame where you want the layer's property to change. You can change one or more of the following properties:

- Modify the transformation to change the rotation or size of the contents of a layer.
- Change the opacity to make the contents of the layer fade in or out.
- Apply a layer effect and then modify the effect so that it will change over time.

Rendering an Animation

You can save your animation either by using the Save For Web & Devices command and creating an animated GIF, or as an image sequence or video. The process of exporting an image sequence or video is called **rendering**, and your animations are saved as movie files. You will be saving your animations as MP4 videos. (*Note:* You can also save your image sequence or video as a PSD file that would allow

Figure 48 *Working with keyframes*

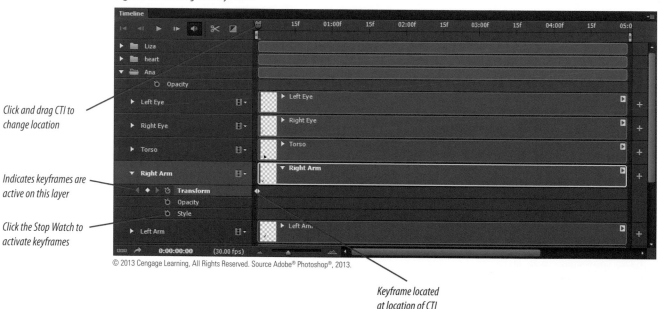

Click and drag CTI to change location

Indicates keyframes are active on this layer

Click the Stop Watch to activate keyframes

© 2013 Cengage Learning, All Rights Reserved. Source Adobe® Photoshop®, 2013.

Keyframe located at location of CTI

Enhancing your Character Using Illustrator and Photoshop

you to import the file into Adobe After Effects, which is beyond the scope of this book.)

Before you export your animation for the web, you should first optimize to allow for better download times in a web browser. Optimizing your animation can be done in two ways:

■ Optimize a frame animation to include only areas that change from frame to frame. This will greatly reduce the size of your animated GIF file.

■ Apply dithering techniques as you would with any GIF image you optimize for the web, dithering applied to an animation will make dither patterns consistent across all frames to avoid flickering when playing the animation.

When you choose to export your animation to a video format using the Render Video command, you can apply compression options in the Render Video dialog box, as shown in Figure 49, which reduces the file size. When you choose to export an H.264 formatted file, the movie has an MP4 extension.

Figure 49 *Render Video dialog box*

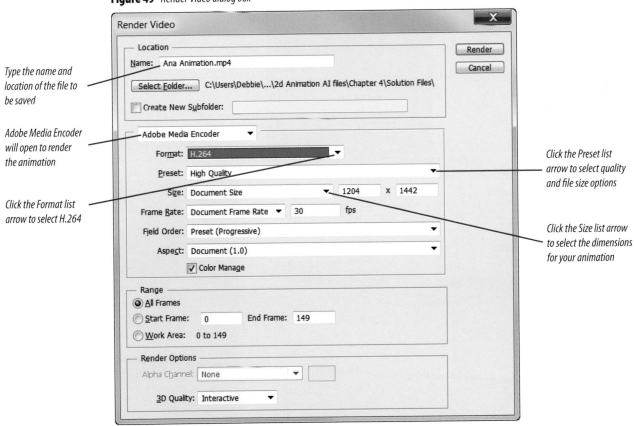

Type the name and location of the file to be saved

Adobe Media Encoder will open to render the animation

Click the Format list arrow to select H.264

Click the Preset list arrow to select quality and file size options

Click the Size list arrow to select the dimensions for your animation

Source Adobe® Photoshop®, 2013.

Prepare an Illustrator file to animate in Photoshop

In this exercise, you will prepare an Illustrator file to animate in Photoshop.

1. Start Illustrator, open 2D 4-2.ai, then save it as **Animated Ana**.

   An image has already been traced for you in Illustrator.

2. Expand the **Liza layer** on the Layers panel.

3. Click the **Selection tool**, then click the **Target icon** on the **right eye sublayer**, as shown in Figure 50.

   The image is grouped and the right eye is selected.

4. Click **Object** on the Menu bar, then click **Rasterize**.

   The Rasterize dialog box opens.

5. Click the **Transparent option button**, as shown in Figure 51, then click **OK**.

   The sublayer is rasterized.

6. Repeat steps 3–5 for the remaining sublayers.

7. Click the **Liza layer**, click the **Layers panel menu button**, then click **Release to Layers (Sequence)**.

   The layers will be separate layers when opened in Photoshop.

(continued)

Figure 50 *Selecting a sublayer with the Target icon*

Target icon on right eye layer selected

Figure 51 *Rasterize dialog box*

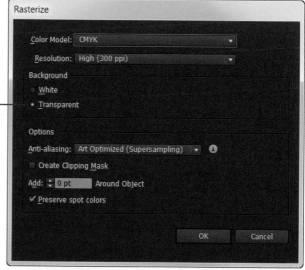

Transparent background option button selected

Enhancing your Character Using Illustrator and Photoshop

Figure 52 *Renamed sublayers*

— *Names are intuitive*

Figure 53 *Exporting an Illustrator file to Photoshop*

Write Layers option button selected —

8. Beginning at the top of the stacking order, rename the sublayers as follows: **right eye**, **left eye**, **left arm**, **right arm**, **torso**, **hair**, **doll**, and **face**, then compare your Layers panel to Figure 52.

   Naming layers helps keep the layers organized when you export the file to Photoshop.

9. Click **File** on the Menu bar, then click **Export**.

   The Export dialog box opens.

10. Click the **Save as type list arrow** (Win) or **Format list arrow** (Mac), click **Photoshop.psd**, then click **Save**.

    The Photoshop Export Options dialog box opens.

11. Verify that the **Write Layers option** is selected, compare your screen to Figure 53, then click **OK**.

12. Save and close your work, then exit Illustrator.

Convert to smart objects

1. Start **Photoshop**, open **Animated Ana.psd**, then set your workspace to **Motion** if necessary.

2. Expand the **Liza group** on the Layers panel, as shown in Figure 54.

   You will convert each of the layers to a smart object.

3. Click the **right eye layer** at the top of the stacking order, click **Layer** on the Menu bar, point to **Smart Objects**, then click **Convert to Smart Object**.

   The layer is converted to a smart object, as shown in Figure 55.

   TIP You can also right-click the layer name and then click Convert to Smart Object.

4. Repeat step 3 for each of the remaining layers in the Liza group.

5. Repeat steps 2–4 for the heart group and the Ana group.

6. Save your work.

Figure 54 *Expanded Liza group*

Click to expand the group

Figure 55 *Layer converted to a smart object*

Layer converted to a smart object

Enhancing your Character Using Illustrator and Photoshop

Figure 56 *Creating a Video Timeline*

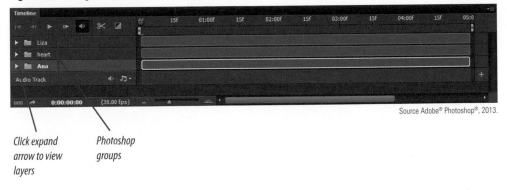

Click expand arrow to view layers

Photoshop groups

Figure 57 *Adjusting the Timeline panel*

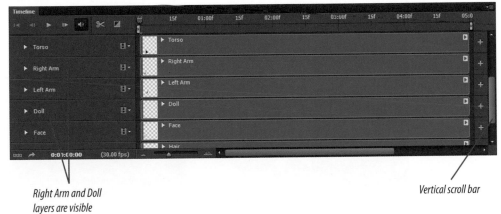

Right Arm and Doll layers are visible

Vertical scroll bar

Animate on the video timeline

1. Click the **Create Video Timeline button** on the Timeline panel, then compare your screen to Figure 56.

   Layers on the Timeline appear. You begin by animating Ana, the character with the purple hair.

2. Click the **Expand arrow** ▶ on the Ana layer.

3. Drag the **vertical scroll bar** so that the Right Arm and Doll layers are visible, as shown in Figure 57.

   You will animate the arm and the doll so that they swing.

TIP You may want to resize the Timeline panel to make it taller.

4. Click the **Expand arrow** ▶ on the Right Arm layer and the Doll layer.

(continued)

5. Verify that the CTI displays 0:00:00:00, then click the **Transform stopwatch icon** ⏱ on the Right Arm layer and the Doll layer, as shown in Figure 58.

   Keyframes are activated for the layers.

   TIP If you do not see Transform, your layer has not been converted to a smart object.

6. Drag the **CTI** 🔻 to **0:00:01:00f**, then click the **keyframe icon** ◆ on the Right Arm layer and the Doll layer.

   A new keyframe appears on each layer.

7. Click the **keyframe** ◆ on the Right Arm layer at **0:00:01:00f**.

   Both layers are selected.

   TIP If both layers are not selected, press and hold [Ctrl] (Win) or ⌘ (Mac), then click the layer that is not highlighted.

8. Click **Edit** on the Menu bar, then click **Free Transform**.

   You will rotate the arm.

   TIP Press and hold [Ctrl][T] (Win) or ⌘ [T] to apply a free transform to the selected layer.

9. Click the **upper-right reference point** on the options bar, drag the **arm** to position it further away from the body, as shown in Figure 59, then click the **Commit transform button** ✓.

   The arm rotates on the point closest to the torso and the doll moves with the arm.

   (continued)

Figure 58 *Activating keyframes*

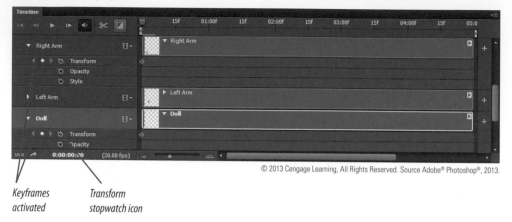

Keyframes activated

Transform stopwatch icon

Figure 59 *Applying a rotation transformation*

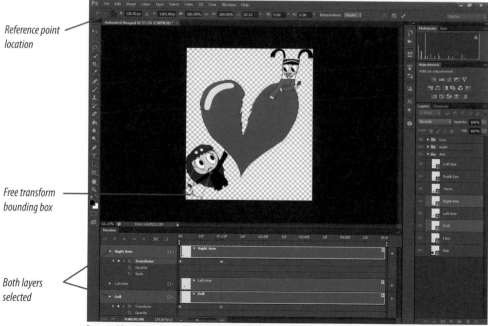

Reference point location

Free transform bounding box

Both layers selected

Enhancing your Character Using Illustrator and Photoshop

Figure 60 *Adding another keyframe*

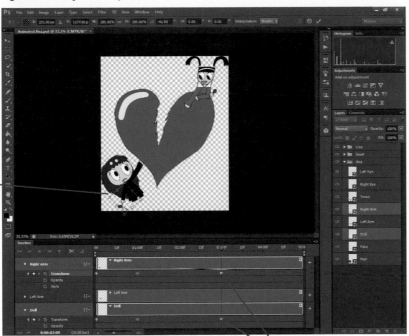

Right arm adjusted down

Courtesy of Raul Gaytan. Source Adobe® Photoshop®, 2013.

New keyframes added

10. Move the **CTI** 🛇 back to **0:00:00:00**, then press **[spacebar]** to preview your animation.

    The arm moves upward away from the body while holding the doll.

TIP If you need to adjust the location of the arm to the torso, click the Go to next keyframe button ▶ to return to the keyframe at 00:00:01:00f.

11. Move the **CTI** 🛇 to **0:00:03:00f**, then repeat steps 7–11 to adjust the arm to swing back towards the body, as shown in Figure 60.

12. Preview your animation.

13. Save your work.

Render an animation

1. Verify that Animated Ana is open.

   You will continue working with your file from the previous set of steps.

2. Click the **Timeline panel menu button** 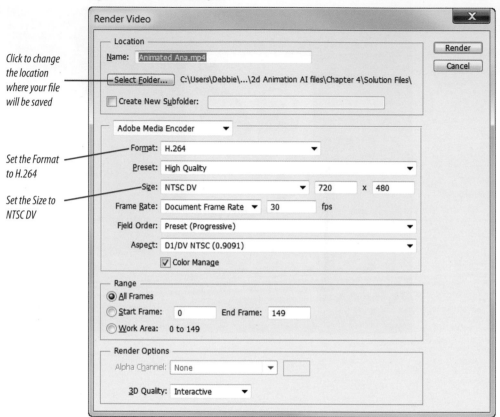, then click **Render Video**.

   The Render Video dialog box opens, as shown in Figure 61.

3. Click the **Format list arrow**, then click **H.264**.

4. Click the **Size list arrow**, then click **NTSC DV**.

   The animation will be resized to 720 px x 480 px.

5. Click **Render**.

   The Progress bar shows the video is created. By default, the video is rendered to the same location as your Photoshop file with the .MP4 file extension.

   TIP Click the Select Folder button to change the location of your final file.

   (continued)

Figure 61 *Render Video dialog box*

Click to change the location where your file will be saved

Set the Format to H.264

Set the Size to NTSC DV

Source Adobe® Illustrator®, 2013.

Enhancing your Character Using Illustrator and Photoshop

Figure 62 *Previewing your animation*

Courtesy of Raul Gaytan. Source Adobe® Photoshop®, 2013.

6. Navigate to the location where you store your Data Files, double-click the **Animated Ana.mp4** file to preview your animation, then compare your screen to Figure 62.

TIP To change the color of the background, add a new layer at the bottom of the stacking order and fill with a color of your choice.

7. Save your work.

Create an Animatic
IN PHOTOSHOP

What You'll Do

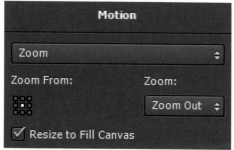

Source Adobe® Photoshop®, 2013.

In this lesson, you will create an animatic in Photoshop.

Creating an Animatic

An **animatic** is a storyboard that has been made into a video and often includes audio. An animatic is used before an animation is drawn in production to be sure the story and the characters make sense and tell a good story. This process saves the studios a great deal of money if changes can be done before the characters are drawn and animated.

You can create an animatic in a variety of ways. When animatics were first created, the method was to film a storyboard that was drawn on paper, edit the footage, and add an audio track. Another method to use is to take stock photographs or stock videos and create an animated storyboard. When stock photographs are used to create an animatic, it is called a **photomatic**. Using stock video is called a **videomatic** or **rip-o-matic**. A final method to use is computer-generated 2D and 3D art. This method eliminates the expense of hiring models to photograph.

You will use the Photoshop timeline to create your animatic from digitized storyboards.

Your storyboard can be created by scanning hand-drawn images or by drawing your images in Illustrator or Photoshop. The storyboard can then be animated in Photoshop. To give the illusion of motion, you will add pan and zoom effects and transitions.

QUICK TIP

Visit http://animatics.greghigh.com to review a variety of animatics online.

Preparing the Timeline

When you create your video timeline, all of the layers are stacked on top of one another and they are all the same length. Therefore, you will need to trim the length of the video layer and then move the video layer so the layers are staggered over time, as shown in Figure 63.

Trimming the video layer involves modifying the In point and Out point. The point at which the video layer begins playing is called the **In point**, and the point at which the video layer finishes playing is called the **Out point**. To adjust the location of an In point or Out point of a video layer, you can perform either of the following:

1. Click and drag the end of the layer.
2. Place the CTI at the location you would like to create a new In point or Out point, point to Move & Trim on the Timeline panel menu, and then select:
   - Trim Layer Start To Current Time, or
   - Trim Layer End To Current Time.

Adjusting the start time of a video layer can be done in one of two ways:

1. Click and drag the video layer.
2. Place the CTI at the location you would like the video layer to begin or end, point to Move & Trim on the Timeline panel menu, and then select:
   - Move Layer In Point To Current Time, or
   - Move Layer End Point To Current Time.

Applying Pan and Zoom Effects

In Photoshop CS6, the video timeline has been redesigned to include transitions and effects to help you create more refined animations. These effects can be applied to text, still images, and smart objects. It is necessary to convert your layers to smart objects, as was discussed in the previous lesson. To apply one of these effects, right-click the clip in the video timeline to access pan, zoom, and rotate presets. The newly created keyframes can then be adjusted on the Timeline to tweak the results.

This effect of panning and zooming has been commonly termed the "Ken Burns Effect."

He popularized the use of the effect in his widely seen Civil War documentary on PBS in the fall of 1990. You can accomplish this by scaling or changing the position or the rotation of the image. Using the "Ken Burns Effect," you can add movement to your illustrations in your animatic. These effects are created using keyframes. Photoshop recognizes the keyframes you have created and fills in the gaps to create a smooth movement between keyframes. This process is called **tweening**, and for this effect to work properly, at least two keyframes need to be created. (*Note*: You will learn much more about tweening in the next chapter when you begin working with Adobe Flash Professional.) Two keyframes are automatically created at the In point and Out point of the selected video layer. After you apply the default pan or zoom effect, you can modify the effect by expanding the video layer and making adjustments at the locations of the Transform keyframes. For example, you may want to increase the amount of zoom to an image by using the Free Transform command to enlarge the image even more.

Figure 63 *Adjusting the duration and placement of video layers*

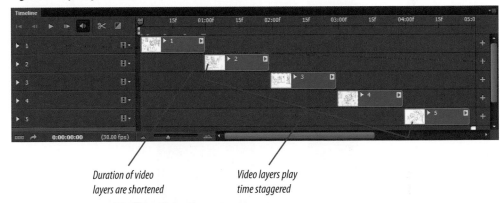

Duration of video layers are shortened

Video layers play time staggered

Adding a soundtrack

A rough soundtrack is usually added to an animatic to establish timing for dialogue and to ensure the story fits within the allotted time. The final soundtrack, which includes voice overs and music, is usually the last elements added to an animatic. Final adjustments are then made to the animation to make certain everything is synchronized. You can add audio files to Photoshop by placing the file on the Audio Track on the Timeline panel. To learn more about this feature, explore Photoshop Help.

Adding Transitions

Transitions can be placed between the video layers at the location of an In point or an Out point to create a professional fade or cross-fade effect. A transition can be added to a video layer by clicking the transitions icon located at the top of the Timeline panel, as shown in Figure 64, and then dragging the transition to the start or end of the clip on the video layer. You can then adjust the length of the transition by dragging its edge on the video layer.

QUICK TIP

If you are familiar with Photoshop, you can also add a layer mask to your video timeline. A layer mask reveals only a portion of the layer's content and allows you to animate the layer mask to reveal different portions of the layer's content over a period of time.

Figure 64 *Adding a transition*

Transition menu

Transition icon

Figure 65 *Video layers trimmed on timeline*

*Video layers trimmed
to location of CTI*

Figure 66 *Video layers staggered over time*

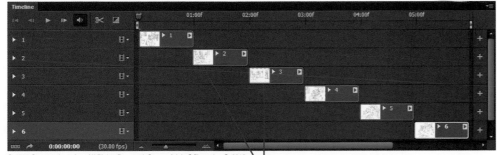

*Video layers staggered to
Out point of previous layer*

Prepare the timeline for an animatic

In this exercise, you will prepare the layers on the Timeline panel to create an animatic.

1. Open 2D 4-3.psd, then save it as **Animatic**.

   A file has been started for you with panels from the Jack and the Beanstalk story; you will create an animatic for the first scene of the story.

2. Expand the **Timeline panel** so you can see all six layers.

   You will trim the length of all of the layers to make it easier to animate.

3. Click **Layer 1** on the Timeline panel, move the **CTI** 🔻 to **00:00:01:00f**, click the **Timeline panel menu button** 📑, point to **Move & Trim**, then click **Trim End at Playhead**.

4. Repeat step 3 for the remaining layers, then compare your Timeline panel to Figure 65.

5. Drag **Layers 2–6** to the locations shown in Figure 66 to stagger them.

6. Save your work.

Apply pan and zoom effects to an animatic

In this exercise, you will add motion to your animatic with pan and zoom effects.

1. Verify that Animatic is open.

2. Select **Layer 1** on the Timeline panel, then verify the **CTI** 🐷 is located at **00:00:00:00**.

   You will apply a zoom effect to this layer.

3. Right-click the **Layer 1 thumbnail** on the Timeline panel, click the **Motion list arrow**, then click **Zoom**.

   The default zoom effect is applied to the layer.

4. Press **[spacebar]** to preview Layer 1.

   The zoom needs to be adjusted.

5. Return the **CTI** 🐷 to **00:00:00:01f**, click the **Expand Arrow** ▶ on Layer 1, then click the **Go to next keyframe icon** ▶ next to the Transform stop watch.

   You need to enlarge the image to increase the zoom effect.

6. Click **Edit** on the Menu bar, click **Free Transform**, press and hold **[Alt] [Shift]** (Win) or **[option] [Shift]** (Mac), drag a **corner transform handle** to resize the illustration, as shown in Figure 67, then click the **Commit transform button** ✓ on the options bar.

   The illustration is enlarged from the center.

7. Right-click the **Layer 2 thumbnail** on the Timeline panel, click the **Motion list arrow**, click **Zoom**, click the **Zoom list arrow**, then click **Zoom Out**, as shown in Figure 68.

   Layer 2 zooms out.

8. Return the **CTI** 🐷 to **00:00:00:00**, then press **[spacebar]** to preview both layers.

   The Layer 2 zoom also needs to be adjusted.

(continued)

Figure 67 *Increasing the zoom effect*

Commit transform button

Selected keyframe

Figure 68 *Applying a Zoom Out effect*

Zoom Out selected

Enhancing your Character Using Illustrator and Photoshop

Figure 69 *Applying a transition*

Fade transition

Transition icon

© 2013 Cengage Learning, All Rights Reserved. Source Adobe® Photoshop®, 2013.

Dragging the
Fade transition

9. Click the **Expand Arrow** ▶ on Layer 2, move to the **second keyframe** of Transform, then resize the illustration to make it approximately **50% smaller**.

TIP You can click and drag the CTI to preview the animation.

10. Right-click the **Layer 3 thumbnail** on the Timeline panel, click the **Motion list arrow**, click **Pan & Zoom**, then type **–180** in the Pan text box.

   The illustration zooms in while panning to the right.

11. Click the **Expand Arrow** ▶ on Layer 3, then adjust the duration to end at **04:00f**.

   The second keyframe adjusts automatically giving more time for the illustration to pan to Jack.

12. Press and hold **[Shift]**, click **Layers 4**, **5**, and **6**, then drag them to the **right** so the In point for Layer 4 begins at **00:00:04:00f**.

   Layers 5 and 6 move with Layer 4.

13. Save your work.

Apply transitions to an animatic

In this exercise, you will add transitions between the illustrations of your animatic.

1. Verify that Animatic is open.

   You will continue working with your file from the previous set of steps.

2. On the Timeline panel, click the **Transition icon** ▨ at the top of the Timeline panel, then drag **Fade** to the end of Layer 3, as shown in Figure 69.

   The transition is a little too long, so you trim the duration.

   (continued)

3. Hover at the **left end** of the transition on Layer 3, then drag it to the **right**, as shown in Figure 70, until the duration shows **00:10**.

4. Apply a **Fade transition** to the beginning of Layer 4, then shorten the duration to **00:05**.

5. Return the **CTI** to **0:00:00:00**, then press **[spacebar]** to preview the animatic.

6. Apply any additional motion effects (pan and/or zoom) and transitions to improve your animatic.

7. Render your animatic as an **H.264**, then set the size to **NTSC DV**.

8. Save and close your work, then exit Photoshop.

Figure 70 *Trimming a transition*

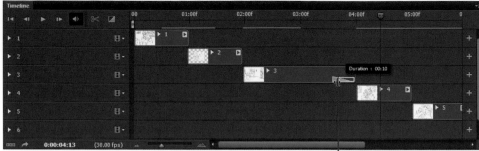

Trimming the duration of a transition

Using the skills learned in Lesson 1 of this chapter, you will create a simple animation.

1. Start Illustrator, open the file of a character you created and traced in a previous chapter, then save the file as **SB1-Simple Animation**.
2. Identify an element of the character you wish to animate.
3. Create a new layer and move the element you will be animating to the new layer, then rename the layer.
4. Duplicate the element you are going to animate and reposition it so that a motion can be applied to the element.
5. Apply the Blend tool to create variations on the element you are applying movement to, then compare your screen to Figure 71.
6. Export your animation as a SWF file. (*Hint*: Remember to select the static layers in the Advanced SWF Options dialog box.)
7. Save and close your work.

Figure 71 *Sample Skill Builder 1*

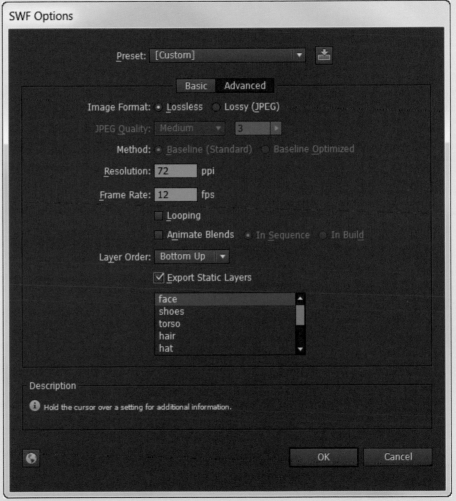

Source Adobe® Illustrator®, 2013.

Using the skills you learned in this chapter, you will create an animation in Photoshop.

1. Start Illustrator, open one of the comic book panels you created in Chapter 2.
2. Group the components of the illustration you want to animate.
3. Rasterize each of the grouped sublayers; be sure to select transparent when rasterizing.
4. Apply the Release to Layers (Sequence) to the layer containing all of the grouped sublayers and name each of the converted sublayers.
5. Export the file as **SB2-PS-Animation.psd**.
6. Open your newly created Photoshop file and convert each of the layers to smart objects.
7. Create a video timeline and add keyframes to the elements you want to animate.
8. Apply the Free Transform command to add movement to your objects, then compare your animation to the sample shown in Figure 72.
9. Render your animation as an H.264 and the size set to NTSC-DV.
10. Save and close your work.

Figure 72 *Sample Skill Builder 2*

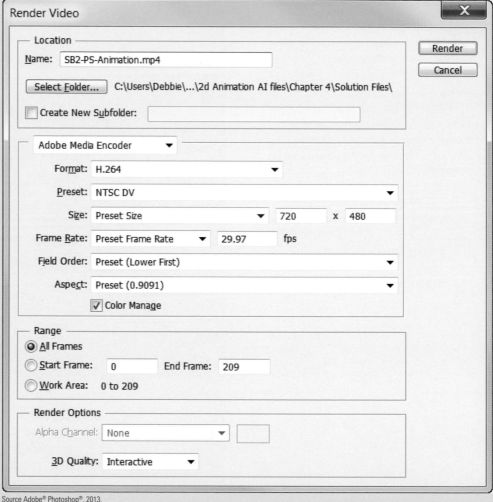

Source Adobe® Photoshop®, 2013.

Create an animatic using the illustrations provided of a scene in the Jack and the Beanstalk story.

1. Start Photoshop, then open a new file named **PP-animatic**.
2. Navigate to where you store your Data Files, then import the files in the PP-animatic sketches folder. (*Hint*: You may need to reorder your layers so the first illustration is at the top of the stacking order.)
3. Convert each layer to a smart object.
4. Create a video timeline.
5. Adjust the layers so one illustration plays after the other.
6. Apply pan and zoom effects to the layers to add motion.
7. Apply and adjust transitions to play between each of the layers, then compare your animation to the sample shown in Figure 73.
8. Render your animation as an H.264 with the size set to NTSC-DV.
9. Save and close your work, then exit Photoshop.

Figure 73 *Sample Completed Portfolio Project*

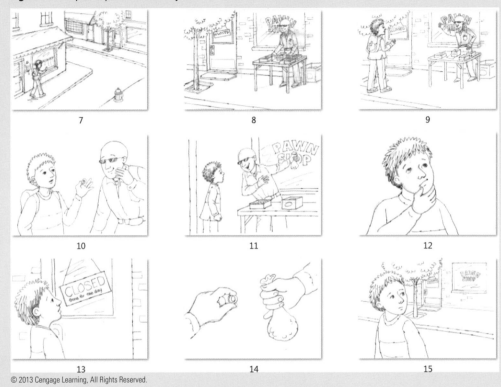

CHAPTER 5 CREATING BASIC ANIMATIONS IN FLASH PROFESSIONAL

1. Review the Flash Professional interface.
2. Create a frame-by-frame animation.
3. Create an animation with tweens.
4. Write basic ActionScript.

CREATING BASIC ANIMATIONS IN
FLASH PROFESSIONAL

Adobe Flash Professional is used to create multimedia content, games, web applications, and animations. Two types of animation that can be created in Flash are frame-by-frame animations and tween animations.

A frame-by-frame animation allows you to create more detail in your animation and is more time-consuming. This type of animation works best when animating a person walking or a person speaking.

A tween animation is simpler to create and relies on Flash to create the changes for you. This type of animation is best used when animating something that fades, rotates, or changes size.

In this chapter, you will work review the Flash Professional workspace, learn about and create frame-by-frame and tween animations, and write basic ActionScript.

TOOLS YOU'LL USE

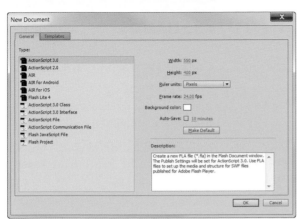

Source Adobe® Flash® Professional, 2013.

© 2013 Cengage Learning, All Rights Reserved. Source Adobe® Flash® Professional, 2013.

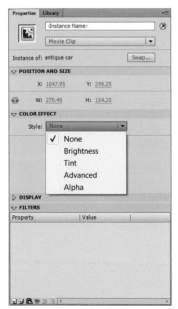

© 2013 Cengage Learning, All Rights Reserved.
Source Adobe® Flash® Professional, 2013.

Source Adobe® Flash® Professional, 2013.

Review the Flash Professional INTERFACE

What You'll Do

Source Adobe® Flash® Professional, 2013.

 In this lesson, you will review the Flash workspace.

Exploring the Flash Workspace

You should already have some familiarity with Flash before beginning this chapter, but you will first briefly review some of the key elements of the Flash workspace. When you create a new document you see the **application window**, which is the main window comprised of various panels. The arrangement of panels in the application window is known as the **workspace**. Flash offers several preformatted workspaces that are designed for specific tasks. Figure 1 shows the default workspace, called **Essentials**. The Essentials workspace, as its name implies, displays the essential panels needed to create a document. You will be using this workspace throughout this book.

You can move individual panels by clicking and dragging the panel tabs. **Panel tabs** display the panel's name and are found at the top of a panel. When you drag a panel, it is removed from the dock and you can place it anywhere on the screen or in a different panel group. When moving a panel to another panel group, a **drop zone** shown as a blue highlighted area, appears, indicating where the panel will be placed when you release the mouse.

You can move a panel group by dragging the title bar for the group. The title bar is the gray area to the left of the panel menu. A collection of panels or panel groups is known as a **dock**.

You can resize panels by dragging any side of the panel or collapse panels by double-clicking the active panel tab. At the top of a dock are the Collapse panel and Expand panel icons. These icons allow you to either collapse the dock to icon view or expand the dock to panel view. When in icon view, you can resize the panel to display or hide the panel names. In icon view, only one expanded panel is visible at a time. By default, Flash has two column

Figure 1 *Flash Essentials workspace (Windows)*

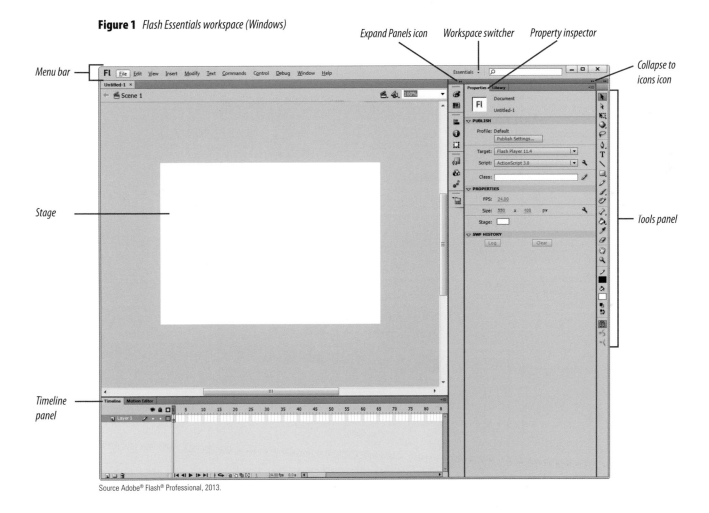

Source Adobe® Flash® Professional, 2013.

docks in the Essentials workspace, with one collapsed to icon view and the other expanded, as shown in Figure 2.

If you want to save a custom workspace, you can do so by clicking the New Workspace command on the Workspace menu, or by clicking the Save Workspace command on the Workspace switcher on the Menu bar. A **custom workspace** is one that has been created by the user and saved with a unique name.

If you want to open or move panels while you are working, you can reset the workspace back to the Essentials workspace using the Workspace switcher. The **Workspace switcher** is a menu on the Menu bar.

Figure 2 *Expanded panel dock*

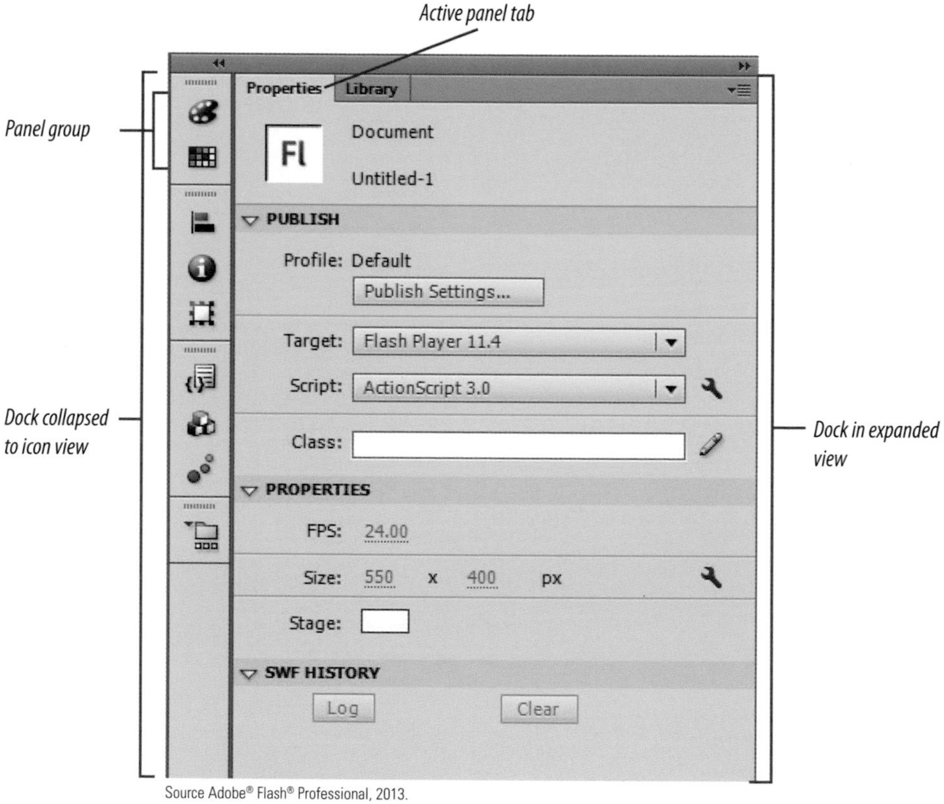

Source Adobe® Flash® Professional, 2013.

Understanding the Welcome Screen

When you open Flash Professional, the Welcome Screen opens by default, as shown in Figure 3. This screen is divided into three columns where you can create a new document from a template, create a new document from scratch, or access Adobe.com to learn more about Flash through the topics available in the third column.

When you use the New command on the File menu, you can also access options to create a new document or create your Flash project from a template. The New Document dialog box has two tabs, General and Templates,

Figure 3 *Flash Welcome Screen*

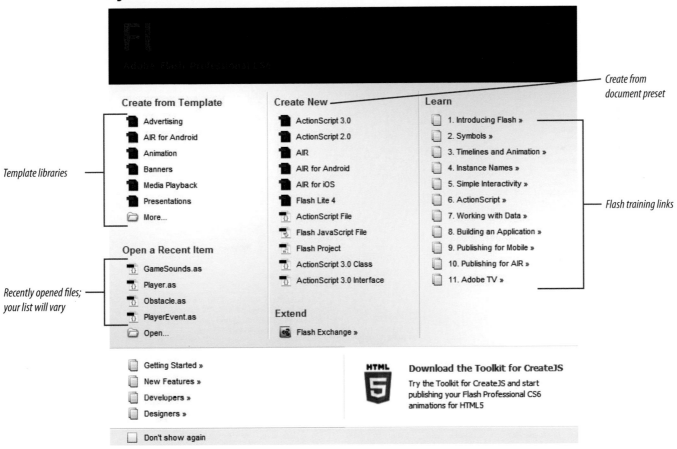

Source Adobe® Flash® Professional, 2013.

which contain the same options available on the Welcome Screen to create a new document from general presets or from a template.

When you create a new document from the New Document dialog box, you can set the width, height, background color, frame rate, ruler units, and set your project to auto-save, as shown in Figure 4. When you create a new project from the Welcome

Figure 4 *New Document dialog box*

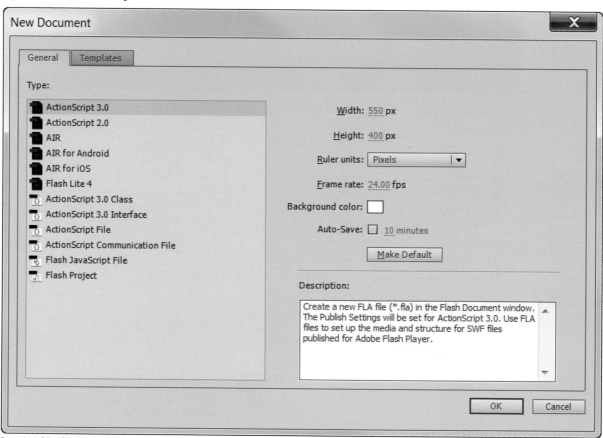

Source Adobe® Flash® Professional, 2013.

Creating Basic Animations in Flash Professional

Screen, you can adjust the project settings after the project is created in the Document Settings dialog box, shown in Figure 5.

The Document Settings dialog box can be accessed by clicking Document on the Modify menu.

When you click a template category in the Create from Template section of the Welcome Screen, the Template tab of the

Figure 5 *Document Settings dialog box*

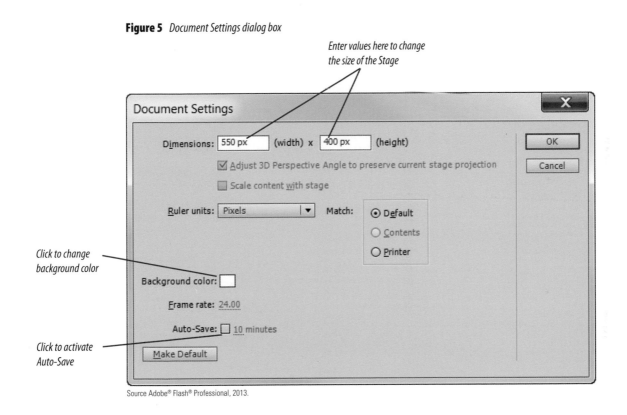

Enter values here to change
the size of the Stage

Click to change
background color

Click to activate
Auto-Save

Source Adobe® Flash® Professional, 2013.

New from Template dialog box opens, where you can preview the templates available in that specific library or category, as shown in Figure 6.

The **Stage** is the viewable area in a Flash project that becomes your published Flash Movie. By default, the Stage is white, the background color.

QUICK TIP

The Stage in Flash is equivalent to the artboard in Illustrator and the canvas in Photoshop.

A Flash project is saved with the FLA file extension, which allows the project to be editable. The project needs to be published before your audience can view it. Publishing options will be discussed later in this chapter.

Figure 6 *New from Template dialog box*

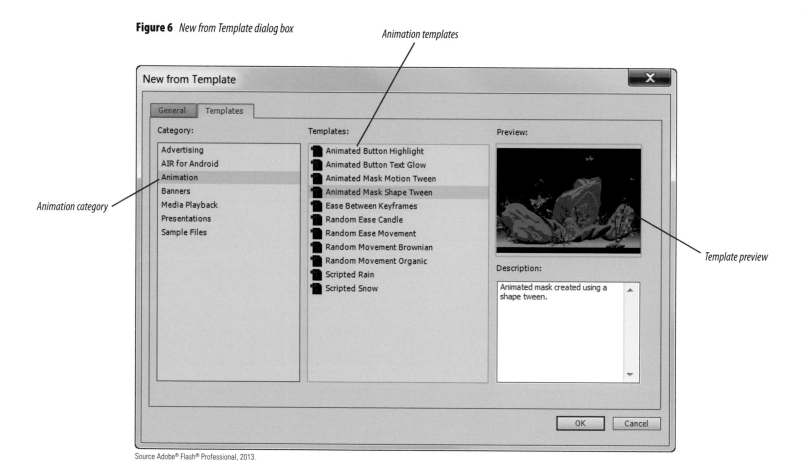

Animation templates

Animation category

Template preview

Source Adobe® Flash® Professional, 2013.

Figure 7 *Document Settings dialog box with default settings*

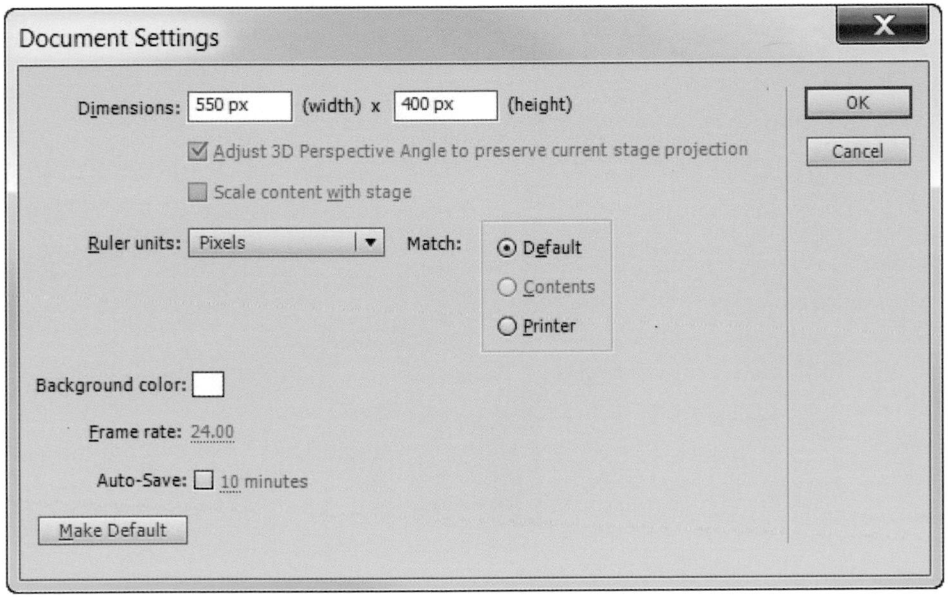

Source Adobe® Flash® Professional, 2013.

Start Flash Professional, create a new document, and explore the workspace

In this exercise, you will explore the Flash Professional workspace.

1. Click the **Start button** 🎯 on the taskbar, point to **All Programs**, then click **Adobe Flash Professional CS6** (Win), or open the **Finder** from the dock, click **Applications** from the sidebar, click the **Adobe Applications folder**, then click **Adobe Flash Professional CS6** (Mac).

   You may need to look in a subfolder if you have installed the Creative Suite.

2. Click **ActionScript 3.0** in the Create New section on the Welcome Screen.

   A new Flash document is created.

TIP Pressing and holding [Alt][Ctrl][Shift] (Win) or [option]⌘[Shift] (Mac) while starting Flash Professional restores default preference settings.

3. Click the **Workspace switcher** on the Menu bar, then click **Essentials**, if necessary.

   The Essentials workspace appears in its original configuration. If a workspace is already selected, you can click Reset <*Workspace*> to reset the current workspace.

4. Click the **Expand Panels icon** ◀◀ at the top of the panel dock.

   The panel dock expands from icon view to panel view.

5. Click the **Collapse to Icons icon** ▶▶ at the top of the Tools panel.

6. Click **Modify** on the Menu bar, then click **Document**.

   The Document Settings dialog box opens, as shown in Figure 7.

   (continued)

TIP You can also access the Document Settings dialog box by clicking the Edit document properties icon 🔧 in the Properties section on the Property inspector.

7. Click the **Background color swatch**, click the **red swatch** in the second column as shown in Figure 8, then click **OK**.

   The Stage color is changed to red.

8. Click **File** on the Menu bar, then click **Save**.

   The Save As dialog box opens, where you can select where to save the file.

9. Type **flash workspace** in the file name text box, navigate to the location where you store your Data Files, then click **Save**.

10. Click **File** on the Menu bar, then click **Close**.

Figure 8 *Changing the Stage color*

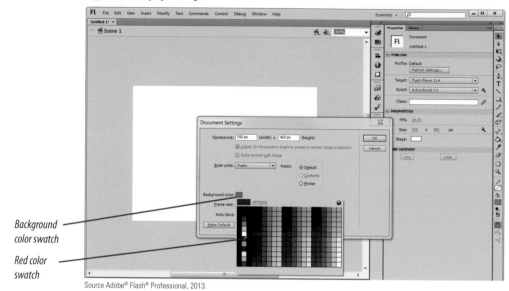

Background color swatch

Red color swatch

Source Adobe® Flash® Professional, 2013.

Create a Frame-by-Frame ANIMATION

What You'll Do

 In this lesson, you will work with the drawing tools and create a frame-by-frame animation.

Working with Flash Layers

Layers are used to organize your artwork, ActionScript, and other assets in your Flash project and are similar to working with layers in Illustrator and Photoshop.

As in other applications in the Adobe Creative Suite, drawing on separate layers allows you to edit and manipulate your artwork without affecting content on other layers. The pencil icon located to the right of the layer's name indicates that the layer is selected. (*Note*: Only one layer can be active at a time, but multiple layers can be selected.) Layers in Flash are located on the Timeline panel, as shown in Figure 9. By default, when you open a new Flash document, Layer 1 is created for you. A layer can be hidden, locked, or rearranged in the stacking order. (*Note*: While the number of layers does not influence the size of your document, the contents of those layers do.)

New layers can be added by clicking on the New Layer icon located at the bottom of the Timeline panel, by using the Layer command on the Timeline submenu on the Modify

Figure 9 *Layers on the Timeline panel*

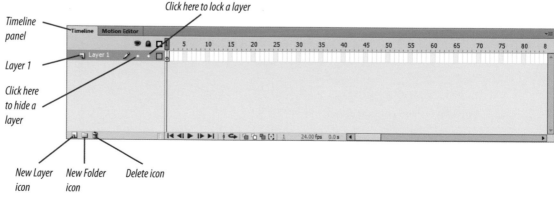

Timeline panel

Click here to lock a layer

Layer 1

Click here to hide a layer

New Layer icon

New Folder icon

Delete icon

Creating Basic Animations in Flash Professional

menu, or by right-clicking the layer's name and clicking Insert Layer from the context-sensitive menu. You can delete a layer with the Delete icon or by right-clicking the layer name and then clicking Delete Layers. The selected layer or layers are removed.

You can also organize layers into folders, similar to how you create groups in Photoshop. This is useful if you are creating a complex animation and using many layers that may contain audio, ActionScript, frame comments, frame labels, or tweens. You can expand or collapse a folder in the Timeline panel without affecting what you see on the Stage.

There are five types of layers you can work with in Flash: normal, mask or masked, guide or guided, motion tween, and armature. A **normal layer** contains most of the artwork in a Flash project file. A **mask layer** contains objects that are used as masks to hide selected portions of the layers below them. A **masked layer** is the layer below the mask layer in the stacking order. A **guide layer** contains strokes that are used as a guide to arrange objects on other layers or to create a classic tween animation. **Guided layers** are those layers associated with the guide layer. Objects on the guided layer can be arranged or animated along the strokes on the guide layer. (*Note:* Guided layers can contain either stationary artwork or classic tweens, motion tweens cannot be created on a guided layer.) A **motion tween** layer contains one or more

animated objects that have a motion tween applied to them. An **armature layer** contains objects that have inverse kinematics applied to them. You will work with some of these layers in this chapter.

Using Flash Professional Drawing Tools

Drawing with the drawing tools in Flash creates vector graphics that help keep your Flash file size small. As you learned previously, a vector graphic is smaller than a bitmap graphic. Many of the drawing tools in Flash behave in a similar manner to the tools you used in Illustrator. Paths also behave as they did in Illustrator.

- Paths are created with anchor points at the end of each line segment.
- A path can be straight, curved, open, or closed.
- The shape of the path can be modified by:
    - Adjusting anchor points.
    - Dragging direction points located on an anchor point.
    - Moving the path segment.
- Anchor points can be either a corner point or a smooth point.

Drawing tools include the Pen, Pencil, Brush, Line, and Deco tools, as shown in Figure 10. In addition, there are several tools available for drawing standard shapes, such as rectangles, circles, lines, stars, and other polygons. The Rectangle tool is the default tool in the shapes tool group on the Tools

panel. To select another tool in the group, click and hold the tool, then click the desired tool. The other tools in the Rectangle tool group are the Oval, Rectangle Primitive, Oval Primitive, and PolyStar tools.

Figure 10 *Flash drawing tools*

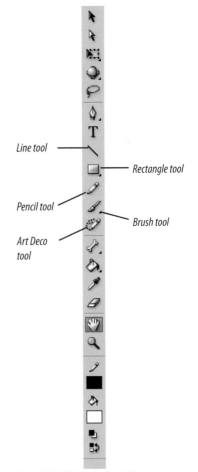

Line tool

Rectangle tool

Pencil tool

Brush tool

Art Deco tool

Source Adobe® Flash® Professional, 2013.

The **Deco tool** makes simple work of drawing complex shapes. The tool includes a variety of buildings, trees, and flowers that you can select from a variety of drawing effects from a pop-up menu on the Property inspector, shown in Figure 11. In addition, there are some animated deco tool drawings, such as drawing fire with the Fire Animation effect. Other drawing effects provide the option to draw the effect on a single frame or to generate an animation, such as creating lightning with the Lightning Brush.

The drawing tools have additional options known as **modifiers** that are available on the Tools panel. (*Note*: If a modifier is available for a specific tool, it will appear below the Fill Color and Stroke Color tools.)

The Brush tool draws brush-like strokes and has modifiers that set the brush size and shape, as shown in Figure 12. If you have a pressure-sensitive tablet, you can activate the Pressure and Tilt modifiers to vary the width and angle of the brush stroke by varying the pressure on the stylus. In addition, the Brush Mode modifier has five different painting modes. The default mode is Paint Normal, which paints over lines and fills on the same layer. The Paint Fill option paints fills and empty areas while not affecting lines.

Figure 11 *Deco tool options on the Property inspector*

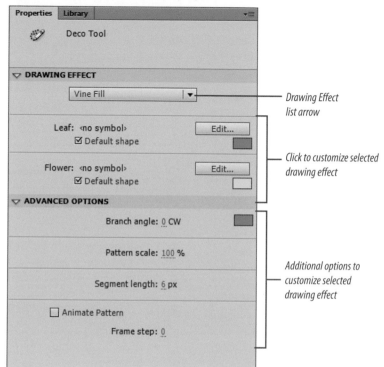

Source Adobe® Flash® Professional, 2013.

Figure 12 *Brush tool modifiers*

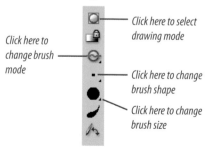

Source Adobe® Flash® Professional, 2013.

The Paints Behind option paints on the same layer behind fills and lines in any blank areas on the Stage, while not affecting both lines and fills. The Paint Selection option is used on a selection and applies the new fill color you select using the Fill Color tool on the Tools panel or the Fill Color icon on the Property inspector. The Paint Inside option paints the fill but does not paint lines, and only works when you paint a fill, not an empty area.

The Paint Bucket tool modifiers ignore a gap when filling an area. You can adjust gap size options (small, medium, and large) or ignore them with the Don't Close Gap option, as shown in Figure 13. The Lock Fill option allows you to fill more than one shape with the same gradient or bitmap so that it extends from one shape to the next.

The Eraser tool removes portions of a shape, and you can use its modifiers to erase fills, strokes, or segments, or select a brush size. The Free Transform tool adjusts the size, proportion, rotation, and distortion of an object and has several modifiers.

Understanding Object and Merge Drawing Modes

Merge drawing mode, the default drawing mode, automatically combines or merges shapes when you overlap them on the same layer. The shape on top cuts away the portion that is overlapped on the shape underneath it, as shown in Figure 14. The stroke and fill of a shape created in Merge drawing mode are separate graphic elements and can be selected and edited individually, as shown

Figure 13 *Filling with the Paint Bucket tool Close Large Gap modifier*

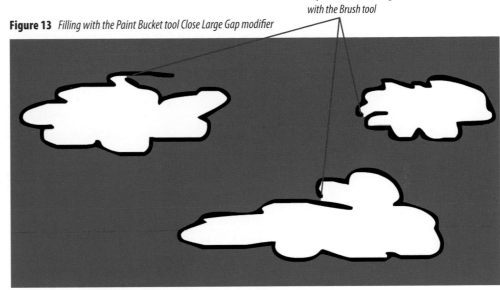

Gaps left when drawing with the Brush tool

Figure 14 *Drawing in merge drawing mode*

Overlapped shapes in merge drawing mode

Area cut away by circle

in Figure 15. When you select a shape that was created in merge drawing mode, dots indicate whether the stroke or fill is selected. If you double-click a shape, you select both the stroke and fill.

When drawing a shape in object drawing mode, you create drawing objects. A **drawing object** is a separate graphic object that does not automatically merge with an overlapping shape. The stroke and fill of a shape are not separate graphic elements. You can overlap shapes without changing their appearance if you move them apart or rearrange their appearance. Flash creates each shape as a separate object that you can individually edit, even if they are on the same layer. When you select a shape that was created in object drawing mode, a rectangular bounding box indicates both the fill and stroke are selected, as shown in Figure 16. The Selection tool moves the drawing object or changes its color. The Free Transform tool resizes, reshapes, or rotates the drawing object. When you double-click a drawing object with the Selection tool or the Free Transform tool, you enter merge drawing mode.

Figure 15 *Making a selection on a shape drawn in merge drawing mode*

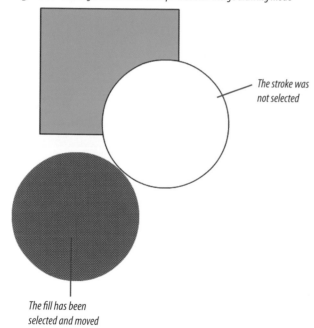

The stroke was not selected

The fill has been selected and moved

Figure 16 *Selecting a shape drawn in object drawing mode*

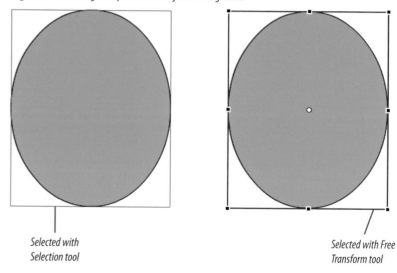

Selected with Selection tool

Selected with Free Transform tool

Working with Graphic Symbols

There are three types of symbols in Flash: movie clip, button, and graphic. Graphic symbols are used to create reusable static images and make creating a frame-by-frame animation much easier.

You can create a new symbol by drawing an object in symbol editing mode or by converting an existing object or shape on the Stage. To create a new symbol, click Insert on the Menu bar, and then click New Symbol. To convert an existing shape or drawing object to a symbol, select all of the elements on the Stage that will make up the symbol, and then click the Convert to Symbol command on the Modify menu. Flash stores and organizes symbols in the Library panel, where you can reuse symbols in the current document or in other Flash documents. Figure 17 shows different symbols in the Library panel.

Figure 17 *Symbols in the Library panel*

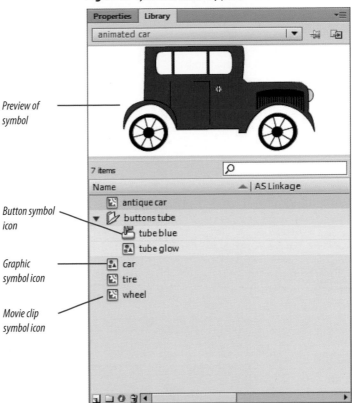

Preview of symbol

Button symbol icon

Graphic symbol icon

Movie clip symbol icon

Understanding Symbols and the Library Panel

You store and organize assets for your Flash project in the Library panel. Assets can include symbols, vector graphics, bitmaps, video, and sound. You can organize library items in folders, see how often an item is used in a Flash project, and sort items by name, type, or date.

Using symbols in your Flash project reduces the file size, improves consistency, simplifies editing, and shares symbols between Flash projects. Symbols can also make your Flash movie interactive. When you place a symbol on the Stage, it is referred to as an **instance** of a symbol.

Editing Symbols and Instances

If you want to edit a symbol on the Stage or in the Library panel, double-click the symbol or select the symbol and then click Edit Symbols on the Edit menu. A breadcrumb trail is created next to the scene in the Edit bar, and a new editing window opens, as shown in Figure 18. When you have finished editing the symbol, click Scene 1 on the Edit bar breadcrumb trail to exit editing mode.

All instances of the symbol will be changed throughout the document. You can modify the brightness, tint, and transparency of a selected instance of a symbol in the Color Effect section of the Property inspector by

Figure 18 *Editing a symbol*

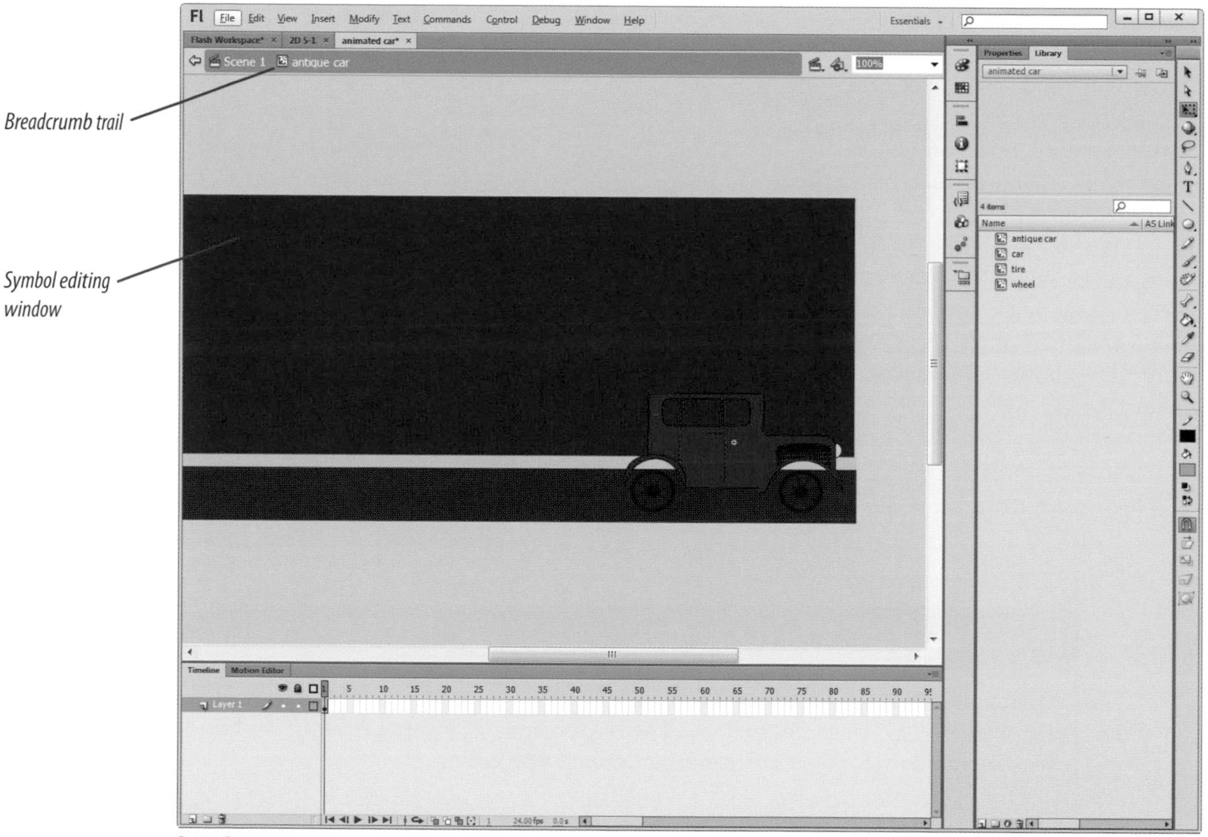

Breadcrumb trail

Symbol editing window

© 2013 Cengage Learning, All Rights Reserved. Source Adobe® Flash® Professional, 2013.

clicking the Color styles list arrow, as shown in Figure 19.

Creating a Frame-by-Frame Animation

The most basic type of animation is **keyframe animation**, also referred to as frame-by-frame animation. You created this type of animation in Photoshop in a previous chapter. Each frame of your animation has unique drawings, and can be compared to a cel animation. This type of animation is perfect for creating complex animations, such as those involving facial expressions.

Every type of animation you work with has frames, keyframes, and blank keyframes. A **frame** displays and organizes content in your Flash movie; the more frames that are used for specific content, the longer the content will appear in the animation. A **blank keyframe** is a placeholder keyframe that does not have any content on it. A **keyframe** indicates that the content on the frame has changed from the previous keyframe. The different types of frames can be added to the Timeline by selecting Timeline on the Insert menu, or by right-clicking a specific frame in the Timeline and then clicking a frame type. To remove any of these frames, click Timeline on the Edit menu or right-click a specific frame in the Timeline and then click a command to cut, clear, or remove the frame. Frames can

be adjusted in the Timeline by clicking and dragging them.

When you create a frame-by-frame animation in Flash, you create a keyframe on each frame so that a different instance of a symbol or shape can be placed on each of those frames.

When creating a frame-by-frame animation, it is often helpful to see the placement of

Figure 19 *Modifying an instance of a symbol*

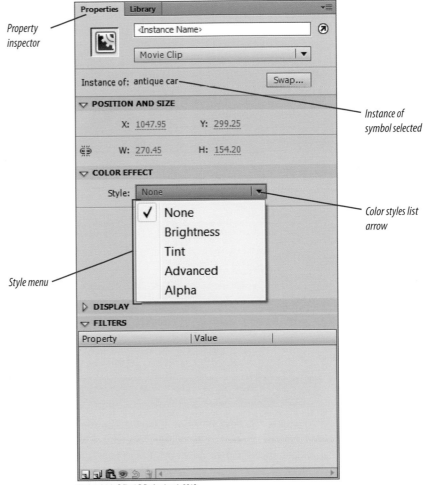

Source Adobe® Flash® Professional, 2013.

the previous object to help position the next object. Enabling **Onion skinning** allows you to see more than one frame at a time, as shown in Figure 20. (*Note*: The Onion skin button is located at the bottom of the Timeline panel.) The frame at the location of the playhead appears in full color, while frames on either side of the playhead are dimmed.

QUICK TIP

Click [F6] to create a keyframe at the location of the playhead on the Timeline.

Figure 20 *Enabling onion skinning*

Previous frame showing faded open eyes

Current frame showing closed eyes with full color

Onion skinning enabled

Playhead

Setting the Speed of an Animation

The frame rate determines the speed the animation is played and is measured in **frames per second (fps)**. The default frame rate for a new Flash project is 24 fps, which usually provides the best results for projects published for the web. Setting a frame rate too slow can make the animation appear to stop and start.

Figure 21 *Template with Content layer selected*

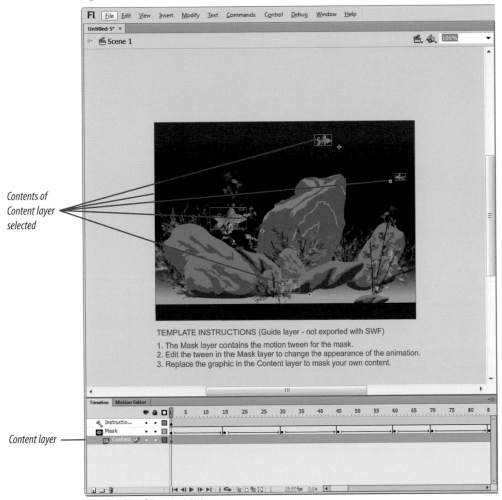

Contents of
Content layer
selected

Content layer

Source Adobe® Flash® Professional, 2013.

Work with Flash layers

In this exercise, you will work with Flash layers.

1. Verify that the Welcome Screen is visible, then click **Animation** in the Create from Template section.

   The New from Template dialog box opens.

   TIP If the Welcome Screen is not visible, click File on the Menu bar, then click New.

2. Click **Animated Mask Shape Tween** in the Templates section, then click **OK**.

   A sample animation has already been created for you.

3. Click the **Content layer** on the Timeline panel, then compare your Timeline panel to Figure 21.

   The fish content in the layer is selected on the Stage.

   (continued)

4. Click **Modify** on the Menu bar, point to **Timeline**, then click **Layer Properties**.

   The Layer Properties dialog box opens.

5. Rename the layer **aquarium**, then click **OK**.

6. Click the **New Layer button** ⊡ on the Timeline panel.

   A new layer, Layer 1, is created above the aquarium layer.

7. Double-click **Layer 1** on the Timeline panel, type **vines**, press **[Enter]** (Win) or **[return]** (Mac), then compare your Timeline panel to Figure 22.

8. Save your project as **animation practice**.

Use the Deco tool

In this exercise, you will use the Deco tool to add some vines to the aquarium.

1. Verify that animation practice is open.

2. Click the **Deco tool** 🖌 on the Tools panel, then show the Property inspector if necessary.

   The Property inspector displays the Deco tool options.

3. Click the **Drawing Effect list arrow**, click **Tree Brush**, click the **Advanced Options list arrow**, click **Vine**, then compare your screen to Figure 23.

   (continued)

Figure 22 *New layers created and named*

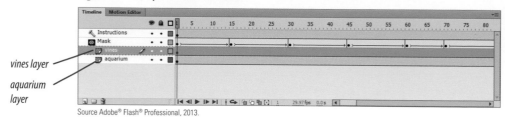

vines layer
aquarium layer

Source Adobe® Flash® Professional, 2013.

Figure 23 *Setting the Deco tool options*

Property inspector with the Deco tool selected

Tree Brush selected on Drawing Effect menu

Vine option selected on the Advanced Options menu

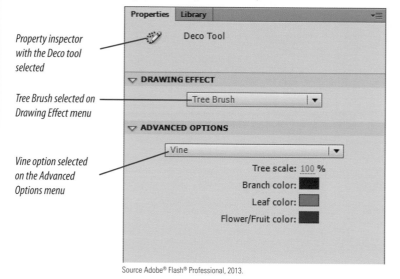

Source Adobe® Flash® Professional, 2013.

Figure 24 *Drawing with the Deco tool*

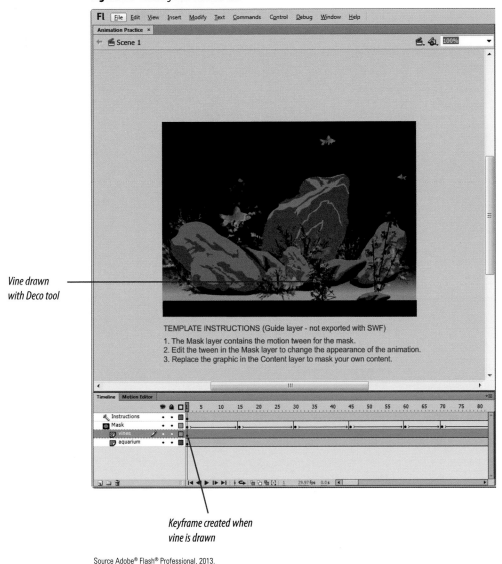

Vine drawn
with Deco tool

Keyframe created when
vine is drawn

Source Adobe® Flash® Professional, 2013.

4. Select the **vines layer** on the Timeline panel, position the **pointer** to the right of the small goldfish at the bottom of the State, then click and drag the **pointer upward** just past the goldfish's dorsal fin.

A random vine is created with a keyframe, as shown in Figure 24.

5. Save your work.

Convert an object to a symbol

In this exercise, you will convert the objects you drew in the previous exercise to symbols.

1. Verify that animation practice is open.

2. Select the **vines layer** on the Timeline panel to select the contents of the layer.

3. Click **Modify** on the Menu bar, then click **Convert to Symbol**, as shown in Figure 25.

   The Convert to Symbol dialog box opens.

4. Type **vine** in the Name text box, verify that **Graphic** is selected on the Type menu, then click **OK**.

5. Click the **Library tab**, and then compare your Library panel to Figure 26.

6. Save your work.

Edit a symbol

In this exercise, you will edit a symbol, a symbol instance, and preview your animation.

1. Verify that animation practice is open.

2. Show the Library panel if necessary, then double-click the **vine graphic symbol**.

   A new editing window opens in symbol editing mode. The scene is not visible.

TIP If you double-click the instance of the symbol on the Stage, the scene is visible in the editing window.

(continued)

Figure 25 *Contents of the Library panel*

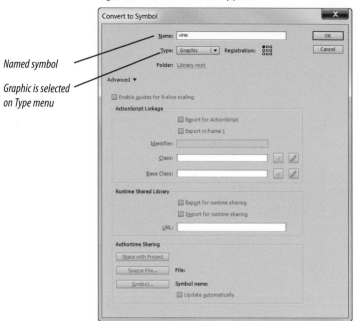

Named symbol

Graphic is selected on Type menu

Source Adobe® Flash® Professional, 2013.

Figure 26 *Contents of the Library panel*

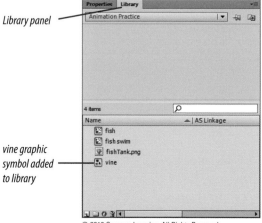

Library panel

vine graphic symbol added to library

© 2013 Cengage Learning, All Rights Reserved.
Source Adobe® Flash® Professional, 2013.

Creating Basic Animations in Flash Professional

Figure 27 *Editing a symbol in symbol editing mode*

Symbol editing mode indicated by bread crumb trail

Two additional vines

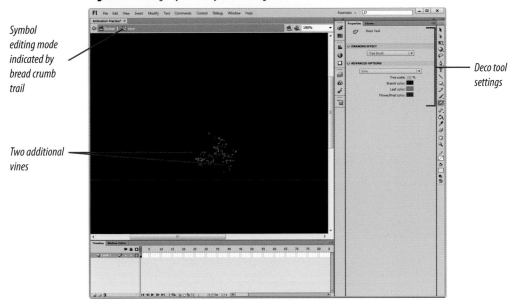

Deco tool settings

Figure 28 *Editing an instance of a graphic symbol*

Tint selected on Style menu

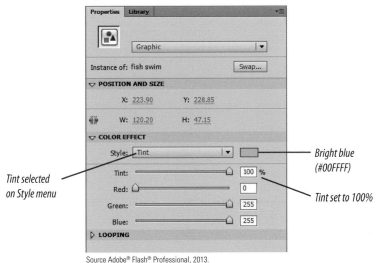

Bright blue (#00FFFF)

Tint set to 100%

3. Click the **Deco tool** on the Tools panel, then draw **two small vines** on either side of the existing vine, as shown in Figure 27.

   Two additional branches are added to the center vine, making it appear thicker.

   TIP A tool retains its settings until you change them or exit Flash.

4. Click **Scene 1** on the Edit bar breadcrumb trail to exit symbol editing mode.

5. Click the **Selection tool** on the Tools panel, then click the **largest goldfish instance** on the Stage.

6. Click the **Properties tab**, expand the Color Effect section if necessary, click the **Color styles list arrow**, then click **Tint**.

7. Click the **Tint color box**, click the **bright turquoise color swatch (#00FFFF)**, then drag the **Tint slider** to **100%**, as shown in Figure 28.

   The color of the goldfish is changed to bright blue.

8. Adjust the **tint** to colors of your choice for the other **two goldfish**.

9. Click **Scene 1** on the Edit bar breadcrumb trail to exit symbol editing mode.

10. Click **Control** on the Menu bar, point to **Test Movie**, then click **Test**.

    Tip You can also press and hold [Ctrl][Enter] (Win) or ⌘ [return] (Mac) to test your animation.

11. Save and close your work.

Create a frame-by-frame animation

In this exercise, you will create a frame-by-frame animation.

1. Open 2D 5-1.fla, then save it as **frame animation**.

   The graphic symbols have already been created for you.

2. Select the **animated eyes layer** on the Timeline panel.

Tip If you cannot see the entire name of the layer, place your pointer between the green box and the blank keyframe, then when the pointer changes to ◀▶, drag to expand the layer label.

3. Show the **Library panel**, drag the **g_open_eyes symbol** to the Stage to the area where the eyes should be, then compare your screen to Figure 29.

   The blank keyframe is converted to a keyframe.

4. Click **Frame 10** on the animated eyes layer.

5. Click **Insert** on the Menu bar, point to **Timeline**, then click **Blank Keyframe**.

   A blank keyframe is placed on frame 10 and the open eyes are no longer visible on the Stage.

TIP You can also right-click a frame and click Insert Blank Keyframe to insert a blank keyframe.

6. Drag an instance of the **g_closed_eyes symbol** to the Stage to the area where the eyes should be.

   To place the closed eyes instance precisely, you turn on onion skinning to match the location to the open eyes instance.

   (continued)

Figure 29 *Editing an instance of a Graphic symbol*

g_open_eyes instance dragged to Stage

g_open_eyes symbol

Animated eyes layer

Keyframe

© 2013 Cengage Learning, All Rights Reserved. Source Adobe® Flash® Professional, 2013.

Figure 30 *Enabling onion skinning*

Eyes visible in both states

Onion skin button

Figure 31 *Timeline panel with frames pasted*

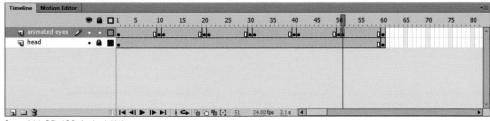

7. Click the **Onion Skin button** 🔲 on the Timeline panel, as shown in Figure 30.

   The opened eyes instance is visible.

8. Adjust the location of the closed eyes instance on the Stage as necessary, then click the **Onion Skin button** 🔲 to turn off onion skinning.

9. Click the **animated eyes layer** on the Timeline panel.

   The frames with content are highlighted.

10. Click **Edit** on the Menu bar, point to **Timeline**, then click **Copy Frames**.

TIP You can also right-click the layer and click Copy Frames to copy frames.

11. Click **Frame 11**, click **Edit** on the Menu bar, point to **Timeline**, then click **Paste Frames**.

    A copy of Frames 1 through 10 is pasted on Frames 11 through 20.

12. Click **Frame 21**, right-click the **frame**, then click **Paste Frames**.

13. Repeat step 12 for **Frames 31**, **41**, and **51**, then compare your Timeline panel to Figure 31.

14. Return the **playhead** ▮ to **Frame 1**, then press **[Enter]** (Win) or **[return]** (Mac) to preview your animation.

    You previewed your animation of the girl blinking without leaving Flash.

15. Save and close your work.

Create an Animation
WITH TWEENS

What You'll Do

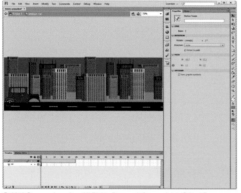

In this lesson, you will create an animation using tweens.

Working with Tweens

In addition to frame-by-frame animation, you can also create a classic tween, motion tween, shape tween, and inverse kinematics poses. A **classic tween** is a keyframe-based motion tween, and is denoted in the Timeline with a purple fill and a continuous arrow. You can animate symbols and editable text with a **motion tween**, which is denoted in the Timeline with a blue fill. You can morph basic shapes with a **shape tween**, which is denoted in the Timeline with a green fill and a continuous arrow. Figure 32 shows the various tweens on the Timeline panel. If there is a dashed line on the layer instead of a solid arrow, the tween is broken. For example, a

dashed line may appear if the final keyframe is missing.

You can create a shape tween by drawing a vector shape on a starting keyframe, and then by changing the shape or by drawing a new shape at the last frame you designate as an ending keyframe. To create a tween, select the first keyframe in the animation and then click Shape Tween on the Insert menu.

A motion tween is created in a similar manner as a shape tween; however, you can only create a motion tween using symbol instances or a text box. When creating a motion tween, you need to have one keyframe on the frame where the tween begins and a blank frame

Figure 32 *Appearance of tweens on the Timeline panel*

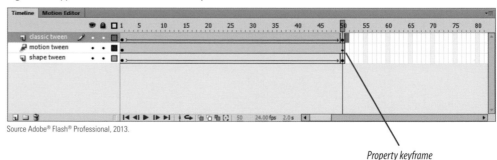

Property keyframe

Creating Basic Animations in Flash Professional

where the animation ends. After you have applied the Motion Tween command, simply move the location of the playhead to where you want to modify the symbol or text field and a property keyframe is created for you. A **property keyframe** is a special keyframe that defines changes to one or more properties, such as position, size, or color tint.

When animating text, you can animate the text as text or as a symbol, or you can break the text apart and animate the text as a shape. If you leave the text as text, all the options on the Property inspector are available, such as the font family. If you choose to break the text apart or convert the text to a symbol, the number of options on the Property inspector is reduced. You will no longer be able to modify properties such as the font family, alignment, and spacing.

If text is converted to a symbol, you can adjust the Alpha option in the Effects section of the Property inspector to change the transparency of the symbol to create a Fade In or Fade Out effect.

QUICK TIP

To create a morphing effect with letters, select the text, and then click the Break Apart command on the Modify menu twice to convert each letter into a shape.

Using Frame Labels

You can place frame labels on frames in the Timeline and then name the frame labels. Naming frames can be more meaningful rather than referring to frame numbers.

Frame labels help identify frames, organize content, provide contents for documentation, and serve as reference anchors when writing ActionScript. A frame label is identified on the frame with a red flag. Frame labels can be added to a frame in the Name text box on the

Using the Motion Editor Panel

The Motion Editor panel, shown in Figure 33, is located next to the Timeline panel, or you can open it by clicking Motion Editor on the Window menu. This panel lets you control in detail motion tween properties that you have created or have applied using a Motion Preset. An expandable list of properties is shown along the left side of the Motion Editor panel. On the right side of the panel, a timeline shows lines and curves that represent the properties as they change over time.

Object-based animation is much easier to work with than working exclusively with keyframes. With object-based animation, keyframes on the Timeline panel are updated automatically as the object is transformed. Transforming the object includes moving, scaling, or rotating the object on the Stage over time across a number of frames. (*Note*: You must first convert an object to a symbol and apply a motion tween to it before object-based animation can be applied.) Bézier controls become available when you click the motion path, which will allow you to adjust the path. The speed of the animation can be adjusted by adding or deleting frames on the animation layer.

Figure 33 *Motion Editor panel with a motion tween applied*

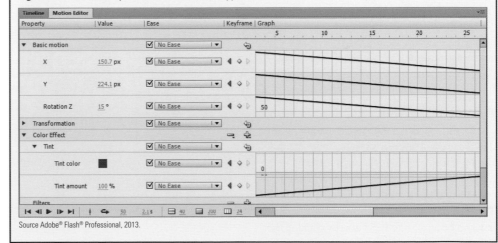

Source Adobe® Flash® Professional, 2013.

Property inspector when a frame is selected, as shown in Figure 34.

Working with Movie Clip Symbols

A movie clip symbol is used when you want the symbol to have its own nested timeline, independent from the main timeline. The nested timeline can be used to create an animation that can be reused; movie clips are also scriptable with ActionScript.

Importing and Using Sound

You can easily add sound to your Flash project by dragging a sound file from the Library panel to the Stage. Flash accepts a variety of audio file formats, including ASND, WAV, AIFF, and MP3. You can use sound to create a soundtrack for an animation, add sound effects to buttons, or any other way you can envision. To import a sound to the Library panel, click File on the Menu bar, point to Import, and then click Import to Library.

There are two types of sound used in Flash: event and stream. An **event sound** must download completely before it begins playing. A **stream sound** begins to play as soon as enough frames have downloaded. A stream sound is coordinated to play with the animation on the Timeline panel. Effects such as fade in and fade out, can be applied to the audio by clicking the Effect list arrow in the Sound section of the Property inspector, as shown in Figure 35.

Figure 34 *Working with Frame labels*

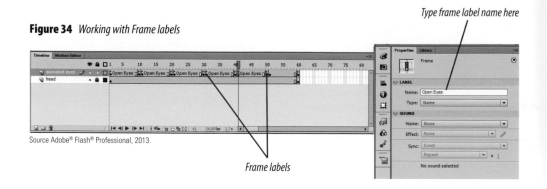

Source Adobe® Flash® Professional, 2013.

Frame labels

Figure 35 *Sound options on the Property inspector*

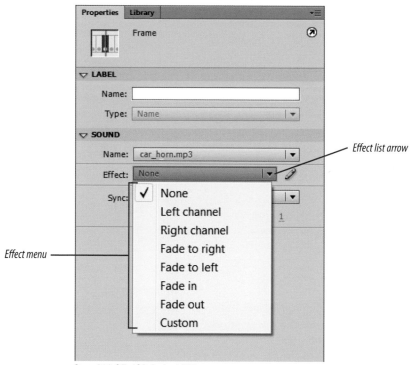

Source Adobe® Flash® Professional, 2013.

Publishing a Flash Document

When publishing your Flash project, you can publish it with an SWF, FLV, or HTML file extension. An **FLA** (.fla) is the native file format for a Flash project file that can only be opened in Flash. A **SWF** (.swf) is an exported or published FLA file that has been optimized for viewing on the web and cannot be edited. It is often used to play animations; and can also be played in a browser with the appropriate Flash Player plug-in. An **FLV** (.flv) video file can be viewed with Flash Player. The **HTML** (.html) extension creates a web page document and SWF file with browser settings that will activate the SWF file when viewed in a browser. By default, the Publish Settings dialog box publishes a SWF and an HTML file. You can also select previous versions for the Flash Player, shown in Figure 36, if you are concerned that your audience may not have the latest version. Flash also publishes an XMP metadata file by default to make metadata available to web search engines. The metadata file has an XMP file extension.

QUICK **TIP**

When you publish a Flash movie to be viewed on the web, it is important to consider adding Flash Player detection so users receive a message if they cannot view the content. A Flash Player Detection Kit can be found at the Adobe website. This kit provides a variety of templates that determine the version of Flash Player installed on a user's computer, and installs the latest version of Flash Player if needed.

Figure 36 *Publishing to previous version of Flash Player*

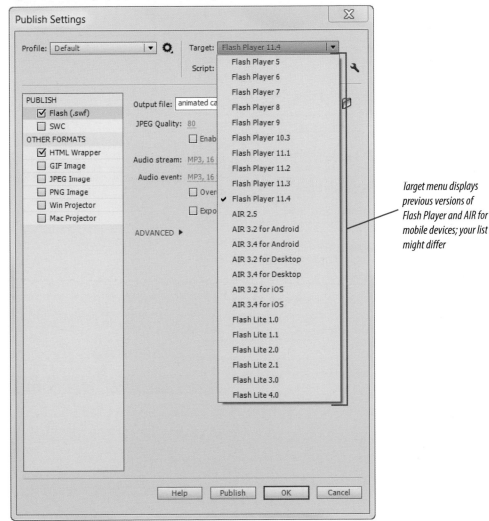

Target menu displays previous versions of Flash Player and AIR for mobile devices; your list might differ

Work with tweens

In this exercise, you will add a motion tween to a road instance.

1. Open 2D 5-2.fla, then save it as **tween animation**.

   A project with movie clip symbols has been created for you.

2. Select the **road instance** on the Stage.

3. Click **Insert** on the Menu bar, then click **Motion Tween**.

   A motion tween is added to the road layer.

4. Move the **playhead** ▯ to **Frame 75**, as shown in Figure 37.

5. Drag the **horizontal scroll bar** to the right until you see the road extending beyond the right edge of the Stage, as shown in Figure 38.

   You need to move the right edge of the road to be even with the Stage.

(continued)

Figure 37 *Adjusting the location of the playhead*

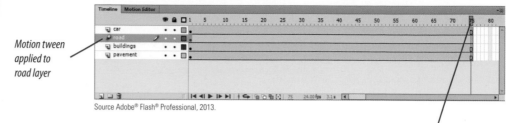

Motion tween applied to road layer

Playhead at Frame 75

Figure 38 *Adjusting the view beyond the Stage*

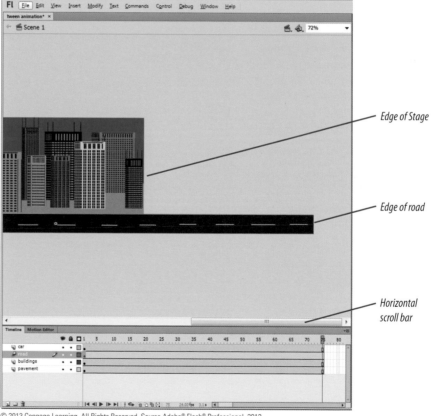

Edge of Stage

Edge of road

Horizontal scroll bar

Figure 39 *Adjusting the end of the road*

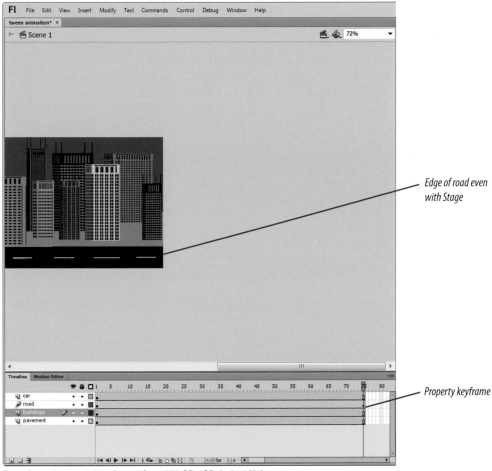

Edge of road even
with Stage

Property keyframe

© 2013 Cengage Learning, All Rights Reserved. Source Adobe® Flash® Professional, 2013.

6. Drag the **road instance** to the left until the **right edge** is even with the Stage, as shown in Figure 39.

   The road extends beyond the left edge of the Stage.

TIP Press and hold [Shift] as you drag the road to constrain its horizontal position.

7. Click **View** on the Menu bar, point to **Magnification**, then click **Fit in Window**.

8. Press **[Enter]** (Win) or **[return]** (Mac) to preview your animation.

   The road is moving across the Stage, but the wheels on the car are not. You will adjust this in the next exercise.

9. Select the **car instance** on the Stage.

10. Click **Insert** on the Menu bar, then click **Motion Tween**.

11. Move the **playhead** to **Frame 75** if necessary.

12. Drag the **car** to the **right edge** of the road so the front edge of the car is near the edge of the road.

13. Press **[Enter]** (Win) or **[return]** (Mac) to preview your animation.

14. Save your work.

Animate a movie symbol

In this exercise, you will animate the tires on the car.

1. Verify that tween animation is still open.

2. Double-click the **car instance** on the Stage.

   The symbol editing mode window opens, as shown in Figure 40. To apply a motion tween to the tire to make it spin, you can only have one instance on a layer.

3. Click the **front tire instance** on the Stage, then press **[Delete]**.

4. Click the **rear tire instance** on the Stage, click **Insert** on the Menu bar, then click **Motion Tween**.

   A motion tween and some additional frames are added to the tire layer.

   (continued)

Figure 40 *Symbol editing mode*

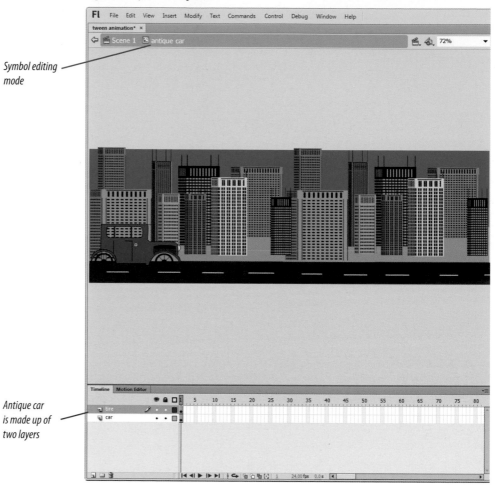

Symbol editing mode

Antique car is made up of two layers

© 2013 Cengage Learning, All Rights Reserved. Source Adobe® Flash® Professional, 2013.

Figure 41 *Motion tween options on the Property inspector*

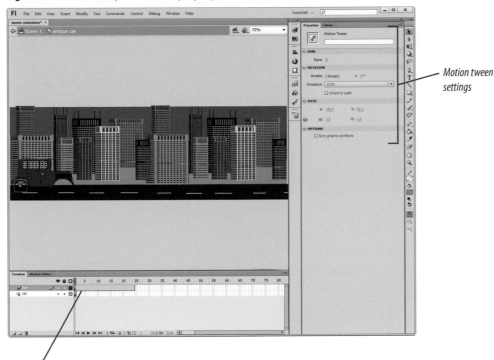

Motion tween settings

Additional frames added

5. Click **Frame 1** on the tire layer, show the Property inspector, click the **Rotate text box**, type **5**, click the **Direction list arrow**, click **CCW**, then compare your screen to Figure 41.

6. Press **[Enter]** (Win) or **[return]** (Mac) to preview your animation, then move the **playhead** to **Frame 1**.

   The rear tire spins, but the car is not visible for the entire animation and you need to add the front tire.

7. Right-click the **tire layer**, then click **Duplicate Layers**.

   A copy of the tire layer appears at the top of the Timeline panel and a copy of the tire instance appears on top of the original instance on the Stage.

8. Drag the **copied tire instance** to the front wheel well on the Stage.

9. Click **Frame 24** on the car layer, right-click the **frame**, then click **Insert Frame**.

10. Click **Scene 1** on the Edit bar breadcrumb trail to exit symbol editing mode.

11. Press **[Enter]** (Win) or **[return]** (Mac) to preview your animation.

    Notice the tires do not move. This is because the tires were rotated on a different timeline. The tire animation is only visible when you test the movie.

    (continued)

12. Click **Control** on the Menu bar, point to **Test Movie**, click **in Flash Professional,** then compare your screen to Figure 42.

The car animation spins down the road.

13. Close Flash Player, then save your work.

Import and use sound

In this exercise, you will add sound to your Flash project.

1. Verify that tween animation is open.

2. Click **File** on the Menu bar, point to **Import**, then click **Import to Library**.

3. Navigate to where you store your Data Files, click **car_horn.mp3**, then click **Open**.

The sound file appears on the Library panel.

4. Click the **New Layer button** 🔲 at the bottom of the Timeline to create a new layer, then rename the layer **car horn**.

5. Click the **Library tab**, verify that the car horn layer is selected, then drag **car_horn.mp3** to the Stage.

The audio waveform for the sound appears on the car horn layer, as shown in Figure 43.

6. Click **Frame 30** on the car horn layer, insert a **blank keyframe**, then repeat for **Frame 55** on the car horn layer.

TIP Press [F7] to insert a blank keyframe on the selected frame.

7. Move the **playhead** ▌ to the blank keyframe on **Frame 30**, then drag another instance of **car_horn.mp3** to the Stage.

8. Repeat step 7 for **Frame 55**, then compare your Timeline panel to Figure 44.

(continued)

Figure 42 *Previewing your animation*

Audio waveform

Figure 43 *Audio waveform on the Timeline*

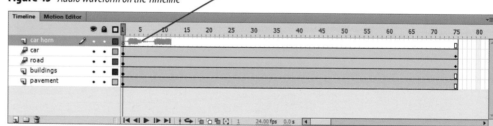

Audio waveform on Frame 30 Audio waveform on Frame 55

Figure 44 *Adding additional instances of a wav file*

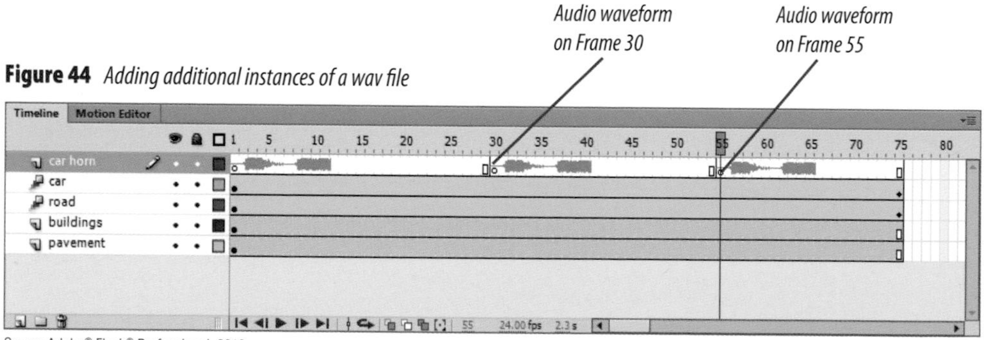

Figure 45 *Export Movie dialog box*

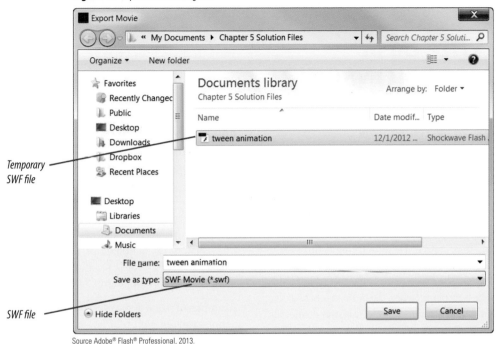

Temporary
SWF file

SWF file

Source Adobe® Flash® Professional, 2013.

9. Click **Control** on the Menu bar, point to **Test Movie**, then click **in Flash Professional**.

   The car horn plays three times throughout the movie.

10. Close Flash Player, then save your work.

Publish a Flash project

In this exercise, you will publish your Flash project.

1. Verify that tween animation is still open.

2. Click **File** on the Menu bar, select **Export**, then click **Export Movie**.

   A temporary SWF file was created earlier where you save your Data Files when you previewed your project using the in Flash Professional command in.

3. Click the **tween animation file**, as shown in Figure 45, (Win) or type **tween animation.fla** in the Format text box (Mac), then click **Save**.

TIP If prompted to replace the file, click Yes (Mac).

4. Click **Yes** in the Confirm Save As dialog box to overwrite the file.

5. Close the document.

Write Basic
ACTIONSCRIPT

What You'll Do

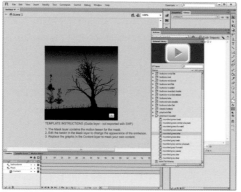

Source Adobe® Flash® Professional, 2013.

 In this lesson, you will work with button symbols and basic ActionScript.

Adding Button Symbols

Button symbols have their own Timeline that consist of four frames representing each of the states of a button: Up, Over, Down, and Hit, as shown in Figure 46. The **Up state** is the first frame; this is the default state displayed when the mouse pointer is not near or over the button. The **Over state** is the second frame; this state is displayed when the mouse pointer is over the button. The **Down state** is the third frame; this state is displayed when the button is clicked. The **Hit state** is the fourth frame; this state defines the area that responds to the mouse pointer or click.

QUICK **TIP**

Buttons can also be made invisible by not adding any elements to an empty symbol. This allows you to assign actions to the various states and place the invisible button on another element on the Stage.

States of a button

Figure 46 *States of a button*

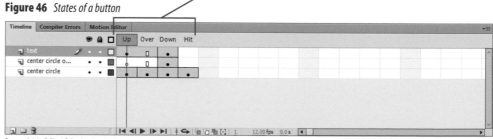

Source Adobe® Flash® Professional, 2013.

Adding Simple Controls with ActionScript 3.0

ActionScript is an object-oriented programming language that allows you to add interactivity or automate animations in your Flash project. Table 1 explains some of the basic concepts of object-oriented programming. The version of ActionScript is determined when you create a new Flash document; the latest version is ActionScript 3.0.

Examples of some of the most used and simple actions are *stop, gotoAndPlay, navigateToURL,* and *SoundMixer.stopALL.* ActionScript is written on the Actions panel.

QUICK **TIP**

Spelling, punctuation and capitalization, also known as syntax, is very important with ActionScript. If not written correctly, your project may not work properly.

Creating Basic Animations in Flash Professional

The **stop action** is used to stop the Flash animation on a specific keyframe. You can place this command on any frame of the Timeline to prevent the animation from playing, or to end the animation or pause it until a user clicks a button to initiate another action. The **gotoAndPlay** action causes the animation to jump from the frame in which the action is placed to another frame in the Flash document; this is most often used to play frames in a nonsequential order. The **SoundMixer.stopALL** action prevents two or more embedded sounds from playing at the same time in your Flash project.

Interactivity is added to a Flash animation using a process called **event handling**. An ActionScript **event** is an interaction in a Flash movie, such as a mouse click causing the playhead to move to a different frame, or the loading of an external sound or movie. Table 2 explains the basic components of event handling.

One method to add code in the Actions panel is by using ScriptAssist mode, shown in Figure 47. ScriptAssist provides prompts for the code and helps you avoid syntax and logic errors.

Figure 47 *Turning on ScriptAssist in the Actions panel*

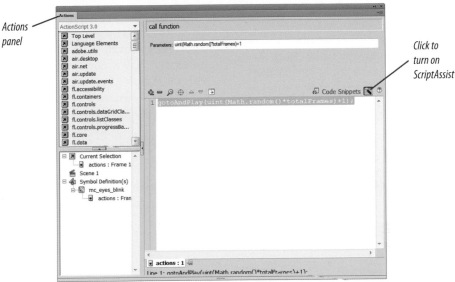

Actions panel

Click to turn on ScriptAssist

Source Adobe® Flash® Professional, 2013.

TABLE 1 BASIC CONCEPTS OF OBJECT-ORIENTED PROGRAMMING	
Term	**Definition**
class	Objects, properties, methods, and events are members of the class; determines the rules that are applied
object	Items in a Flash document that can be manipulated, such as movie clips, buttons, graphics, and text fields
method	The action an object can do
property	Characteristics applied to an object on the Property inspector
variable	A method of storing data; data may change or be altered during the running of the Flash movie
function	A block of code that is named so that it can be reused; analogous to creating a CSS style in Dreamweaver

© 2013 Cengage Learning, All Rights Reserved.

TABLE 2 ACTIONSCRIPT 3.0 EVENT-HANDLING CONCEPTS	
Term	**Definition**
Event source	The object the event will happen to
Event listener	A function written to react to an event, such as the click of the mouse
Listener function	Where an action is specified

© 2013 Cengage Learning, All Rights Reserved.

The easiest method to add actions to your Flash project is with the Code Snippets panel, shown in Figure 48. Code snippets are divided into six categories: actions, timeline navigation, animation, load and unload, audio and video, and event handlers. Additional code snippets for designing for mobile devices include Mobile Touch Events, Mobile Gesture Events, Mobile Actions, AIR for Mobile, and AIR. These collections include commonly used code blocks, which can be added to your Flash animation. The following are examples of the contents of these categories:

- Actions contains common actions, including play a movie clip, stop a movie clip, and timers.
- Timeline Navigation contains code to navigate to various frames.
- Animation contains code to fade a movie clip in or out, navigate with the keyboard, and rotate.
- Load and Unload provides codes to load images from the Library panel and external text.
- Audio and Video provides code to play, pause, rewind, and stop audio or video.
- Event Handlers includes code for mouse or keyboard interactivity.

The snippets include comments for implementing the code, as shown in Figure 49. These are very helpful if you are new to writing ActionScript.

Code Snippets panel

Figure 48 *Code Snippets panel*

Code Snippet categories

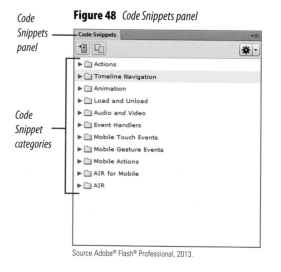

Source Adobe® Flash® Professional, 2013.

Figure 49 *Example code snippet in Actions panel*

Code snippet instructions

```
//, /* */ : Indicates one or more lines of script comments.

Comment:  Click to Go to Frame and Stop
√ Multiline  Clicking on the specified symbol instance moves the playhead to the specified frame in the timeline and stops the movie.
          Can be used on the main timeline or on movie clip timelines.

          Instructions:
          1. Replace the number 5 in the code below with the frame number you would like the playhead to move to when the symbol instance is clicked.
```

```
51  }
52
53
54  // sound file finished while playing, set position to start and change button appearance
55  function soundCompleteHandler(e:Event):void {
56      //stop the sound, set sound position to beginning
57      soundCnl.stop();
58      currPos = 0.00;
59
60      //change the appearance of the buttons
61      playpause_mc.gotoAndStop("play")
62  }
63
64  /* Click to Go to Frame and Stop
65  Clicking on the specified symbol instance moves the playhead to the specified frame in the
    timeline and stops the movie.
66  Can be used on the main timeline or on movie clip timelines.
67
68  Instructions:
69  1. Replace the number 5 in the code below with the frame number you would like the
    playhead to move to when the symbol instance is
    clickedplaypause_mc.addEventListener(MouseEvent.CLICK,fl_ClickToGoToAndStopAtFrame);
    AtFrame);
70
71  function fl_ClickToGoToAndStopAtFrame(event:MouseEvent):void
72  {
73      gotoAndStop(5);
74  }
75
```

Actions : 1
Line 62: /* Click to Go to Frame and Stop

Source Adobe® Flash® Professional, 2013.

Creating Basic Animations in Flash Professional

Figure 50 *Adding a stop action to the Actions panel*

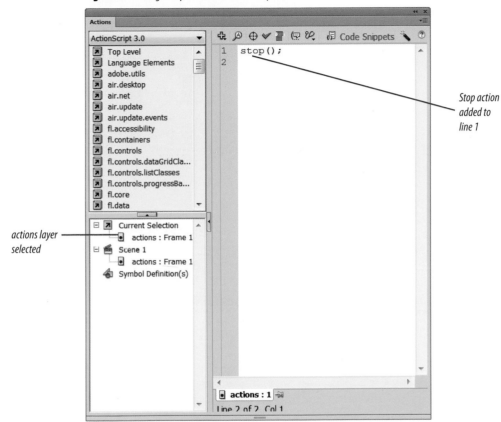

actions layer selected

Stop action added to line 1

Source Adobe® Flash® Professional, 2013.

Working with buttons

In this exercise, you will create buttons and add ActionScript to control your animation.

1. Click **File** on the Menu bar, then click **New**.

2. Click the **Templates tab**, click **Animation**, click **Animated Mask Motion Tween**, then click **OK**.

3. Press **[Ctrl][Enter]** (Win) or ⌘ **[return]** (Mac) to preview the animation.

   You add a button to control the animation.

4. Click **Window** on the Menu bar, click **Actions**, then adjust the panel so you can still see the Stage.

   The Actions panel opens.

   TIP You can also press [F9] (Win) or [option][F9] (Mac) to open the Actions panel.

5. Click the **Instructions layer**, click the **New Layer button** ⬚ at the bottom of the Timeline panel, then name the layer **actions**.

6. Click **line 1** in the Actions panel, type **stop();**, then press **[Enter]** (Win) or **[return]** (Mac), as shown in Figure 50.

   TIP It is helpful to turn off ScriptAssist when you are writing simple code.

7. Click **Control** on the Menu bar, point to **Test Movie**, then click **in Flash Professional**.

   The movie is paused and does not play.

8. Close the Flash Player.

(continued)

9. Click **Window**, point to **Common Libraries**, then click **Buttons**.

   The Buttons common library opens. You can use a button from the common library to apply ActionScript to control the animation.

10. Click the **Expand arrow** ▷ next to playback rounded, drag an instance of **rounded green play** to the bottom-right corner of the Stage, as shown in Figure 51, then close the External Library panel.

11. Click the **rounded green play button** on the Stage if necessary, then click the **Code Snippets button** 🗐 on the Actions panel toolbar.

   The Code Snippets panel opens.

12. Click the **Expand arrow** ▷ next to Timeline Navigation, then double-click **Click to Go to Frame and Play**.

13. Type **play_button** in the Set Instance Name dialog box, click **OK**, then close the Code Snippets panel.

(continued)

Figure 51 *Using the Button common library*

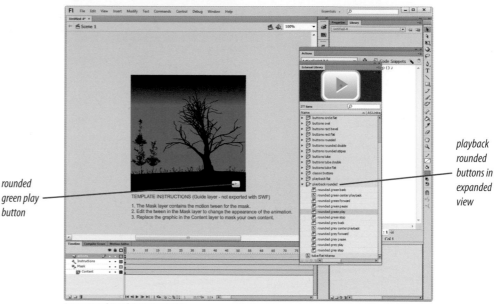

rounded green play button

playback rounded buttons in expanded view

Source Adobe® Flash® Professional, 2013.

Figure 52 *Code snippet added to the Actions panel*

Code snippet instructions

Go to Frame and Play code snippet

Replace frame 5 with frame 1

Source Adobe® Flash® Professional, 2013.

14. Click a blank area of the Actions panel to deselect the code snippet.

The code is inserted in the Actions panel, as shown in Figure 52.

15. Select **5** on line 15, then type **1**.

The button is clicked and the playhead returns to Frame 1 of the animation.

16. Click **Control** on the Menu bar, point to **Test Movie**, click **in Flash Professional**, then test the button.

The animation plays one time and returns to Frame 1, where it is paused.

17. Save your work as **play button**, then close the file.

Working with ActionScript 3.0

In this exercise, you will add ActionScript to your Flash project to make the eyes blink.

1. Open 2D 5-3.fla, save it as **random eye blink**, then reset the Essentials workspace, if necessary.

2. Press **[Ctrl][Enter]** (Win) or ⌘ **[return]** (Mac) to preview the animation, then close the Flash Player.

   Notice the eyes blink at a steady rhythm. The frame animation has only one frame.

3. Double-click the **mc_eyes_blink instance** on the Stage.

   You will add ActionScript to the Timeline inside the movie clip.

4. Click **Window** on the Menu bar, then click **Actions**.

5. Verify that the actions layer is selected on the Timeline panel.

6. Click **line 1**, type **gotoAndPlay(uint(Math .random()*totalFrames)+1);**, then press **[Enter]** (Win) or **[return]** (Mac), as shown in Figure 53.

   TIP The words in this syntax appear in blue and the number in black. If your words are black, you have made a typing error.

7. Click **Control** on the Menu bar, point to **Test Movie**, then click **in Flash Professional**.

   The eyes blink randomly.

8. Save and close your work, then exit Flash.

Figure 53 *Typing ActionScript on the actions layers*

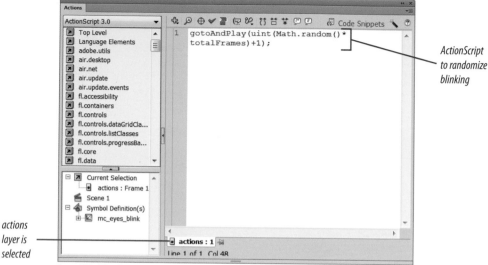

ActionScript to randomize blinking

actions layer is selected

Source Adobe® Flash® Professional, 2013.

Creating Basic Animations in Flash Professional

Create a frame-by-frame animation of a cartoon face drawn from the frontal view. Your character can be either female or male depending on the audio file that you select. Create an eye blink before and after your character begins speaking.

1. Conduct an Internet search using the phrase *lip sync mouth chart* to help you with creating the basic mouth shapes.
2. Create a new Flash document named **Lip Sync**.
3. Create a graphic symbol for each mouth shape on the chart you have selected; be sure to name the symbols with the letters representing the shape of the mouth for that symbol so they make sense, e.g., mouth_EH or mouth_MBP.
4. Create a graphic symbol for the eyes open and the eyes closed.
5. Draw your character on its own layer named **head** without the mouth or eyes.
6. Create three layers above the head layer: **audio**, **mouth**, and **eyes**.
7. Select the audio layer, then import into the Library either 2D 5-SB1-m.wav or 2D 5-SB1-f.wav from where you store your Data Files.
8. On the mouth layer, create blank keyframes, then place your mouth graphic symbols to lip sync to the audio file.
9. On the eyes layer, add a blink before and after your character speaks.
10. Test your animation as you work.
11. When you have finished, publish your animation as a SWF file, then compare your animation to the sample shown in Figure 54.
12. Save and close your work.

Figure 54 *Sample Completed Skill Builder 1*

Create an animation based on a children's story of your choice. If you need help with story ideas, visit the World of Tales website at *http://worldoftales.com*.

1. Create a new Flash document and name it after the story you have selected.
2. Draw your characters as movie clips so that you can add motion tweens to animate them.
3. Name your movie clips and layers as you work to stay organized.
4. Test your animation as you work.
5. When you have finished, publish your animation as a SWF file, then compare your animation to the sample shown in Figure 55.
6. Save and close your work.

Figure 55 *Sample Completed Skill Builder 2*

Courtesy of Julianna Trevino.

Using what you have learned in this chapter, create a bouncing ball animation that demonstrates three different types of balls. Review Lesson 3 in Chapter 3 for the principles behind a bouncing ball. You may want to combine frame-by-frame with motion tweens to create this animation. You will animate a volleyball, a basketball, and a tennis ball. Each ball should resemble and react as a real ball.

1. Create a new Flash document and name it **bouncing ball**.
2. Create graphic symbols and movie clip symbols as needed.
3. Create separate layers for each animation.
4. Add a rotation to at least one ball inside a movie clip symbol to make it rotate while it is bouncing.
5. Test your animation as you work.
6. When you have finished, publish your animation as a SWF file, then compare your animation to the sample shown in Figure 56.
7. Save and close your work, then exit Flash.

Figure 56 *Sample Completed Portfolio Project*

CHAPTER 6

ANIMATING WITH ILLUSTRATOR AND PHOTOSHOP FILES IN FLASH PROFESSIONAL

1. Animate Illustrator files in Flash.
2. Animate a Photoshop file in Flash.
3. Animate with inverse kinematics.

CHAPTER 6
ANIMATING WITH ILLUSTRATOR AND PHOTOSHOP FILES IN FLASH PROFESSIONAL

You may have found drawing in Flash Professional restrictive compared to the artwork you created in Illustrator and Photoshop. Fortunately, Flash Professional supports both Illustrator and Photoshop documents, allowing you to still create your artwork without limitations and then animate it in Flash Professional.

In this chapter, you will animate Illustrator and Photoshop files in Flash Professional. You will also learn how to work with the Bone tool and create animations using inverse kinematics, a type of animation that utilizes an armature.

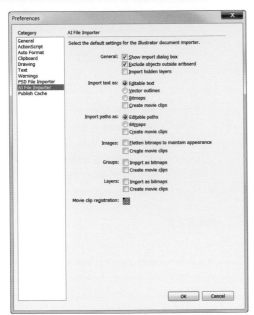

Source Adobe® Flash® Professional, 2013.

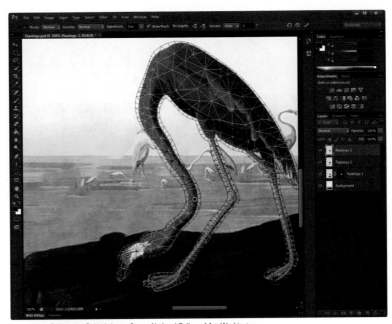

Source Adobe® Photoshop®, 2013. Image Source National Gallery of Art, Washington

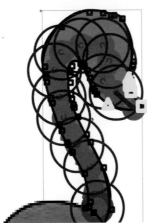

Animate Illustrator
FILES IN FLASH

What You'll Do

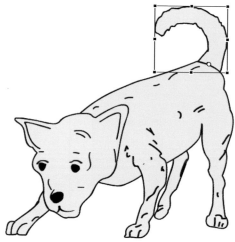

© 2013 Cengage Learning, All Rights Reserved. Source Adobe® Illustrator®, 2013.

 In this lesson, you will animate an Illustrator document in Flash.

Preparing an Illustrator File to Animate in Flash

You can create your artwork in Adobe Illustrator and import it into Flash while preserving the majority of its editability. The AI File Importer settings, found in the Flash Preferences dialog box, allow you to determine how your artwork will be imported; specifically, how objects will be treated when imported, as shown in Figure 1. Illustrator paths can be imported as a bitmap or as an editable path. Illustrator objects that have been grouped can be imported as a bitmap. Illustrator layers can also be imported as a bitmap, flattening all of the sublayers into a single image. You also have the option to create a movie clip from any of these objects, which saves time when you animate the artwork later in Flash.

To have the greatest flexibility with Illustrator in Flash, it is important to follow these steps in Illustrator:

1. Separate the parts of your illustration that you will want to animate into their own sublayers.
2. Group each of the sublayers.

3. Name the layers; this makes them easier to work with when you are importing the file into Flash. (*Note*: Names will be preserved during the import process.)
4. Set the document color mode to RGB.
5. Save your Illustrator File.

> **QUICK TIP**
>
> You can also copy and paste between Illustrator and Flash Pro. The Paste dialog box provides options to paste the selection as a bitmap or paste using the AI File Importer preferences. (*Note*: You will not be able to override any preferences.) You can also choose to resolve incompatibilities and to maintain layers.

Importing an Illustrator File into Flash

Flash has two options to importing an Illustrator file: Import to Stage and Import to Library. Both, of course, place the objects in the Library, and give you various import options. The Import to Stage option resizes your Flash document to match the Illustrator artboard when the objects are placed on the Stage. The Import to Library option creates a flattened bitmap of the file, as shown in Figure 2.

The selection column, located to the left of the layer, controls whether or not the object will be imported. The object type column, located to the right of the layer, displays an icon indicating its object type.

In addition, an Illustrator file that has layers can be imported as Flash layers, a single Flash layer, or Flash frames by selecting the correct option from the Convert layers to menu.

- Flash Layers translates each of the Illustrator layers to its own Flash layer.

- Single Flash Layers flattens all of the Illustrator layers into a single Flash layer.
- Keyframes translates each of the Illustrator layers to a keyframe on the same Flash layer.

Figure 1 *AI File Importer preferences*

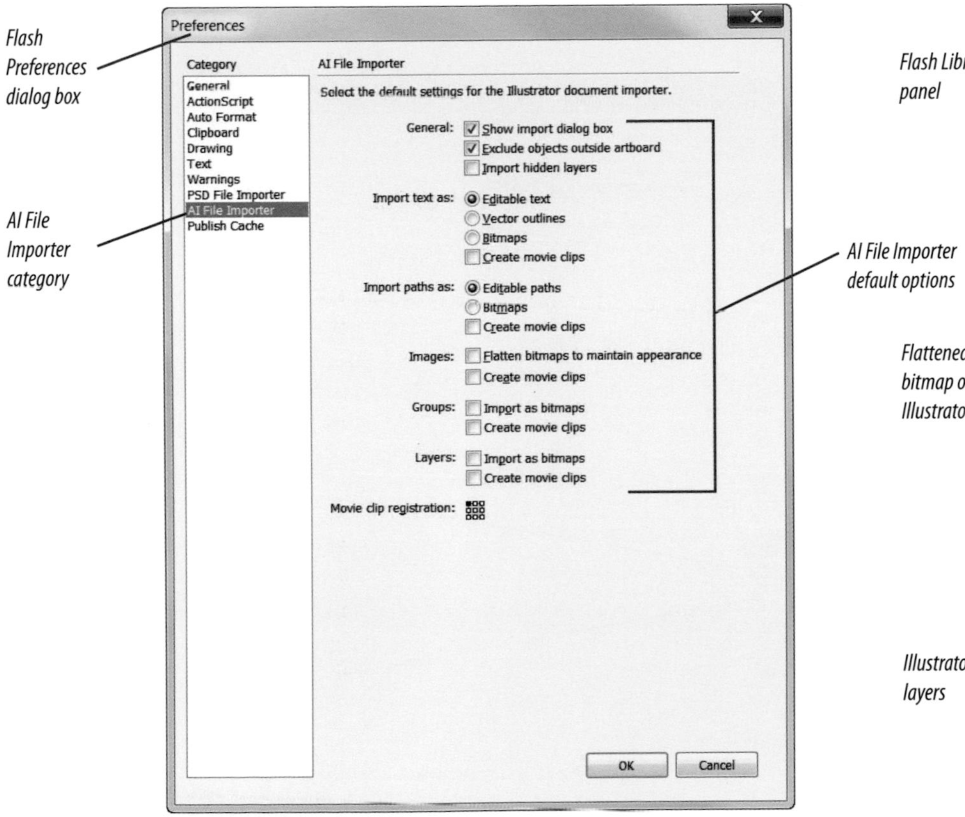

Flash Preferences dialog box

AI File Importer category

AI File Importer default options

Source Adobe® Flash® Professional, 2013.

Figure 2 *Object type icons in Import dialog box*

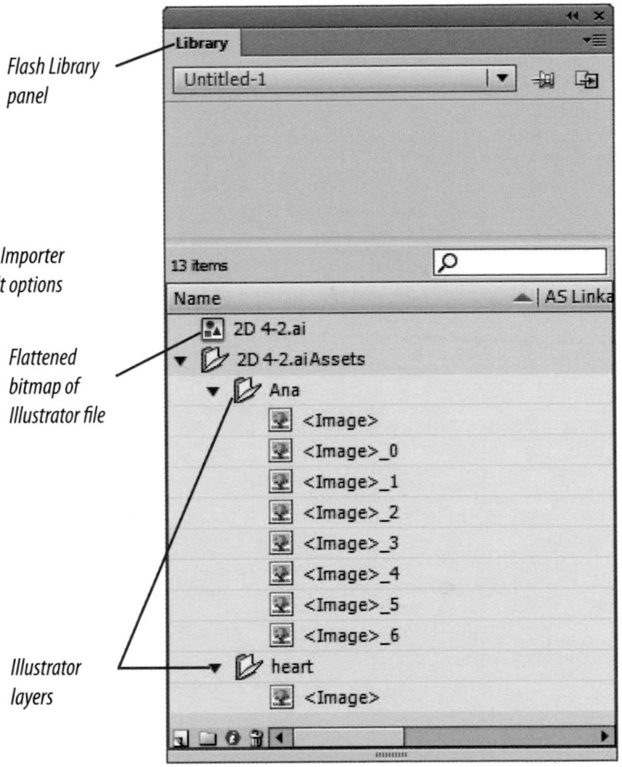

Flash Library panel

Flattened bitmap of Illustrator file

Illustrator layers

Source Adobe® Flash® Professional, 2013.

Figure 3 shows the Import dialog box for an Illustrator file used in a previous chapter. As you may recall, the heart and Ana sublayers were rasterized for you, while the Liza layer objects were grouped. When importing this same file into Flash, notice that each of the Liza sublayers shows the group icon and the grouped objects, when expanded, are paths, while those sublayers that had been rasterized are bitmaps.

You can choose to import each Illustrator layer as a flattened bitmap or select each sublayer or object individually and then identify the import options specific for that type of object. Importing an object as a path keeps the path editable in Flash, which is the default setting. You can permanently override this option in the Preferences panel or during the import

Figure 3 *Overriding default options during import*

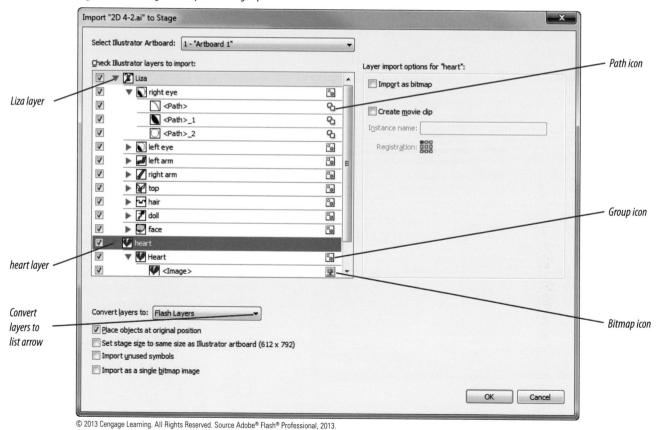

© 2013 Cengage Learning. All Rights Reserved. Source Adobe® Flash® Professional, 2013.

process, as shown in Figure 4. Importing a path as an editable path will create an editable vector path maintaining blend modes, effects, and transparency if applied. If imported as a bitmap, the exact appearance of the path will be maintained but the path will no longer be editable.

The bitmap icon identifies an object that has been rasterized in Illustrator, as shown in Figure 4. Converting the file to a bitmap in Flash will maintain the appearance of the Illustrator bitmap. Importing an object identified as a group as a flattened bitmap will remove the option to import the elements of the group as editable paths.

Figure 4 *Import to Stage dialog box*

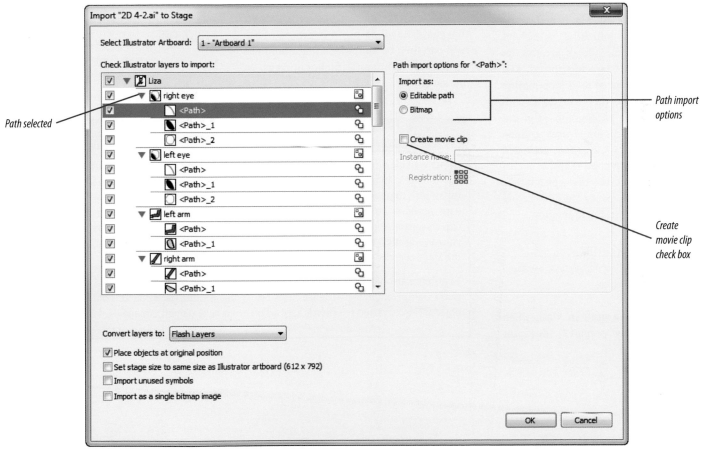

Creating a Cut-Out Style Animation in Flash

Artwork created in Illustrator can be imported into Flash and animated using the cut-out style of animating. A **cut-out style animation** is a method of creating an animation using flat characters, props, and backgrounds, also referred to as **stop-motion animation**. Originally, this was done with paper, stiff fabric, or photographs. Cut-out style animation on a computer uses scanned images or vector graphics. The animated comedy *South Park* is a good example of cut-out animation; in fact, the first episode was actually created with paper cutouts before moving to computer cut-out animation.

This technique can be used in Flash when importing a properly prepared Illustrator file, as discussed earlier. You will want to take advantage of the setting options in the Import to Stage dialog box to import your artwork to a single Flash layer and to create the movie clips of the components that will be animated. Completing these steps during the import process makes it easier to separate the parts of your animation onto separate layers. The layers will automatically be named for you with the same name as the movie clip you created during this process. Each layer can then be animated using traditional keyframing techniques, motion tweens, or motion guides.

When you name your movie clip, there are some basic naming conventions you should follow: Do not use spaces or special characters except for the underscore, and begin the name with a lowercase letter. Following these suggestions will make writing ActionScript much easier. Also, give your movie clip, or any symbol, a name that is descriptive to make it easier to locate in the Library.

Applying the Rasterize Command

Before working with an Illustrator file in Photoshop, you must rasterize your artwork. When applying the rasterize command, the selection converts into a bitmap image on its own sublayer. If you choose to rasterize components of your artwork so they can be animated in Flash it is important to rasterize each individual object rather than rasterizing the entire document. Rasterizing each object keeps the objects separated on a single layer, allowing you to work with them in Flash. When imported into Flash, you can edit as if it were drawn in object drawing mode, which allows you to manipulate each object on the Stage or convert it to a symbol.

To rasterize an object, select the object, click Object on the Menu bar, then select Rasterize. Be sure to select Transparent in the Rasterize check box so that a white background is not added to each of the objects. The converted selection is appears on a new layer named <Image>.

Figure 5 *Results of grouping objects*

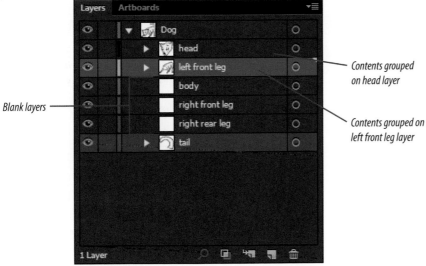

Blank layers

Contents grouped
on head layer

Contents grouped on
left front leg layer

Prepare an Illustrator file for animation in Flash

In this exercise, you will prepare an Illustrator file for importing into Flash and then animate it.

1. Start Illustrator, navigate to where you store your Data Files, open 2D 6-1.ai, then save it as **Dog.ai**. Artwork has already been created for you.

Tip Set the Essentials workspace if necessary.

2. Show the **Layers panel**, then click the **Expand icon** ▶ on the Dog layer if necessary.

3. Press and hold **[Shift]**, click the **Target icon** ○ on the body layer, then click the **Target icon** ○ on the right front leg layer. Both layers are selected.

4. Click **Object** on the Menu bar, then click **Group**. The two objects are grouped on the body layer.

Tip You can also press and hold [Ctrl][G] (Win) or ⌘[G] (Mac) to group selected objects.

5. Click the **Target icon** ○ on the body layer to reselect it, then repeat steps 3 and 4 to select and group the **body**, **left front leg**, and **right rear leg layers**.

The objects are grouped on the left front leg layer, as shown in Figure 5.

6. Click the **Target icon** ○ on the tail layer, click **Object** on the Menu bar, then click **Group** to group the objects on the tail layer.

(continued)

7. Select the **body, right front leg**, and **right rear leg layers**, then click the **Delete Selection icon** 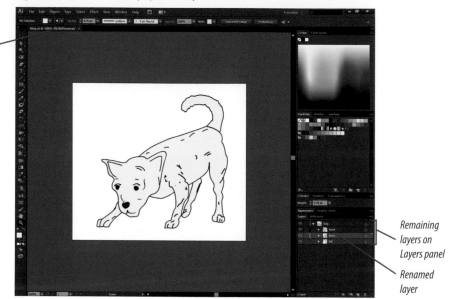 at the bottom of the Layers panel.

8. Rename the left front leg layer **body**.

9. Click **File** on the Menu bar, click **Document Color Mode**, click **RGB Color**, then compare your screen to Figure 6.

   RGB color mode appears on the document title tab next to the filename. RGB makes the file compatible with Flash.

10. Click **File** on the Menu bar, click **Save**, then click **Close**.

Import an Illustrator file into Flash

In this exercise, you will import an Illustrator file into Flash.

1. Start Flash, click **ActionScript 3.0** on the Welcome Screen to open a new file, then save your file as **Animated Dog**.

2. Click **File** on the Menu bar, click **Import**, then click **Import to Stage**.

   The Import dialog box opens.

   (continued)

Figure 6 *Illustrator document prepared to import into Flash*

RGB color mode

Remaining layers on Layers panel

Renamed layer

Figure 7 *Import "Dog.ai" to Stage dialog box*

Named layers

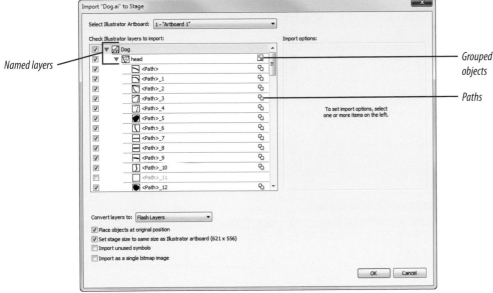

Grouped objects

Paths

3. Navigate to where you store your Data Files, click **Dog.ai**, then click **Open**.

   The Import "Dog.ai" to Stage dialog box opens, as shown in Figure 7.

4. Verify that the Set stage size to same size as Illustrator artboard (621 × 556) check box is selected and that Flash Layers is selected in the Convert layers to menu.

5. Click the **Collapse icon** ▼ next to the **head**, **body**, and **tail layers**.

6. Select the **head layer**, click the **Create movie clip check box**, then type **head** in the Instance name text box.

7. Repeat step 6 for the **body** and **tail layers**, then click **OK**.

   All of the movie clips are created on the Dog layer on the Timeline.

   (continued)

8. With the movie clips still selected, click **Modify** on the Menu bar, point to **Timeline**, then click **Distribute to Layers**.

   The movie clips are placed on their own layers, which have the same names as the movie clips, as shown in Figure 8.

TIP If your movie clips are not selected on the Stage, select the keyframe in Frame 1 on the Dog layer.

9. Click the **Dog layer**, then click the **Delete button** on the Timeline panel.

10. Save your work.

Create a cut-out style animation in Flash

In this exercise, you will create a simple animation with an Illustrator file using the cut-out style.

1. Click **Frame 60** on the head layer, press and hold **[Shift]**, then click **Frame 60** on the tail layer, as shown in Figure 9.

   Frame 60 is selected on all three layers.

2. Press **F5** to insert a new frame in Frame 60 in all three layers.

   Additional frames are added to the selected layers up to Frame 60.

3. Select the **tail layer**.

4. Click **Insert** on the Menu bar, then click **Motion Tween**.

   A motion tween is added to the tail layer.

5. Verify that the tail layer is selected, then move the **playhead** to **Frame 20**, as shown in Figure 10.

(continued)

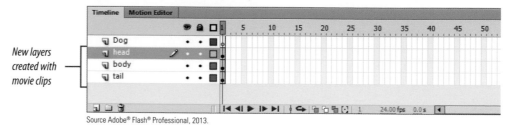

Figure 8 *Movie clips distributed across layers*

New layers created with movie clips

Source Adobe® Flash® Professional, 2013.

Figure 9 *Selecting a frame across multiple layers*

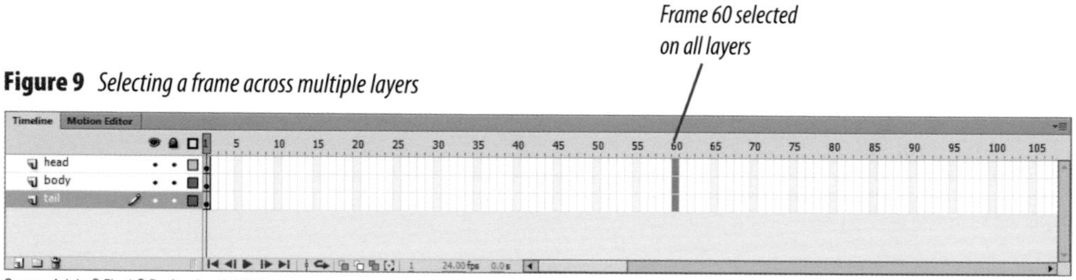

Frame 60 selected on all layers

Source Adobe® Flash® Professional, 2013.

Figure 10 *Adjusting the playhead*

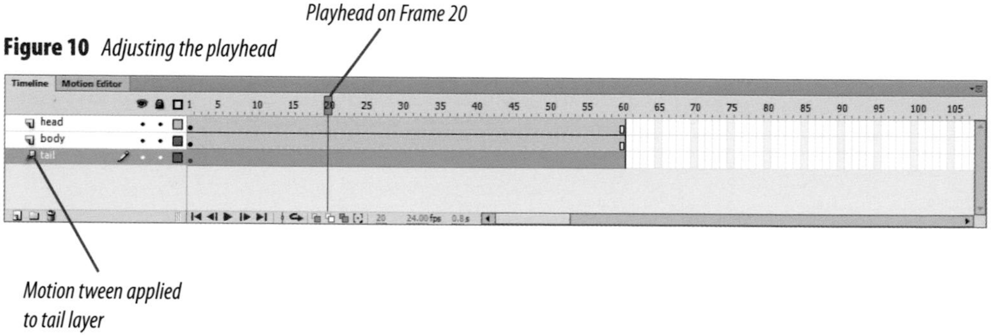

Playhead on Frame 20

Motion tween applied to tail layer

Source Adobe® Flash® Professional, 2013.

Figure 11 *Adjusting the reference point*

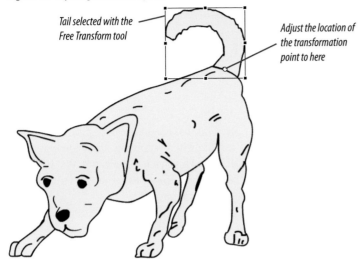

Tail selected with the Free Transform tool

Adjust the location of the transformation point to here

Figure 12 *Rotating the dog's tail*

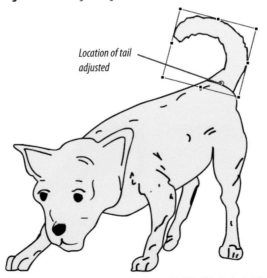

Location of tail adjusted

6. Select the **Free Transform tool** on the Tools panel.

   The free transform bounding box surrounds the tail of the dog.

7. Click and drag the **Transformation point** to the **base of the dog's tail**, as shown in Figure 11.

   The tail will rotate on this point.

8. Place the **rotation pointer** over a corner of the bounding box, rotate the **tail** to the **right**, then adjust the **location** of the tail so it stays behind the dog, as shown in Figure 12.

   A keyframe is created in Frame 20 on the tail layer.

9. Repeat step 8 on **Frame 40**, rotating the **tail** to the **left**.

   Remember to adjust the location of the playhead before rotating the tail, if necessary.

10. Click **Control** on the Menu bar, click **Test Movie**, then click **Test** to preview your animation.

    The tail wags back and forth.

11. Click **File** on the Menu bar, click **Save**, then click **Close**.

Animate a Photoshop FILE IN FLASH

What You'll Do

Image Source National Gallery of Art, Washington. Source Adobe® Photoshop®, 2013.

 In this lesson, you will prepare a Photoshop document and then animate it in Flash.

Using Content-Aware Fill

Photoshop introduced a feature called content-aware fill in CS5 that removes the contents of a selection replacing it with content based on nearby pixels. The best results when applying this command are achieved by creating a selection that is slightly larger than the object you are removing, as shown in Figure 13.

Figure 13 *Making a selection to use with content-aware fill*

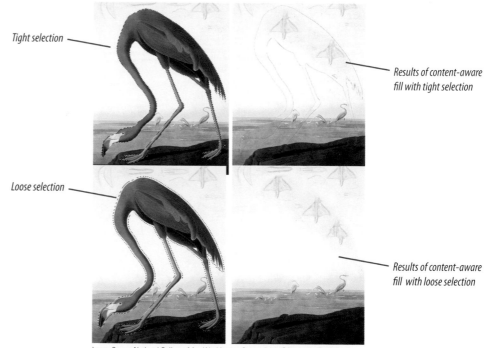

Tight selection

Results of content-aware fill with tight selection

Loose selection

Results of content-aware fill with loose selection

Image Source National Gallery of Art, Washington. Source Adobe® Photoshop®, 2013.

After selecting the object you want to remove from an image, select Fill from the Edit menu. The content-aware command is found in the Fill dialog box on the Use menu, as shown in Figure 14.

Using Puppet Warp

The Puppet Warp feature, located on the Edit menu, was also introduced in Photoshop CS5 and allows you to make adjustments to an image such as repositioning an arm on a person or a tail on an animal. This feature works best if you first remove the background from the image you want to adjust.

A mesh appears on the object, shown in Figure 15, which allows you to set pins to the parts of the image you want to transform and to the parts you want to anchor in the original position. To distort the image, drag the pins.

The options bar, as shown in Figure 16, displays the options available when working with Puppet Warp. The Mode setting sets the overall flexibility of the mesh. You can select Normal, Distort, or Rigid. Normal, the default setting, applies a standard

Figure 15 *The puppet warp mesh*

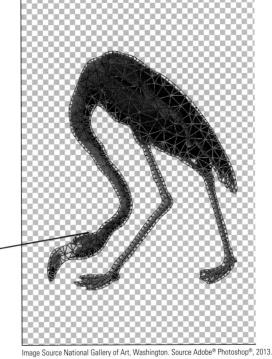

Image Source National Gallery of Art, Washington. Source Adobe® Photoshop®, 2013.

Puppet Warp mesh

Figure 14 *Fill dialog box*

Content-Aware selected on Use menu

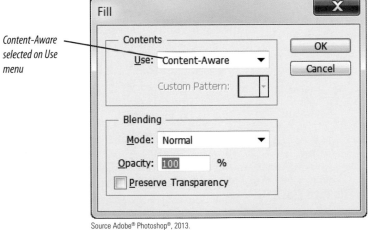

Source Adobe® Photoshop®, 2013.

Figure 16 *Puppet Warp options bar*

Remove all pins icon   Commit Puppet Warp

Source Adobe® Photoshop®, 2013.

Mode list arrow   Density list arrow   Rotate list arrow   Cancel Puppet Warp

amount of flexibility between each of the pins as you move them. Distort mode warps the image at the location of the pin as you drag the pin, while the Rigid mode is more inflexible and would work well on hands. The Density setting sets the space between mesh points. Choosing More Points increases the amount of mesh and therefore the accuracy that can be created with pins and requires more processing time. Fewer Points reduces accuracy and takes less time to process. The Expansion setting expands or contracts the outside edge of the mesh. The Show Mesh check box is selected by default; deselecting this option will show only the adjustment pins making it easier to see your transformations. When you create a pin, the Rotate menu is set to Auto by default. Selecting the pin and changing the Rotate menu to Fixed anchors the pin so it does not move. The options bar also allows you to remove all of the pins, cancel the puppet warp, or commit to your changes. You will need to either cancel your puppet warp or commit to your puppet warp before you are able to continue working with Photoshop.

QUICK **TIP**

Puppet Warp can be applied in a nondestructive image by first making your image a Smart Object.

Preparing a Photoshop File to be Animated in Flash

You may find that using Photoshop's drawing and selection tools gives you more flexibility and control than the tools in Flash. Fortunately, importing a Photoshop file into Flash is similar to importing an Illustrator file. As with Illustrator, Flash can maintain the elements of the Photoshop document and by bringing them into Flash, you can create animated elements.

When preparing your Photoshop file to be imported into Flash, consider the following best practices:

- Verify your color mode is set to RGB; this can be done by selecting Mode on the Image menu.
- Separate content you want to animate onto their own layers.
- Name your layers.

QUICK **TIP**

Smart objects will be rasterized when imported into Flash.

Importing a Photoshop File into Flash

Importing a Photoshop file into Flash shares many core features as importing an Illustrator file. You can use Import to Stage or Import to Library commands to select the layers you want to import (based on whether the layer was visible in Photoshop).

The Import to Library option places the assets in a folder in the Library panel. Each layer is brought in as an editable bitmap or a flattened bitmap. You can also choose to bring the layer in as a movie clip symbol. In addition, a flattened bitmap of the Photoshop document is also placed in the Library panel.

The Import to Stage option places the Photoshop layers on the Stage. You can choose to convert the Photoshop layers to Flash layers or to keyframes on the same Flash layer. You also have the option to resize the Stage to the same size as the Photoshop document you are importing.

As with Illustrator, there is an Import dialog box PSD file importer, as shown in Figure 17. When importing a Photoshop document into Flash, Flash will recognize image layers, text layers, shape layers, layer groups, and merged bitmaps. You have the option to import image, text, and shape layers so they are still editable as a flattened bitmap. You can also choose to create these layers into movie clips. By default, the import options are set to create flattened bitmaps from these layers. If you choose to copy and paste or click and drag layers between Photoshop and Flash, the default settings will be applied. These default settings can be modified in the PSD file importer options found in the Flash Preferences, shown in Figure 17.

The Publish Setting option lets you determine the amount of compression and the quality that will be applied when the image is published as a SWF file. (*Note*: These settings will have no effect on the imported image when it is placed on the Stage or in the Library.)

The compression options available are lossy or lossless. **Lossy** compression compresses the image to the JPEG file format. If you want to use the settings specified by the imported image, choose Use publish settings. If you would like to customize the quality, select Custom and set the value between 1 and 100. The larger the number, the greater the integrity of the image and the larger the file size. Lossless compresses the image to the PNG or GIF file format and does not discard any data from the image.

QUICK TIP

For images such as photographs that have complex color and tonal variations, use the lossy compression. For images with simple shapes and few colors, use the lossless compression.

Figure 17 *PSD File Importer preferences*

PSD File Importer

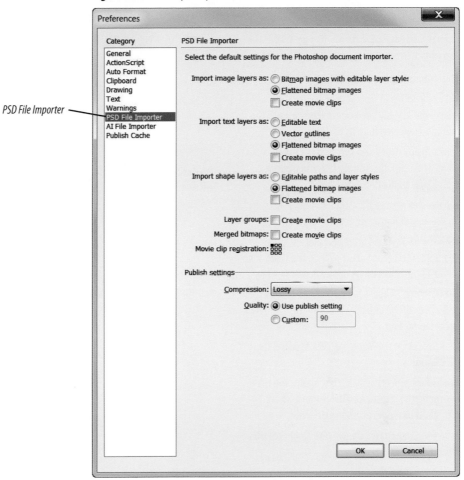

© 2013 Cengage Learning, All Rights Reserved. Source Adobe® Photoshop®, 2013.

Use content-aware fill

In this exercise, you will use the content-aware fill command to remove an image from the background.

1. Start Photoshop, open 2D 6-2.psd, then save it as **Flamingo.psd**.

   A layer has already been created for you with the flamingo removed from its background.

2. Select the **background layer** on the Layers panel, then click the **Toggle layer visibility icon** ⊙ on the flamingo 1 layer.

   You need to remove the flamingo from the image on the background layer.

3. With the background layer still selected, press and hold **[Ctrl]** (Win) or ⌘ (Mac), then click the **Layer thumbnail mask** on the flamingo 1 layer.

   The flamingo image is selected on the canvas and a copy of the image appears on the background layer.

4. Click **Select** on the Menu bar, click **Modify**, then click **Expand**.

   The Expand Selection dialog box opens. You need to expand the selection so the content-aware fill command has some pixels to work with.

5. Type **4** in the **Expand By** text box, then click **OK**.

   The selection around the flamingo expands, as shown in Figure 18.

6. Click **Edit** on the Menu bar, then click **Fill**.

   The Fill dialog box opens.

   (continued)

Figure 18 *Expanding a selection*

Image Source National Gallery of Art, Washington. Source Adobe® Photoshop®, 2013.

Hidden flamingo 1 layer

Layer thumbnail mask

Expanded selection

Selected background layer

Figure 19 *Effects of the content-aware fill command*

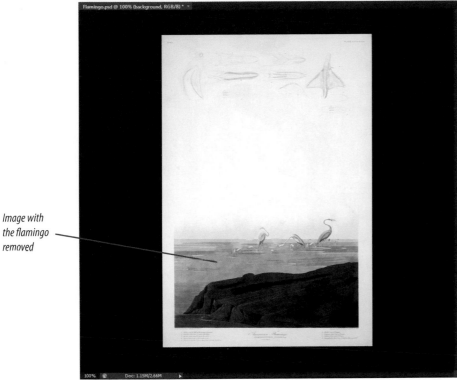

Flamingo.psd @ 100% (background, RGB/8) *

Image with the flamingo removed

100%   Doc: 1.15M/2.66M

Image Source National Gallery of Art, Washington. Source Adobe® Photoshop®, 2013.

7. Click the **Use list arrow**, click **Content-Aware** if necessary, then click **OK**.

   The selected flamingo is replaced with the background content.

8. Click **Select** on the Menu bar, then click **Deselect** to remove the selection, as shown in Figure 19.

9. Select the **flamingo 1 layer**, then click the **Indicates layer visibility icon** to show the flamingo 1 layer.

   The flamingo is visible on the canvas and the Layer thumbnail is selected on the layer.

TIP   Make sure the Layer mask thumbnail is not selected.

(continued)

10. Click **Edit** on the Menu bar, then click **Free Transform**.

A bounding box surrounds the entire image. You need to resize the flamingo to prepare the image when you change the position of the head.

11. Press and hold **[Shift]**, drag the **upper-right sizing handle** down to resize the flamingo to approximately one quarter of its original size, as shown in Figure 20, then press **[Enter]** (Win) or **[return]** (Mac).

12. Save your work.

Figure 20 *Resizing the flamingo*

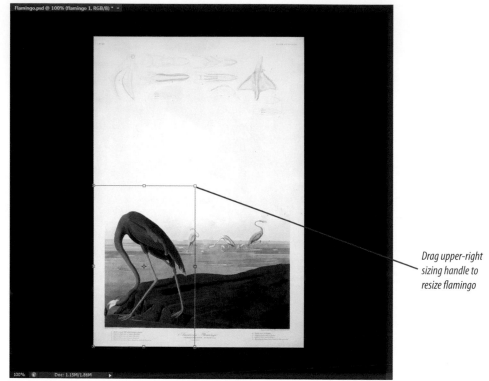

Drag upper-right
sizing handle to
resize flamingo

Image Source National Gallery of Art, Washington. Source Adobe® Photoshop®, 2013.

Animating with Illustrator and Photoshop Files in Flash Professional

Figure 21 *Adjusting the location of the resized flamingo*

Move flamingo here

Image Source National Gallery of Art, Washington. Source Adobe® Photoshop®, 2013.

Use Puppet Warp to prepare the Photoshop file for Flash

In this exercise, you will use the puppet warp feature to adjust the location of the flamingo's head.

1. Verify that Flamingo.psd is open.

2. Make sure the flamingo 1 layer is selected, click the **Move tool** ▶⊕ on the Tools panel, then move the flamingo to the **center of the grassy area**, as shown in Figure 21.

3. Press and hold **[Ctrl]** (Win) or ⌘ (Mac), then click the **Layer thumbnail mask** on the flamingo 1 layer.

4. Click **Edit** on the Menu bar, then click **Copy**.

   A copy of the flamingo is placed on the clipboard.

5. Click the **Create a new layer icon** 🔳 on the bottom of the Layers panel.

   A new layer, Layer 1, is created.

   (continued)

6. Click **Edit** on the Menu bar, then click **Paste**.

   A copy of the flamingo without the background is placed on the new layer, as shown in Figure 22.

7. Rename Layer 1 **flamingo 2**.

8. Right-click the **flamingo 2 layer**, then click **Duplicate Layer**.

   The Duplicate Layer dialog box opens.

9. Type **flamingo 3**, then click **OK**.

   Three copies of the flamingo appear on separate layers on the Layers panel.

   (continued)

Figure 22 *Creating a copy of the flamingo*

Copy of flamingo on new layer

Image Source National Gallery of Art, Washington. Source Adobe® Photoshop®, 2013.

Animating with Illustrator and Photoshop Files in Flash Professional

Figure 23 *Placing pins with Puppet Warp*

Rotate menu

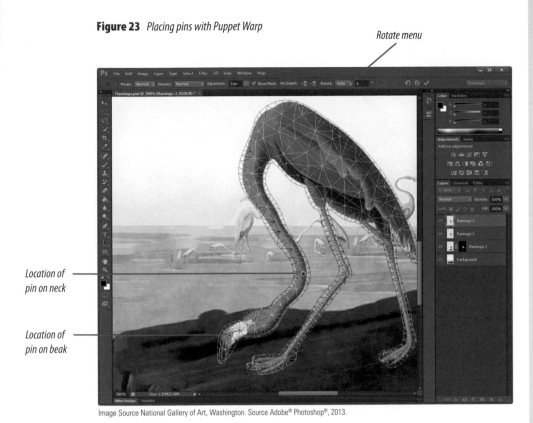

Location of pin on neck

Location of pin on beak

Image Source National Gallery of Art, Washington. Source Adobe® Photoshop®, 2013.

10. Make sure the flamingo 3 layer is selected, click **Edit** on the Menu bar, then click **Puppet Warp**.

A mesh is placed on the flamingo. You will place two pins to adjust the location of the flamingo's head.

11. Click the **curve of the flamingo's neck** and **beak** to place pins as shown in Figure 23.

TIP Zoom in as necessary.

(continued)

12. Click the **pin on the flamingo's neck** to select it, click the **Rotate list arrow** on the options bar, then click **Fixed**.

    Selecting Fixed allows you to move the flamingo's head but not move the rest of the neck.

13. Click the **pin on the flamingo's beak**, drag the **beak up**, as shown in Figure 24, leaving enough room for another copy of the head, which will fit between the two visible heads, then click the **Commit Puppet Warp button** 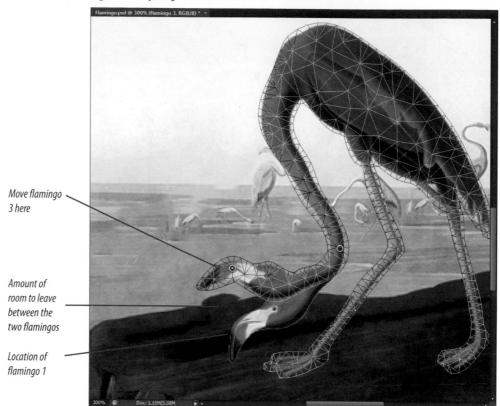 on the options bar.

    (continued)

Figure 24 *Adjusting the location of the head*

Move flamingo 3 here

Amount of room to leave between the two flamingos

Location of flamingo 1

Image Source National Gallery of Art, Washington. Source Adobe® Photoshop®, 2013.

Animating with Illustrator and Photoshop Files in Flash Professional

Figure 25 *Locations of the flamingo's head*

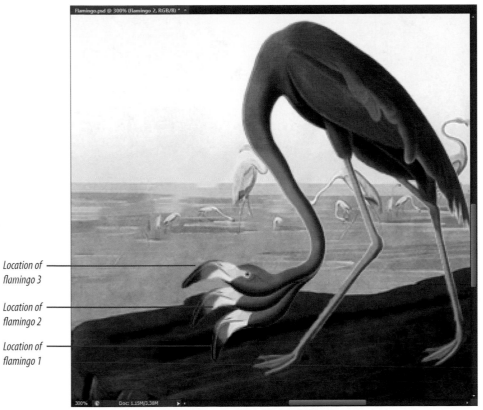

Location of
flamingo 3

Location of
flamingo 2

Location of
flamingo 1

Image Source National Gallery of Art, Washington. Source Adobe® Photoshop®, 2013.

14. Select **flamingo 2** on the Layers panel, repeat steps 11–12, click the **pin on the flamingo's beak**, then drag the **beak up** between the other two, as shown in Figure 25.

15. Save your work, then exit Photoshop.

Import a Photoshop file into Flash

In this exercise, you will import a Photoshop file into Flash and animate the image.

1. Start Flash, click **ActionScript 3.0** on the Welcome Screen to open a new file, then save it as **Animated Flamingo**.

2. Click **File** on the Menu bar, click **Import**, then click **Import to Stage**.

The Import dialog box opens.

(continued)

3. In the Import dialog box, click **Flamingo.psd**, then click **Open**.

   The Import "Flamingo.psd" to Stage dialog box opens, as shown in Figure 26.

4. Check the **Set stage size to same size as Photoshop canvas (524 × 770) check box**, then click **OK**.

   The canvas is resized for the Photoshop document and the Photoshop layers appear on their own Flash layers, as shown in Figure 27.

   (continued)

Figure 26 *Import "Flamingo.psd" to Stage dialog box*

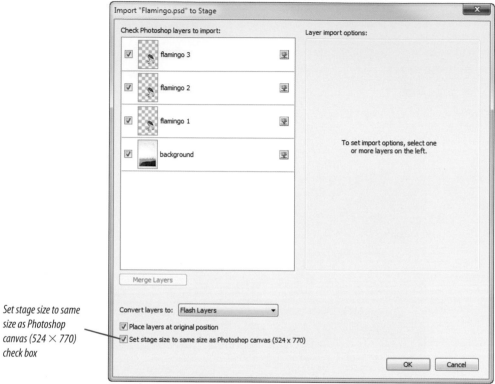

Set stage size to same size as Photoshop canvas (524 × 770) check box

Figure 27 *Flamingo layers in Timeline panel*

Flash layers automatically named with Photoshop layer names

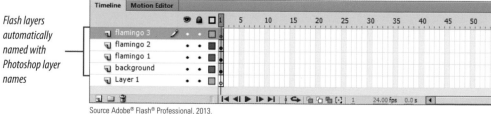

Animating with Illustrator and Photoshop Files in Flash Professional

Figure 28 *Frame 60 selected*

Frame 60 selected
on multiple layers

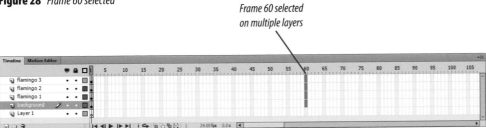

Source Adobe® Flash® Professional, 2013.

Figure 29 *Location of keyframes on the flamingo layers*

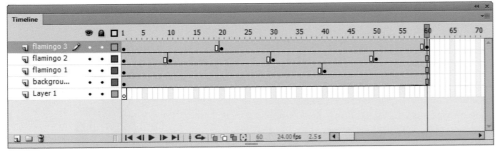

Source Adobe® Flash® Professional, 2013.

Figure 30 *Location of blank keyframes on the flamingo layers*

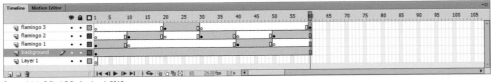

Source Adobe® Flash® Professional, 2013.

5. Click **Frame 60** on the flamingo 3 layer, press **[Shift]**, then click on **Frame 60** on the background layer, as shown in Figure 28.

   Frame 60 on the four imported layers is selected.

6. Press **F5** to insert a new frame in Frame 60 on all four layers.

   Additional frames are added to the selected layers up to Frame 60.

7. Click **Frame 40** on the flamingo 1 layer, then press **F6**.

   A keyframe is added to Frame 40.

8. Click **Frame 10** on the flamingo 2 layer, press **F6**, then repeat for **Frames 30** and **50**.

9. Click **Frame 20** on the flamingo 3 layer, press **F6**, repeat for **Frame 60**, then compare your Timeline to Figure 29.

10. Click **Frame 10** on the flamingo 1 layer, press **F7**, then repeat for **Frame 50**.

   A blank keyframe is added to Frames 10 and 50.

11. Click **Frame 1** on the flamingo 2 layer, press **Delete**, then repeat for **Frames 20** and **40**.

12. Click **Frame 1** on the flamingo 3 layer, press **Delete**, repeat for **Frame 30**, then compare your Timeline to Figure 30.

13. Click **Control** on the Menu bar, click **Test Movie**, then click **Test** to preview your animation.

14. Save your document, then exit Flash.

Animate with Inverse
KINEMATICS

What You'll Do

 In this lesson, you will create an animation using inverse kinematics.

Working with Inverse Kinematics

Inverse kinematics uses bones to adjust or animate parts of a shape, eliminating the need to draw separate versions of an object to represent different movements. This technique can be combined with the other types of animations you have already learned: frame-by-frame, tween, and cut-out. The series of bones created to simulate the movement of characters is referred to as the **armature**, as shown in Figure 31. When one bone moves, any connected bones also move. There are two tools in Flash that are used when creating an armature, the Bone tool and the Bind tool, which are used to connect objects and edit those connections.

The Bone tool is used to create the bones that make up the armature. Bones can connect symbol instances or shapes. Connected objects can then be posed at various locations on the Timeline to create your animation. To create and connect objects or shapes, place the pointer over the first object or shape and then when you see a plus sign, click and drag to the second object or shape. A new layer, the armature layer, is created automatically. You can continue to connect objects in the same manner. Keep in mind you always need at least two items to connect.

Figure 31 *Sample armature*

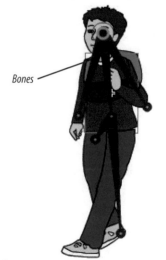

Bones

The Bind tool can be used to edit the connections between each bone and to shape the **control points**. By default, control points are connected to the nearest bone. This may cause problems when you move a bone because the shape may look distorted. When you select your armature with the Bind tool, control points are highlighted in yellow and the selected bone is highlighted in red. Control points connected to only one bone are displayed as squares; those connected to more than one bone are displayed as triangles, as shown in Figure 32.

Other tools you can use when working with inverse kinematics include the Selection tool, the Subselection tool, the Pen tool, and the Free Transform tool. The Selection tool selects and moves bones to adjust the pose of the armature. The Subselection tool moves the joints of bones by making them shorter or rotating them. The Pen tool adds or removes control points to a shape. The Free Transform tool adjusts the starting points of any bones that are a part of a symbol-based armature.

Figure 32 *Using the Bind tool*

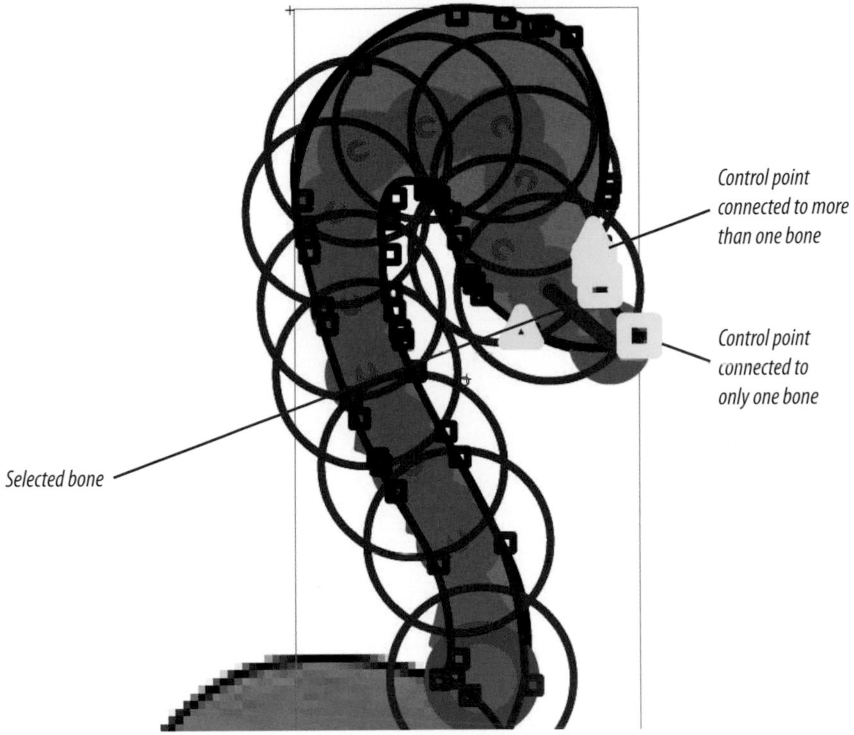

Control point connected to more than one bone

Control point connected to only one bone

Selected bone

© 2013 Cengage Learning, All Rights Reserved. Source Adobe® Flash® Professional, 2013.

Working with the Bind Tool

Multiple control points can be bound to one bone and multiple bones can be bound to one control point.

- To add control points to a selected bone, press and hold [Shift], then click a control point that is not highlighted, or press and hold [Shift], then drag a bounding box around multiple control points to add to the selected bone.
- To remove a control point from the bone, press and hold [Ctrl] (Win) or [option] (Mac), then click a control point that is highlighted in yellow. To remove multiple control points from the selected bone, press and hold [Ctrl] (Win) or [option] (Mac), then drag a bounding box around multiple controls points.
- To highlight the bones connected to a control point, select the Bind tool, then click the control point.
- To add bones to the selected control point, press and hold [Shift], then click a bone.
- To remove a bone from the selected control point, press and hold [Ctrl] (Win) or [option] (Mac), then click a bone that is highlighted in yellow.

Lesson 3   Animate with Inverse Kinematics

2D ANIMATION 6-29

Creating an Animation with Inverse Kinematics

After you create your armature, you can add motion to your character. First, it is important to verify that the armature and all of the necessary elements are located on the armature layer. If items are missing from the armature layer, they are not connected by any bones. If you need to start over, you can remove the armature by right-clicking a frame in the Timeline and then clicking Remove Armature.

You can perform the following steps to animate an armature:

1. Press F5 on the frame of the armature layer to set the length of your animation.
2. Move the playhead to where you want to adjust the armature.
3. Use the Selection tool to adjust the pose of the armature. (*Note*: A keyframe will be created automatically.)
4. Move the playhead to the location for each pose.
5. To copy a pose, right-click the keyframe for the pose, click Copy Pose, right-click the frame where you want the pose duplicated, and then click Paste Pose. (*Note*: Do not select the frame first.)

Editing an Animation Using Inverse Kinematics

There are many ways to adjust or edit the bones after you create an armature. You may want to reposition the bones and their associated objects, move a bone within an object, change the length of a bone, delete a bone, and edit the objects that contain

the bones. (*Note*: You should edit the bones before you start creating poses.)

Bones can be selected with the Selection tool; double-clicking one of the bones selects all of them, pressing and holding [Shift] and clicking individual bones selects multiple bones.

Once you have a bone(s) selected you can:

- Delete a bone by pressing [Delete].
- Edit the properties of the bone in the Property inspector.

There are five parameters available in the Property inspector that can be defined for each bone or set of bones, as shown in Figure 33.

Figure 33 *Bone tool properties in the Property inspector*

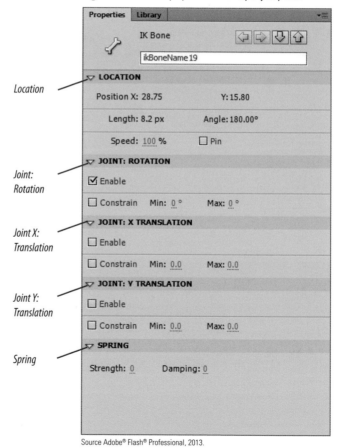

Source Adobe® Flash® Professional, 2013.

You can adjust bone properties, select the Bone tool, then click a bone. In the Location section of the Property inspector, you can pin a bone to the Stage so it cannot move. The Joint properties can be used to restrict the amount of rotation on a bone or the direction it can move on the x- or y-axis. Restricting the rotation or direction that a bone can move helps you create more realistic animations, such as restricting the motion of an arm. The Spring properties can also assist in creating more realistic movements by adding springiness to your armature. The strength of a spring adds stiffness to the spring; the higher the value, the stiffer the effect. The damping parameter adjusts the rate of decay of the spring over time; the higher the number, the quicker the decay.

The armature layer also has its own Property inspector, shown in Figure 34, where you can change some of its properties. (*Note*: The properties you change here affect the entire armature on the layer, not specific bones.) The ease parameter adjusts the speed at which the animation begins and ends. The options parameter configures your armature to respond to ActionScript by selecting the type. The style option changes how the bones are displayed: solid, wire, line, or none.

Figure 34 *Armature properties in the Property inspector*

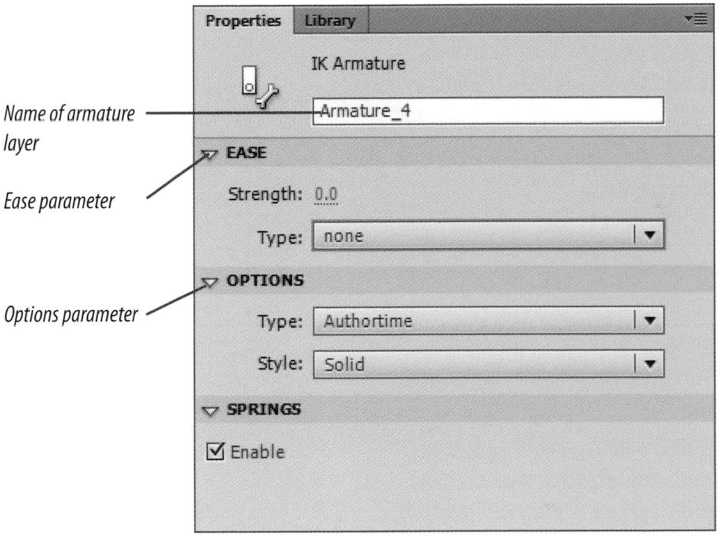

Source Adobe® Flash® Professional, 2013.

Import an Illustrator file into Flash

In this exercise, you will import the Illustrator file to be animated with inverse kinematics.

1. Create a new Flash document with default ActionScript 3.0 settings, then save it as **Animated Lion**.

2. Click **File** on the Menu bar, click **Import**, then click **Import to Stage**.

   The Import dialog box opens. You import an Illustrator file that has already been created for you.

3. Navigate to where you store your Data Files, click **2D 6-3.ai**, then click **Open**.

   The Import "2D 6-3.ai" to Stage dialog box opens.

4. Collapse all the **layers** below the lion layer, then compare your screen to Figure 35.

5. Click the **head layer**, click the **Create movie clip check box**, then type **head** in the Instance name text box.

6. Repeat step 5 for the **body**, **right front**, **right back**, **left front**, and **left back layers**, typing an **underscore _** in place of spaces as necessary.

   (continued)

Figure 35 *Layers collapsed*

Collapse all layers except lion

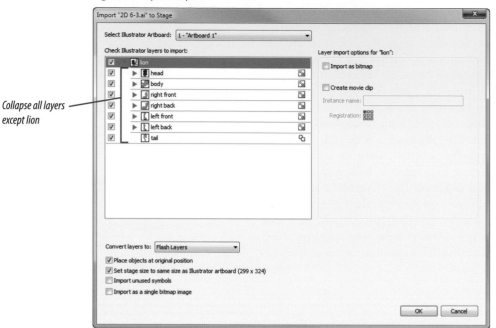

© 2013 Cengage Learning, All Rights Reserved. Source Adobe® Flash® Professional, 2013.

Figure 36 *Import options for tail layer*

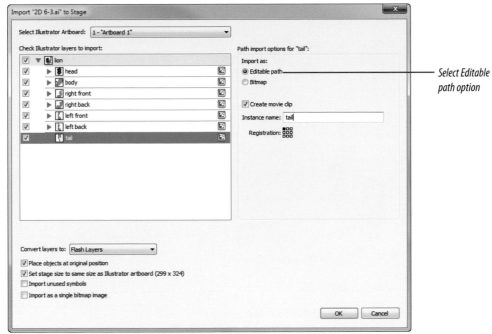

Select Editable path option

7. Click the **tail layer**, make sure the Editable path check box is selected, click the **Create movie clip check box**, then type **tail** in the Instance name text box, as shown in Figure 36.

   You will edit the tail in Flash before animating it.

8. Click the **Convert layers to list arrow**, then click **Single Flash Layer**.

9. Verify that the Place objects at original position and the Set stage size to same size as Illustrator artboard (299 × 324) check boxes are selected.

10. Click **OK**.

11. Save your work.

Work with inverse kinematics on a shape

In this exercise, you will animate the tail using inverse kinematics.

1. Verify that Animated Lion.fla is open.

2. Click the **Selection tool** ▸ on the Tools panel, then double-click the **tail instance** on the Stage to enter movie clip editing mode for the lion instance.

3. Double-click the **tail instance** to enter movie clip editing mode just for the tail instance, as shown in Figure 37.

(continued)

Figure 37 *Editing mode for the instance of the tail*

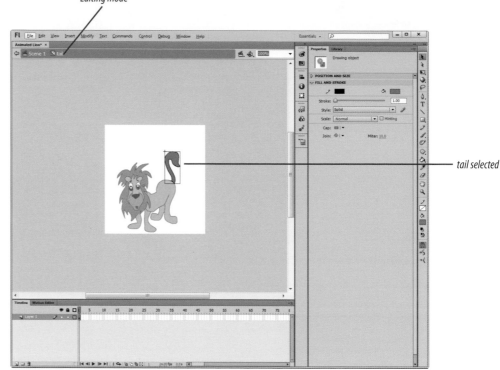

Editing mode

tail selected

Figure 38 *Setting the first bone*

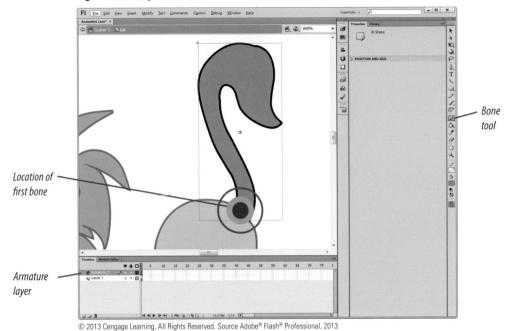

Location of
first bone

Armature
layer

Bone
tool

4. Zoom in on the tail as necessary.
5. Click the **Bone tool** ![bone icon] on the Tools panel, then click **the base of the tail**, as shown in Figure 38.

TIP Be careful that you do not click the stroke.

(continued)

6. Following the shape of the tail, click and drag to create **several short bones**, as shown in Figure 39.

   Twelve bones were created in the figure.

7. Insert a **keyframe** in Frame 60 on the Armature layer.

   An identical version of the tail appears on Frame 60.

8. Move the **playhead** to Frame 20, click the **Selection tool** on the Tools panel, click the **tail**, then drag the **bone on the tip of the tail** out and to the right.

   The thickest part of the tail needs to be adjusted to move with the tip of the tail.

TIP Drag the playhead back and forth to preview your animation.

(continued)

Figure 39 *Twelve bones added to tail*

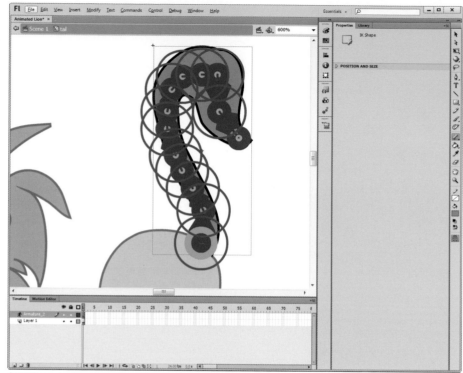

© 2013 Cengage Learning, All Rights Reserved. Source Adobe® Flash® Professional, 2013.

Animating with Illustrator and Photoshop Files in Flash Professional

Figure 40 *Adjusting the pose of the tail*

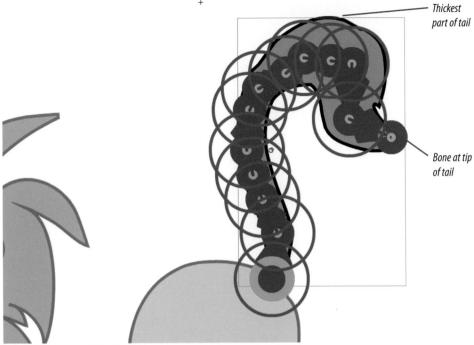

Thickest part of tail

Bone at tip of tail

9. Make sure the playhead ▮ is on Frame 20, drag a **bone** on the **thickest part of the tail** to the right, then compare your screen to Figure 40.

TIP If you need to make adjustments, press and hold [Ctrl][Z] (Win) or ⌘[Z] (Mac) to undo an action, then recreate a bone segment.

10. Insert a **keyframe** on Frame 40, then repeat steps 8 and 9, moving the tail to the **left**.

   You may choose to adjust different bones than you did on Frame 20.

   (continued)

11. Open the Property inspector if necessary, then click the **bone on the tip of the tail**, as shown in Figure 41.

    You need to make the tail move in a more natural manner.

12. Click the **Expand icon** 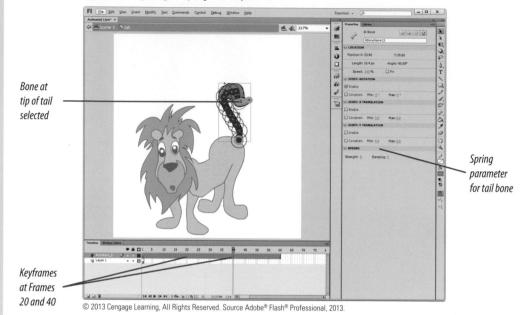 in the Spring section on the Property inspector, then adjust the Strength to **8** and the Damping to **4**.

13. Click **Scene 1** on the Edit bar to exit editing mode.

14. Click **Control** on the Menu bar, click **Test Movie**, then click **Test**, to preview your animation.

15. Save your work.

Figure 41 *Adjusting the spring on the tip of the tail*

Bone at tip of tail selected

Spring parameter for tail bone

Keyframes at Frames 20 and 40

© 2013 Cengage Learning, All Rights Reserved. Source Adobe® Flash® Professional, 2013.

Figure 42 *Creating an armature on the front legs*

Begin bone here

Figure 43 *Creating a second armature on the hind legs*

Rear leg armature

Work with inverse kinematics on movie clips

In this exercise, you will animate the legs of the lion using inverse kinematics.

1. Verify that Animated Lion.fla is open and you have exited edit mode.

   You will create two separate armatures, one for the front legs and the other for the rear legs.

2. Click the **Bone tool** 🦴 on the Tools panel, click the lion's **mouth**, then drag a **bone** to the lion's **right paw**, as shown in Figure 42.

   A new armature layer is created.

3. Hover over the mouth, when the pointer changes to ✛, click and drag a **bone** to the lion's **left paw**.

   The lion's left paw moves in front of the lion's mane.

4. Click the **Selection tool** ▶, click a blank area of the Stage, right-click the lion's **left front leg**, click **Arrange**, then click **Send to Back**.

5. Click the **Bone tool** 🦴, click the lion's **rear end**, then drag a **bone** to the **heel of its right rear paw**.

TIP Be careful not to drag the bone to an overlapping movie clip.

   A new armature layer is created.

6. Repeat step 5 but drag the bone to the **toe of the left rear paw**, arrange the **rear legs** to be behind the lion's body, then compare your screen to Figure 43.

(continued)

7. Rename the appropriate armature layers **front legs** and **rear legs**.

TIP You may need to reorder your armature layers so that the front legs layer is at the top of the stacking order.

8. Select **Frame 60** for all three layers, then press **F6** to insert a keyframe.

   A keyframe is inserted in Frame 60 for all three layers.

9. Move the playhead ▊ to **Frame 20**.

10. Select the **front legs layer**, click the **Selection tool** ▶, then move the lion's **left front leg** slightly to the left.

    A new keyframe is created.

11. Move the playhead ▊ to **Frame 30**.

12. Move the lion's **right front leg** slightly to the left.

TIP If you want to remove a pose, right-click a keyframe, then click Clear Pose.

13. Move the playhead ▊ to **Frame 10**.

14. Select the **rear legs layer**, click the **Selection tool** ▶, then move the lion's **right rear leg** slightly to the left.

15. Move the playhead ▊ to **Frame 40**.

16. Move the lion's **left rear leg** slightly to the right, then compare your screen to Figure 44.

17. Click **Control** on the Menu bar, click **Test Movie**, then click **Test**, to preview your animation.

18. Save your work, then exit Flash.

Figure 44 *Final workspace for lion armature*

Renamed armature layers

© 2013 Cengage Learning, All Rights Reserved. Source Adobe® Flash® Professional, 2013.

Using one of the comic panels from the Jack comic book, create a cut-out style animation for that scene of the story. You will first need to prepare the Illustrator file for import into Flash to be animated.

1. Open 2D6-SB1.ai and rename it **SB1 Cut_Out**.
2. Determine which elements of the scene you want to animate and which parts will remain still.
3. Prepare the file so that it can be imported into Flash in order to be animated.
   - Group necessary elements.
   - Distribute to layer.
   - Name layers.
4. Compare your screen to the sample shown in Figure 45, then save your document.
5. Create a new Flash document and name it **SB1 Cut_Out**.
6. Import your SB1 Cut_Out.ai file into Flash.
   - Verify the settings that work best for your project.
   - Create and name movie clips.
7. Separate items onto layers as needed to animate.
   - Consider creating some of the animated elements inside a movie clip.
8. When you are satisfied with your work, save the file and publish it as a SWF file.
9. Close your file.

Figure 45 *Sample Completed Skill Builder 1*

© 2013 Cengage Learning, All Rights Reserved. Source Adobe® Illustrator®, 2013.

Using the skills you learned in this chapter, create two versions of a walk cycle—a person walking a dog. The first using cut-out style animation and the other using inverse kinematics. Explore the Flash IK example before you create your walk cycle. Create your characters in Illustrator, being sure to prepare your document to be imported into Flash for animation.

View the sample

1. Start Flash, click More in the Create from Template section on the Welcome Screen, click Sample Files in the Category section, then click IK Stick Man Sample in the Template section.
2. Experiment with adjusting the various bones to add motion to this armature, then save or close the file as you wish.
3. Start Illustrator, then create a document named **SB2 Walk Cycle**.
4. Before drawing your characters, consider which character you will animate with the cut-out style and which will be animated with inverse kinematics.

   ■ Be sure to overlap elements of your character to allow for movement so that gaps will not appear.
   ■ Consider which objects will need to be imported as movie clips and which will be imported as editable paths.
   ■ Group necessary elements, distribute to layers and name layers.

5. Create a new Flash document titled **SB2 Walk Cycle**.
6. Import your Illustrator document into Flash.

   ■ Verify the settings that work best for your project.

   ■ Create and name movie clips.
   ■ Apply the editable paths option to layers that will be animated as a shape.

7. Separate items onto layers as needed to animate.

   ■ Consider creating your animation inside a movie clip for the cut-out animation.

Figure 46 *Sample Inverse Kinematics Animation*

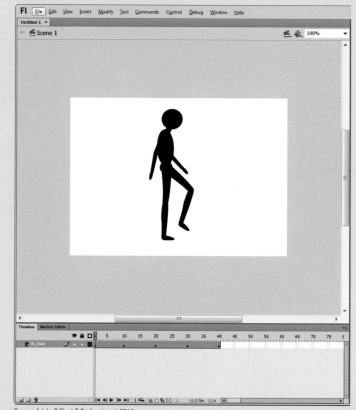

Source Adobe® Flash® Professional, 2013.

8. Save your work and publish it as a SWF file when you are satisfied with your work. Compare your screen to the sample shown in Figure 46.
9. Close your file.

You have been asked to create an animation of a man trying to fall asleep and counting sheep. During the story, the sheep occasionally get into a huddle to come up with more creative ways to get the man to fall asleep. As time passes, the sheep get sleepy themselves and finally decide to drop an anvil on the man's head to help him fall asleep. Sketches have been provided for you. Use Illustrator or Photoshop to trace the artwork so that you can then animate it in Flash using the various types of animation techniques. (*Note*: You may not need all of the sketches provided to tell your story.)

1. Create a new Illustrator or Photoshop document named **PP Sheep**.
2. Before drawing your characters, consider which character you will animate with the cut-out style, which will be animated with inverse kinematics, and which will be animated with frame-by-frame animation.
   - Be sure to overlap elements of your character to allow for movement so that gaps will not appear.
   - Consider which objects will need to be imported as movie clips, graphic symbols, or editable paths.
   - Group necessary elements, distribute to layers, and name layers.
3. Compare your screen to the sample shown in Figure 47, then save and close your document.
4. Create a new Flash document titled **PP Sheep**.

5. Import your Illustrator or Photoshop document into Flash.
   - Verify the settings that work best for your project.
   - Create and name movie clips.
   - Apply the editable paths option to layers that will be animated as a shape.

6. Separate items onto layers as needed to animate.
   - Consider creating parts of your animation inside movie clips.
7. When you are satisfied with your work, save the file and publish it as a SWF file.
8. Close your file, then exit Illustrator or Photoshop and Flash.

Figure 47 *Sample Completed Portfolio Project*

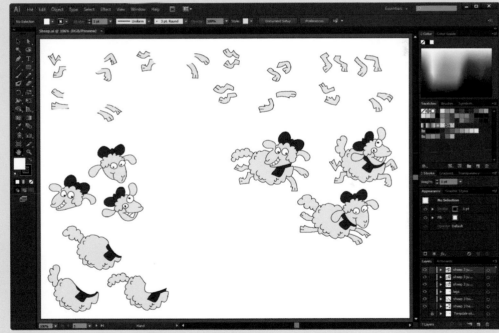

The Children's Publishing Group has begun publishing a series of informative picture books for children aged 6–9. These books are designed with contemporary style characters to teach a variety of lessons.

The series is written covering the following topics:

- Honesty
- Responsibility
- Sharing
- Caring
- Respect
- Individuality
- Manners
- Perseverance
- Death
- Environment

You will write and illustrate a book for the series in Illustrator with the following project specifications:

Technical Specifications:

- Color mode: CMYK
- Units of measure: Inches
- Document dimensions: 6.5" × 9"
- ½-inch margins
- Font size for pages: 20 pt
- Paragraph spacing: 6 pt
- Published as a PDF
- Number of pages: 10–12 (not including the cover)

Design Specifications:

- Cover should include artwork, title, and author (you are the author).
- Each page of the story should have both artwork and words.
- The font and style should be easy to read and consistent throughout the book.

(*Hint*: Remember to leave a blank artboard after the cover to allow for two-sided printing.)

The Children's Publishing Group has decided to create a series of fractured fairy tales created in Flash for their website. The target audience will be children ages 10–14. You can fracture the fairy tale in any of the following ways:

- Change the main character
- Change the setting
- Tell the story from a different character's point of view
- Alter the ending of the story

Locate a fairy tale you would like to fracture, then use Illustrator or Photoshop to illustrate your characters. Create the animation in Flash with the following project specifications:

Technical Specifications:

- Color mode: RGB
- Units of measure: Pixels
- Document dimensions: 550 × 400
- Duration: 30 seconds
- Frames per second: 15
- Published as a SWF

Design Specifications:

- Add a title to introduce animation.
- Create tween and frame-by-frame animations.
- Create symbols as needed.
- Describe the story well; add movement to characters and scenes.
- Provide credits to the original fairy tale's author.

You want to study animation and have begun applying to animation schools. You want to add another animation to your portfolio for your application. While looking for ideas for your final portfolio piece, you discovered The National Gallery website in London. Here college students collaborate with the museum to create 2D Flash animations inspired by paintings.

View the animations at The National Gallery: http://www.nationalgallery.org.uk/learning/inspired-by-the-collection/2d-animation/.

Through your research, you found the National Gallery of Art website in Washington, DC that provides open access to a variety of artwork that is now in the public domain. You have decided to use a painting to create your own animation. Because the work is in the public domain, you can safely create a new work that will not violate copyright law.

Choose a painting at https://images.nga.gov/en/page/show_home_page.html.

In this project, you will step through all the following phases of creating an animation:

- Brainstorming
- Conducting research
- Developing a story
- Developing characters
- Creating an animation using Illustrator, Photoshop, and Flash

Decide how to add "new life" to an "old" painting. Will you:

- Tell a story around that moment in time captured by the painting?
- Create your own interpretation of the painting?
- Incorporate the methods used by the artist?

Technical Specifications:

- Color mode: RGB
- Units of measure: Pixels
- Document dimensions: 550 × 400
- Published as a SWF

Other Specifications:

- Include the original painting at the beginning or end of the animation. Include a credit line for the artist.
- Add enough characters to tell the story effectively.
- Include an explanation to explain your approach to the creation of the animation.

DATA FILES LIST

2D ANIMATION			
Chapter	**Data File Supplied**	**Student Created File**	**Used In**
Chapter 1	None	Illustrator Workspace.ai	Lesson 1
	2D 1-1.ai	Illustrator Drawing Practice.ai	Lesson 2
	2D 1-2.ai	Illustrator Pen Practice 1.ai	Lesson 3
	2D 1-3.ai	Illustrator Pen Practice 2.ai	
	None	Jack.ai	Lesson 6
	None	Character Practice SB1.ai	Skill Builder 1
	2D 1-SB2.tif	Jack SB2.ai	Skill Builder 2
	None	Portfolio Project-Character Analysis	Portfolio Project
Chapter 2	None	Story Idea	Lesson 1
	None	Story Outline	
	2D 2-1.ai	Jack Comic Book.ai	Lesson 2, Lesson 3, Lesson 4
	Jack-Cover.tif		
	Jack Symbols.ai		
	speech_bubbles.tif	speech bubbles.ai	Lesson 3
	*Jack Comic Book.ai	Jack Comic Book SB1.ai	Skill Builder 1
	*Jack Comic Book SB1.ai	Jack Comic Book SB2.ai	Skill Builder 2
	**Chapter 1 characters	Portfolio Project-Comic.ai	Portfolio Project
Chapter 3	None	Photoshop Workspace.psd	Lesson 1
	None	Photoshop Drawing Practice.psd	
	2D 3-1.psd	Photoshop Painting Practice.psd	
	None	Walk Cycle.psd	Lesson 2
	None	hard bouncing ball scan.pdf	Lesson 3
	* hard bouncing ball scan.pdf	hard bouncing ball scan.gif	
	None	hard bouncing ball.psd	
	None	"Twelve Principles of Animation applied"	Skill Builder 1

* Created in a previous Lesson, Skill Builder, or Portfolio Project in the current chapter
** Created in a previous chapter

2D ANIMATION			
Chapter	**Data File Supplied**	**Student Created File**	**Used In**
Chapter 3, continued	None	Walk Cycle SB2.psd	Skill Builder 2
	*Walk Cycle SB2.psd	Walk Cycle PP.psd	Portfolio Project
Chapter 4	2D 4-1.ai	Pierre Animation.ai	Lesson 1
		Pierre Animation.swf	
	2D 4-2.ai	Animated Ana.ai	Lesson 2
	*Animated Ana.ai	Animated Ana.psd	
	*Animated Ana.psd	Animated Ana.mp4	
	2D 4-3.psd	Animatic.psd	Lesson 3
		Animatic.mp4	
	**Chapters 1-3 character	SB1-Simple Animation.ai	Skill Builder 1
		SB1-Simple Animation.swf	
	**Chapter 2 panel	SB2-PS-Animation.psd	Skill Builder 2
		SB2-PS-Animation.mp4	
	PP-animatic sketches folder	PP-animatic.psd	Portfolio Project
		PP-animatic.mp4	
Chapter 5	None	flash workspace.fla	Lesson 1
	None	animation practice.fla	Lesson 2
		animation practice.swf	
	2D 5-1.fla	frame animation.fla	
	2D 5-2.fla	tween animation.fla	Lesson 3
		tween animation.swf	
	None	play button.fla	Lesson 4
	2D 5-3.fla	random eye blink.fla	
		random eye blink.swf	

* Created in a previous Lesson, Skill Builder, or Portfolio Project in the current chapter
** Created in a previous chapter

DATA FILES LIST

(CONTINUED)

2D ANIMATION			
Chapter	**Data File Supplied**	**Student Created File**	**Used In**
Chapter 5, continued	2D 5-SB1-f.mp3 or	Lip Sync.fla	Skill Builder 1
	2D 5-SB1-m.mp3	Lip Sync.swf	
	None	*Student-named-file.fla*	Skill Builder 2
		Student-named-file.swf	
	None	bouncing ball.fla	Portfolio Project
		bouncing ball.swf	
Chapter 6	2D 6-1.ai	Dog.ai	Lesson 1
	*Dog.ai	Animated Dog.fla	
		Animated Dog.swf	
	2D 6-2.psd	Flamingo.psd	Lesson 2
	*Flamingo.psd	Animated Flamingo.fla	
		Animated Flamingo.swf	
	2D 6-3.ai	Animated Lion.fla	Lesson 3
		Animated Lion.swf	
	2D 6-SB1.ai	SB1 Cut_Out.ai	Skill Builder 1
	*SB1 Cut_Out.ai	SB1 Cut_Out.fla	
		SB1 Cut_Out.swf	
	None	SB2 Walk Cycle.ai	Skill Builder 2
	*SB2 Walk Cycle.ai	SB2 Walk Cycle.fla	
		SB2 Walk Cycle.swf	
	Sheep Sketches	PP Sheep.ai or PP Sheep.psd	Portfolio Project
	*PP Sheep.ai or PP Sheep.psd	PP Sheep.fla	
		PP Sheep. swf	

* Created in a previous Lesson, Skill Builder, or Portfolio Project in the current chapter

A

ActionScript event
An interaction in a Flash movie, such as a mouse click causing the playhead to move to a different frame, or the loading of an external sound or movie.

Anchor point
The point between each line segment that can either be a smooth anchor point or a corner anchor point. This point determines whether the line is straight or curved.

Application window
The main window comprised of various panels.

Arc principle
One of the 12 principles of animation that improves realism; the trajectory an object would follow while in that particular motion, such as the movement of a head or an arm.

Armature
The series of bones created to simulate the movement of characters.

Armature layer
This layer contains objects that have inverse kinematics applied to them.

Artboard
The printable region of your document.

B

Bitmap
An image, technically known as a raster image, that is represented by pixels in a grid layout; each pixel contains color information for the image.

Blank keyframe
A placeholder keyframe that does not have any content on it.

Bounding box
A solid-lined rectangle that appears around the selection.

Brush Definition
A tool that applies a unique stroke to a path using one of five types of brushes: calligraphic, scatter, art, bristle, or pattern.

C

Camera angle
The way the panel's layout is composed.

Canvas
The white area in the center of the workspace.

Cel
A transparent celluloid sheet that contains a drawing and is then overlapped with other celluloid sheets.

Cel animation
A type of animation that uses transparent celluloid sheets (cels); each cel represents one frame in an animation.

Character arc
The path of growth a character develops as the story is told and follows the flow of the story structure.

Character development
The process of developing a character.

Classic tween
A keyframe-based motion tween that is denoted in the Timeline with a purple fill and a continuous arrow.

Climax
The part of the story that involves the final conflict that addresses your character's goals.

Clipping Mask
This selection hides everything outside the shape used to create the mask.

Clipping Set
This selection includes the clipping mask and the objects that are included in the mask.

CMYK
The color mode used for creating an illustration for print; uses cyan, magenta, yellow, and black to create various colors.

Compound path
This path appears in the Layers panel as <Compound Path> and is created by two or more paths; a hole appears where the shapes overlap.

Compound shape
This path is displayed in the Layers panel as <Compound Shape> and is created by two or more objects.

Control points
The connections between each bone; these can be edited with the Bind tool in Flash.

Copyright
A category of intellectual property law providing protection to the authors of "original works of authorship," including literary, dramatic, musical, artistic, and certain other intellectual works.

Corner point
A point that may have one, two, or no direction lines.

Current time indicator (CTI)
A light blue triangle in the ruler with a vertical red line extending through the video and audio tracks indicating the current frame being displayed. Also known as a playhead.

Custom workspace
A workspace that has been created by the user and saved with a unique name.

Cut-out style animation
A method of creating an animation using flat characters, props, and backgrounds. Also referred to as stop-motion animation.

——————— **D** ———————

Deco tool
This tool makes simple work of drawing complex shapes.

Derivative work
A work based on one or more existing works (and previously published).

Direction handle
This feature is comprised of a direction line and a direction point and is the green line with a green dot on the end that extends from an anchor point.

Direction line
The blue line.

Direction Point
The blue dot at the end of the direction line.

Dock
A collection of panels or panel groups.

Down state
The third frame; this state is displayed when the button is clicked.

Draw Behind
A drawing mode that allows you to draw behind all artwork on a selected layer, if no selections are made.

Draw Inside
A drawing mode that allows you to draw inside a selected object.

Draw Normal
The default drawing mode in Illustrator.

Drawing modes
A method of drawing shapes in Photoshop; there are three drawing modes: shape layers, paths, or fill pixels.

Drawing object
This object is a separate graphic object that does not automatically merge with an overlapping shape.

Drop zone
A feature that appears when moving one panel to another panel group, indicating where the panel will be placed when you release the mouse.

────────── **E** ──────────

Essentials
The default workspace that displays the essential panels needed to create a document.

Event handling
A process used to add interactivity to a Flash animation.

Event sound
A sound option in Flash that must download completely before it begins playing.

────────── **F** ──────────

Fair use doctrine
A law that allows copyrighted work to be reproduced for a variety of reasons, including news reporting, teaching, parody, and research.

Final output
How you intend to use the document when you are finished.

Fill pixels mode
This mode allows you to create the shape on the selected layer.

FLA
The native file format for a Flash project file that can only be opened in Flash.

Flick book
Images are drawn on pages of a book with each image differing slightly so that when you flip the pages, the image appears to move across the page. Also known as a flip book.

Flip book
Images are drawn on pages of a book with each image differing slightly so that when you flip the pages, the image appears to move across the page. Also known as a flick book.

Flip-style animation
A style of hand-drawn animation. The first animation to use a linear sequence of images.

FLV
A video file that can be viewed with Flash Player.

Frame
A frame displays and organizes content in your Flash movie; the more frames that are used for specific content, the longer the content will appear in the animation.

Frame-by-frame animations
Flip style animations that are created using the Frame mode.

Frames per second (fps)
The way the speed of animation is played and measured.

────────── **G** ──────────

gotoAndPlay action
This action causes the animation to jump from the frame in which the action is placed to another frame in the Flash document; most often used to play frames in a nonsequential order.

Guide layer
This layer contains strokes that are used as a guide to arrange objects on other layers or to create a classic tween animation.

Guided layers
Those layers associated with the guide layer.

Gradient
A blending of colors, which is defined by a series of color stops along a gradient slider.

Gradient annotator
This tool allows you to customize a gradient in the same way you can in the Gradient panel. In addition, you can also adjust the size and location of the gradient in relation to the object.

Gradient mesh
A tool that allows you to create complex gradients by creating a custom mesh object on which you can customize the colors of the mesh points located at intersecting lines.

———————— **H** ————————

Hit state
The fourth frame; this state defines the area that responds to the mouse pointer or click.

HTML
This extension creates a web page document and SWF file with browser settings that will activate the SWF file when viewed in a browser.

———————— **I** ————————

In-between animator
Title given to the animator that draws the in-between frames.

Inbetweener
Title given to the animator that draws the in-between frames.

Inbetweening
The in-between frames that show the transition from one keyframe to the next keyframe. Also known as tweening.

Instance
The action of dragging a symbol to the artboard.

Intellectual property
Creations of the mind and may include copyrights, trademarks, patents, industrial design rights, and trade secrets.

Intermediate frames
When an animator draws various stages of the animation. Also known as a keyframe.

Interpolation
A process done when you create more than one keyframe. Photoshop determines what needs to be done to the layer to make it change from one keyframe to the next.

In point
The point at which the video layer begins playing.

Inverse kinematics
The use of bones to adjust or animate parts of a shape eliminating the need to draw separate versions of an object to represent different movements.

———————— **K** ————————

Key animator
Title given to the animator that draws the intermediate frames or keyframes. Also known as a Lead Animator.

Keyframe
An instruction that tells Photoshop how you want your layer to appear at that time. Photoshop will interpolate the changes in values at the locations of keyframes over time to animate the object; indicated by a black circle.

Keyframe animation
The most basic type of animation. Also known as frame-by-frame animation.

Keyframes
When an animator draws various stages of the animation. Also known as an intermediate frame.

Kineograph
The name of the first flip book that was patented in 1868 by John Barnes Linnett.

———————— **L** ————————

Lead animator
Title given to the animator that draws the intermediate frames or keyframes. Also known as a Key Animator.

Living Pictures or Living Photograph
A new style of flip book with photographs that was made at end of the 19th century.

Lossy
Compression method that compresses the image to the JPEG file format.

M

Mask layer
This layer contains objects that are used as masks to hide selected portions of the layers below them.

Masked layer
The layer below the mask layer in the stacking order.

Middle
Part of the story that shows the development of the story through a sequence of obstacles, which ultimately leads to a climax.

Modifiers
Additional options available for drawing tools on the Flash Tools panel.

Motion tween
This type of tween allows you to set the properties, such as the position and alpha transparency, for an object at the location of a keyframe. Flash will then interpolate the values overtime to animate the object.

N

Normal layer
This layer contains most of the artwork in a Flash project file.

O

Objects
A term used in Illustrator to describe parts of a vector drawing that are comprised of paths and anchor points.

Onion skinning
This feature allows you to see more than one frame at a time.

Out point
The point at which the video layer finishes playing.

Over state
The second frame; this state is displayed when the mouse pointer is over the button.

P

Panel tab
This feature displays the panel's name and is found at the top of a panel.

Pathfinder
A tool that creates new shapes from overlapping objects. (*Note*: Additional Pathfinders can be found on the Effect menu.)

Paths
A sequence of line and curve segments that have anchor points at either end.

Paths mode
This mode allows you to create a work path on the current layer.

Photomatic
When stock photographs are used to create an animatic.

Pose-to-pose
This drawing method draws only the main poses in the animation.

Property keyframe
A special keyframe in Flash that defines changes to one or more properties, such as position, size, or color tint.

Public domain
A work that is no longer protected by copyright, or whose intellectual property rights have expired.

R

Rendering
The process of exporting an image sequence or video.

Resolution
The part of the story that ties up any loose ends of your story and usually ends the story quickly.

RGB
The color mode used on computer displays, television screens, and mobile devices such as smartphones and tablets; uses red, green, and blue in various combinations to create the colors you see.

Rip-o-matic
When stock video is used to create an animatic. Also known as a videomatic.

S

Selected art indicator
The colored square in the selection column of the Illustrator Layers panel that indicates whether any items are selected on the layer.

Selection marquee
The arrow that creates a single bounding box around the selected objects.

Set-up
The beginning of the story.

Shape layers mode
This mode allows you to create a shape on a separate layer.

Shape modes
The four options in the top row of the Pathfinder that create compound paths.

Shape tween
A tool that allows you to morph basic shapes and is denoted in the Timeline with a green fill and a continuous arrow.

Smart object
A layer that contains image data from raster or vector images, such as Photoshop or Illustrator files.

Smooth point
A point that has two direction lines.

SoundMixer.stopALL action
This action is used to prevent two or more embedded sounds from playing at the same time in your Flash project.

Squash and stretch principle
One of the 12 principles of animation that gives the impression of weight, volume, and flexibility as the character or object moves.

Stacking order
The arrangement of items on the artboard.

Stream sound
A sound option in Adobe Flash that begins to play as soon as enough frames have downloaded.

Stop-motion animation
A type of animation that takes pictures of real objects that are repositioned for each picture, then puts them together in a sequence to create the illusion of motion. Claymation is one of the most common types of stop-motion animation.

Storyboard
A series of pictures used to show a story in a sequence using drawings, direction, and dialogue.

Straight ahead
A drawing method that draws the scene from the beginning to the end.

SWF
An exported or published FLA file that has been optimized for viewing on the web and cannot be edited.

T

Target icon
The hollow circle to the right of the layer's name in Illustrator.

Thaumatrope
From the Victorian era, this form of animation blends two images that were on opposite sides of a spinning disc. Using the phenomenon known as persistence of vision, the two images appeared to merge into one image.

Timing principle
One of the 12 principles of animation used to add interest to a scene; varied timing can help establish mood.

Tweening
The in-between frames that show the transition from one keyframe to the next keyframe. Also known as inbetweening.

U

Up state
The first frame; the default state displayed when the mouse pointer is not near or over the button.

V

Variable Width Profile
A tool that changes the shape of the stroke in Illustrator.

Vector drawing
A drawing made up of objects that are created by a series of paths.

Videomatic
When stock video is used to create an animatic. Also known as a rip-o-matic.

Volume principle
A principle of animation that indicates the mass of the ball should not change when the ball squashes or stretches.

W

Walk cycle
The foundation concept in animation of drawing the character walking.

Work path
This path is temporary and you can use it to create a mask, fill and/or stroke, or to make a selection.

Workspace
The arrangement of panels in the application window.

Workspace switcher
This command, available on the Menu bar, allows you to reset your current workspace to default settings, switch to other available workspaces, or create your own custom workspace.

Z

Zoetrope
This form of animation produced the illusion of motion by using a cylinder on which a series of static pictures were placed. Spinning the zoetrope made the image appear to move.